Royal
Audience

Royal Audience

70 YEARS, 13 PRESIDENTS—
ONE QUEEN'S SPECIAL
RELATIONSHIP WITH
AMERICA

&

DAVID CHARTER

G. P. PUTNAM'S SONS
NEW YORK

PUTNAM
— EST. 1838 —

G. P. PUTNAM'S SONS
Publishers Since 1838
An imprint of Penguin Random House LLC
penguinrandomhouse.com

ISBN 9780593712870

Printed in the United States of America
1st Printing

While the author has made every effort to provide accurate telephone
numbers, internet addresses, and other contact information at the time of
publication, neither the publisher nor the author assumes any
responsibility for errors, or for changes that occur after publication.
Further, the publisher does not have any control over and does not assume
any responsibility for author or third-party websites or their content.

To Michelle, Leo, and Kim,

with love

CONTENTS

Introduction
1

Chapter 1
11

Chapter 2
21

Chapter 3
42

Chapter 4
62

Chapter 5
80

Chapter 6
97

Chapter 7
122

Chapter 8
135

Chapter 9
158

CONTENTS

Chapter 10
177

Chapter 11
194

Chapter 12
214

Chapter 13
235

Chapter 14
254

Conclusion
272

Acknowledgments
281

Notes
284

Photo Credits
315

Index
316

INTRODUCTION

"Tiny Princess Born Yesterday to House of York May One Day Occupy British Throne"

—*Los Angeles Times*, April 22, 1926

The birth of a daughter to Albert, the Duke of York, second son of King George V, made news around the English-speaking world, including the royal-obsessed United States of America. The new baby, Elizabeth Alexandra Mary, was third in the line of succession at her birth on April 21, 1926—behind her father and his older brother. But the chances of her assuming the throne seemed dim at best. A brother would take precedence under male-line primogeniture laws not abolished until 2011. The unimaginable abdication crisis that would lead to her ascension was still ten years away, and her uncle Edward, the playboy heir to the imperial throne of "Britain, Ireland and the British Dominions beyond the Seas," could foreseeably yet settle down and start a family of his own. There were, however, already early signs pointing to Elizabeth's accession, from her difficult birth by Caesarean section, which indicated that she would not have many siblings, to Edward's fondness for travel, including two high-profile American tours, which suggested a yearning to distance himself from the fate decreed for him as king emperor.

The US would have an unexpectedly decisive say in that.

Baby Elizabeth was born into a dynasty that oversaw a vast empire but that was always careful to maintain close links with the very first colony to break away. It had been fifteen decades since America declared Elizabeth's great-great-great-great-grandfather a "tyrant" and rejected the monarchy in the Declaration of Independence of 1776. George III continues to be demonized in popular US culture for his role in prosecuting the Revolutionary War (see: the Broadway musical *Hamilton*), but the first ambassador to London from the new republic found the King unfailingly polite and optimistic about future relations.

John Adams, the future second president, presented his credentials to King George on June 1, 1785, twenty-one months after the end of the hostilities, declaring to the King that his aim was "restoring an entire esteem, confidence, and affection, or, in better words, the old good nature and the old good humor between people, who, though separated by an ocean, and under different governments, have the same language, a similar religion, and kindred blood."

The King responded magnanimously: "I will be very frank with you. I was the last to consent to the separation; but the separation having been made, and having become inevitable, I have always said, as I say now, that I would be the first to meet the friendship of the United States as an independent power." In the decades and centuries after a war to escape from royal rule, it was ironically the powers of the American president that would prove far more durable than those of British kings and queens.

George III was still nominally on the throne when British soldiers invaded Washington, DC, burning down the Capitol and the White House during the War of 1812—a conflict much better known today in the US than in the UK. His duties were by then in the hands of his son, who as prince regent took little interest in the policies of his ministers. By 1830, relations had improved to the point where Andrew Jackson, the seventh president, wrote a letter in fond terms to the new king, William IV: "I have received with deep regret the doleful intelligence of the decease of your august Sovereign George the 4th and offer you my sincere condolence. . . . I feel confident that the people of England will find all the blessings of the succeeding reign." These warm words were from a former general who had defeated British forces just fifteen years earlier, at the Battle of New Orleans.

American interest in the British monarchy reached a new peak when William's eighteen-year-old niece, Victoria, came to the throne in 1837. She wasted no time in writing to Martin Van Buren, the eighth US president, expressing "Our most earnest desire to cultivate and maintain the Relations of Friendship and good Understanding which so happily subsist between the Two Countries" and signing the letter "Your Good Friend, Victoria R." Van Buren sent his son John to the coronation, kindling rumors that the widowed president might even seek Victoria's hand, despite being thirty-six years her senior. Such was the fascination with the teenage Queen that the American press also speculated about the chances of John—a mere nine years older than Victoria—marrying into the royal dynasty that his republican forebears had rejected. After sharing a dance with Victoria at a ball, the president's son earned the nickname "Prince John."

Eventually, though, the American media had to concede defeat when the young Queen proposed to a real prince: "At one time, it was neck and neck between Prince Albert of Saxe-Coburg and Gotha, and Prince John—the one being of a high Dutch breed from Germany—the other low Dutch," wrote the celebrated American publisher James Gordon Bennett. "Unfortunately for the progress of liberty and democracy in England, Baroness Lehzen [Victoria's governess and companion], an old woman in the palace, gave the casting vote for the high Dutchman, and Prince John returned to the country to finish his land speculations."

Although Victoria never visited the United States in her sixty-three-year reign, American interest in British royalty reached another crescendo when she sent her eighteen-year-old son and heir, Albert Edward, for a month-long tour of the United States in the fall of 1860. This followed three months in Canada and included a three-day stay with President James Buchanan at the White House. As would become a staple of later royal visits, the Prince of Wales went to Mount Vernon, the first president's former estate, to pay homage. He was ogled by huge crowds wherever he went.

In her speech at the state opening of Parliament in February 1861, Queen Victoria remarked that her son's visit brought the two nations closer . . . but warned that she could not ignore the storm clouds gathering in America after the secession of seven states. "It is impossible for me to look without great concern upon any events which can affect the happiness and welfare of a people purely allied to my subjects by descent," she said. "My heartfelt wish is that these differences may be susceptible of satisfactory adjustment."

Both sides in the American Civil War would seek British royal support. President Abraham Lincoln penned a long letter of condolence to Victoria upon the death of Albert, her consort, in December 1861, stressing, "The People of the United States are kindred of the People of Great Britain," but he was also keen to underline that his concern for her "irreparable bereavement . . . emanates from only virtuous motives and natural affection."

The Queen would turn consoler after Lincoln's assassination with a letter to his widow, Mary Todd Lincoln, declaring, "No one can better appreciate than I can, who am myself utterly broken hearted by the loss of my own beloved husband, who was the light of my life—my stay—my all, what your own sufferings must be." Mrs. Lincoln replied that she was "deeply grateful" for Victoria's "expressions of tender sympathy." It was the first time the British sovereign corresponded with an American First Lady and suggested a special level of closeness between the two nations that Victoria was careful to nurture.

She welcomed Ulysses Grant for an overnight stay at Windsor Castle in June 1877 on his post-presidential world tour, and in 1880 she sent President Hayes the gift of a desk made from the timbers of HMS *Resolute*, a lost Arctic exploration ship retrieved by the US and restored in 1856 as a gesture of goodwill. The Resolute Desk was used by Hayes and by various presidents in different areas of the White House before being installed in the Oval Office by President John F. Kennedy, removed by his successor Lyndon B. Johnson, and brought back by Jimmy Carter.

Victoria's son, who finally came to the throne as King Edward VII after her death in 1901, followed her lead, congratulating Theodore Roosevelt on his 1904 reelection and noting, "You, Mr President, and I have been called upon to superintend the destinies of the two great branches of the Anglo-Saxon race." Roosevelt wrote back, agreeing that "the larger interests of the two nations are the same; and the fundamental, underlying traits of their characters are also the same." The twenty-sixth president planned to travel to meet his royal pen pal a year after leaving office, but fate intervened, and instead Roosevelt became the first former president to attend a British monarch's funeral.

While the new king, George V, was less interested in America, he became the first British sovereign to host a sitting US president when Woodrow Wilson visited on Boxing Day 1918, on a stopover before the Paris Peace Conference of the victorious First World War allies. Tens of thousands flocked to central London to see the two heads of state take a horse-drawn carriage from Charing Cross Station to Buckingham Palace. Reporting Wilson's reception by Londoners, *The Guardian* wrote, "All the gaiety pent up through the cruel four and a half years seemed to be released in the great noise of cheering that rose round the leader of the world's peace." His visit was also a sentimental one—Wilson went to view Carlisle in northern England, where his mother was born—highlighting the close cultural and ancestral ties as well as the political bond between the countries.

In the revolutionary atmosphere that saw kings and emperors ousted across Europe, George V—the future Elizabeth II's grandfather—decided to follow the example of his own grandmother, Queen Victoria, in dispatching his son, the Prince of Wales, to tour Canada and the United States. The trip was made partly to burnish the royal family's modern credentials and partly as a test of the monarchy's popularity abroad in the English-speaking world. The dashing Prince Edward, aged twenty-five, was well-suited to the task—he smoked, danced, and enjoyed jazz. He was the very picture of a contemporary young royal.

Calling in at the White House, he found Wilson propped up in bed, recovering from a stroke, but the president's personal physician reported that the two had "a fine old time" conversing for twenty minutes. They talked about the president's enormous old bed in the Lincoln Bedroom, where the prince's grandfather slept in 1860. Like him, Edward laid a wreath at George Washington's Mount Vernon tomb and attracted huge interest both from the US media and not a few young women. His reputation as Europe's most eligible bachelor preceded him, and by the time of a return visit in 1924, speculation was beginning about whether he would ever settle down. He would . . . much to his family's dismay.

In January 1931, at a country house party, Edward was introduced to Wallis Simpson, a married American who would change the course of history. The relationship that developed between them was ignored by the British press but covered

extensively in the US; even when his father died in January
1936 and he came to the throne as Edward VIII, most of the
British public was unaware of his love for a woman who applied
for her second divorce only after he became king. His adamant
desire to marry Simpson, against strong opposition from the
Church of England (which frowned on divorce) and senior establishment figures, led Edward to "renounce the Throne for
Myself and for My descendants."

The abdication rocked the monarchy to its core, but the institution pivoted quickly. In short order, Edward's younger
brother Albert was crowned as King George VI, making his
ten-year-old daughter, Elizabeth, heiress presumptive—provided
a brother did not appear. The day after the abdication, a message for the new king arrived from President Franklin D. Roosevelt: "On behalf of the people and the government of the
United States, I extend to Your Majesty sincere good wishes for
a long and happy reign."

Roosevelt won reelection in 1940, proclaiming to American
families, "Your boys are not going to be sent into a foreign
war"—even as bombs were raining down on London and European nations were already falling like dominos in the face of
Adolf Hitler's advance. Privately, though, Roosevelt had already foreseen that America could very well be dragged into
the conflict. He had cannily invited King George VI to become the first reigning British monarch to visit the US, along
with his consort, Queen Elizabeth, in June 1939, on the eve of
war, to remind Americans how much they liked the British.

Much to the relief of Britain and the White House, huge crowds turned out to testify to the continuing royal allure, including half a million in Washington, DC, when the royals arrived at Union Station by train from Canada.

At the state dinner that week, the King toasted to the hope that "our great nations may ever in the future walk together along the path of friendship in a world of peace." The most important meal, however, took place at FDR's Hyde Park estate in New York State, where the president laid out a picnic and served the King and Queen hot dogs for the first time in their lives. He also invited the estate's staff and their families to mingle with the royals to portray them as "regular people." The result was a PR triumph. "King Tries Hot Dog and Asks for More," ran the *New York Times* headline.

Even if Americans generally were not aware of the trip's true purpose, it was not lost on the British—who knew that US wartime support would be invaluable and marveled at the president's gift for creating positive publicity out of his royal audience. It underlined how important the royals had become for Britain's standing abroad and the crucial modern role this ancient institution could play in diplomacy and public relations, setting a pattern for the future Queen.

CHAPTER 1

When I was a little boy I read about a Fairy Princess—and there she is.

—Harry S. Truman, October 31, 1951

Princess Elizabeth, Duchess of Edinburgh, was twenty-five years old and much closer than she desired to her destiny of inheriting the British throne when she became the first member of the royal family to fly across the Atlantic. Her historic transatlantic flight on October 8, 1951, together with her dashing naval officer husband, Philip, was not, however, part of the original plan for the young royals' first North American tour. They were initially scheduled to travel on an ocean liner like her father, George VI, and mother, Queen Elizabeth, had done twelve years earlier. But the Edinburghs' departure was dramatically postponed just two days before they were due to set sail when the King's doctors decided that he should undergo an emergency lung operation. This caused them to delay the trip and saw Elizabeth's role as heiress presumptive thrust into the spotlight, as she joined a council of state with other senior royals to work out how to relieve her father of official duties during his

convalescence. Wartime searchlights shone a victory *V* over
Whitehall after the King survived a "lung resection," but neither the nation nor, initially, the monarch himself were told that
cancer had been diagnosed. Nor was the public informed that
the operation entailed the removal of the King's entire left lung.

Three days afterward, Buckingham Palace issued a bulletin
warning that "although no complications have arisen so far,
there will inevitably be a period of some anxiety for the next
week or ten days." It was progress enough for Elizabeth's North
American trip to go ahead, and her itinerary ended up being
pushed back by just one week thanks to a flight on a Boeing
Stratocruiser operated by the British Overseas Airways Corporation. This modern advance required extra security measures:
Royal Navy warships patrolled the Atlantic every seven hundred miles along the flight path.

It was clear even before the King's operation that Elizabeth
was being readied for her future role as Queen: she had started to
receive confidential governmental papers in June 1950. Throughout the visit *The Times* of London arrived by airmail daily so she
could keep up-to-date with current affairs. The fifty-five-year-
old King's fragile condition was always in the background, while
articles in the Canadian press pointing out that she looked "a
bit wan" and that "her broad, flashing smile wasn't so much in
evidence" suggested the pressures building on the young princess. Her father had been too sick to see her off at the airport
when she bade farewell to her two infant children, Charles and
Anne. In his briefcase Martin Charteris, the princess's private
secretary, carried paperwork for the accession should it become
necessary. It was a time of upheaval for the United Kingdom at
home and abroad: not only was the King in perilous health, but

his empire was crumbling, and while Elizabeth was on her travels, the postwar socialist British government of Clement Attlee was unexpectedly ejected in a snap election. Wartime prime minister Sir Winston Churchill was back and would prove a pillar of support when the accession came.

Truman was an admirer of Churchill, whom he hosted in 1946 for one of his most famous speeches warning of the "Iron Curtain" of Soviet dominance over central and eastern Europe. It was also in this speech that Churchill argued for the core importance to world peace of "a Special Relationship between the British Commonwealth and Empire and the United States." This he envisaged as cooperation "in the air, on the sea, all over the globe and in science and in industry, and in moral force" to provide "an overwhelming assurance of security." The phrase stuck, and from that moment on, the strength of the "Special Relationship" became the defining yardstick of transatlantic ties.

The stage for Princess Elizabeth's Washington sojourn was set that summer when Margaret Truman, the twenty-seven-year-old only child of the president, visited London. Charming and fashionable, Margaret was hailed as "America's Princess Margaret" by some British commentators, who saw parallels with the flamboyant younger daughter of King George VI. Margaret Truman was introduced to Princess Elizabeth and her twenty-year-old sister at a US embassy party—where, American reporters noted, she gave "a deep and lovely curtsy." A couple of days later she watched, entranced, from diplomatic seats at Horse Guards Parade in central London as Elizabeth, riding sidesaddle, received the royal salute and inspected the troops for the first time at the Trooping the Colour ceremony while standing in for her ailing father, in another sign of George VI's growing frailty.

"I have never seen anything so thrilling or so perfect," the president's daughter said afterward.

Clifton Truman Daniel, Margaret's son, remembers his mother telling him how she was invited to lunch with Princess Elizabeth where Philip proceeded to feed the corgis under the table when his wife was not looking.

That October, the glamorous young royal couple's tour across Canada in their ten-carriage special train drew larger and larger crowds as they went along: a million people turned out in Toronto—twice the number drawn by the King and Queen in 1939—while in Montreal the total attendance of spectators along the couple's motorcade route through the city was estimated at 1.5 million. Following the publication of a photograph of Princess Elizabeth in Canada wearing "sensible brogues" for a walkabout, there was a run on the footwear at Saks Fifth Avenue.

As expectation built in the US, the princess was paid the ultimate tribute by one of the queens of Hollywood, gossip columnist Hedda Hopper, whose words were syndicated to a readership of thirty-five million Americans. "She's doing a superb public relations job," Hopper wrote of Elizabeth twelve days into the Canadian tour. "I'd never know she was the same girl I met in London in '45. Then she was shy, aloof, unsmiling but very gracious. . . . Elizabeth and Philip are like a storybook couple, and this disillusioned old world can use one such pair."

All was not well with the fading British Empire and its sickly king, however. Less than forty-eight hours after the young couple arrived in Canada, Buckingham Palace announced that Elizabeth and Philip would stand in for George VI on his planned tour of Australia early the following year, due to his continued need for rest. A week before their arrival in Washington, DC, an Italian doctor privy to secret details of the King's operation revealed in the press what many had suspected and feared—that Elizabeth's father had lung cancer.

After flying into the US capital from Montreal with the Royal Canadian Air Force, Elizabeth descended the steps from the plane first, followed by Philip, to be met by the president, First Lady Bess Truman, and their daughter. She received a twenty-one-gun salute—not an honor that she was entitled to but, as the American media enthusiastically reported, "the US gave it to her anyway just in the name of romance." During his formal greeting at the airport Truman suggested a longer visit next time, more like the extensive tour of Canada. "I am sure that would make our good relations and our strong friendship with the British people even better than they are now," he said.

The president had met King George VI on two occasions: on the six-day royal tour of the US in 1939, during the presidency of Franklin D. Roosevelt, and again in the southern British port of Plymouth in 1945, when Truman, by then president, was on the way back from the Potsdam conference of victorious wartime leaders. But on this day the talk was less of war and more of family matters. Truman told the princess: "I was most happy to hear that the King had recovered so promptly, so that you could make this trip." He departed from his prepared words to ad-lib: "Margaret tells me that whenever anyone becomes acquainted with you, they immediately fall in love with you."

Elizabeth, sticking to her prepared script, told the sixty-seven-year-old president and millions more watching on TV and listening live on radio, "Free men everywhere look towards the United States with affection and with hope. The message that has gone out from this great capital city has brought hope and courage to a troubled world."

She was also grateful for the kind words about the King. "I want you all to know how deeply my family and our whole country was moved by the sympathy—and might I say affection—shown to my father, the King, by the people and press of the United States during his recent illness." *The Des Moines Register* recorded that at the end of her speech, Truman "gave her a fatherly smile and said, 'Thank you, dear.'" It added that "husky" Prince Philip wore his naval attire while "petite" Elizabeth, in a dark red suit, black hat, and black accessories "seemed to hit it off with the president immediately . . . they chatted together cheerfully as they walked together reviewing the troops."

Not everyone was impressed. The front page of *The Washington Times-Herald* carried a cartoon showing "Liz and Phil" flying on a Halloween broomstick with the caption "Trick or Treat?" (the royal couple arrived on October 31). It combined old colonial disdain for royalty with a dig at Britain's reliance on handouts of American candy.

The estimated 550,000 people who turned out to line the route of the presidential convoy bringing Elizabeth and Philip into the capital suggested that Americans were generally over feelings of contempt for the British monarchy—although the ranks of spectators on the streets were swelled by thousands of government workers allowed by Truman to leave their desks early to view the arrival. The American press gushed about the enthusiastic welcome and emphasized the youthfulness of the couple.

"From the moment of their dramatic arrival at National airport at 4 o'clock, their eyes sparkled with small girl-and-boy wonderment at the welcome, American style. They were to stay here forty-five hours," the Associated Press reported.

Elizabeth and Philip stayed at Blair House, a residence for state guests dating back to 1824 just across Pennsylvania Avenue from the White House, where the Trumans were also living during extensive renovations of the presidential mansion. During the trip, Truman took the couple up to the top floor to meet his elderly mother-in-law, Margaret Wallace, who was practically deaf and bedridden.

"Mother! I've bought Princess Elizabeth to see you!" he shouted. Confused and having heard that Churchill was back in office, she responded: "I'm so glad your father's been re-elected."

After a change of costume for the princess into a green-gold cocktail dress and gray fur cape, the royal couple attended a reception with the US press where there was not one bow or curtsy but, as throughout Canada, they were showered with gifts for their two infant children, including an "Indian bonnet with eagle feathers" for Prince Charles (aged almost three) and an "Indian doll" for Princess Anne (aged one). *The Des Moines Register* found Elizabeth up close appeared "nervous and fatigued" after two dozen days on tour through Canada, while Philip, on the other hand, "was booming with vigor and wisecracks as befits a royal salesman for the beleaguered British empire. . . . Philip, to tell the truth, almost stole the show from his wife during the couple's first hours in Washington. Thousands of women along the line of the motorcade shrieked, 'There he is' as the big blond boy with the big smile waved to the crowds."

Elizabeth had the last laugh on the press corps. Once she was back in Canada, the princess used her talent for mimicry to mock US news reporters while she did some filming of her own—a hobby of the couple's. As she pointed a camera at her husband, she cried out in a nasal American voice, "Hey! You there! Hey, Dook! Look this way a sec! Dat's it! Thanks a lot!"

Elizabeth and Philip departed from a capital "completely captivated by their youthful charm and grace," according to the United Press news agency. This was a coup for the British and showed just what a royal visitation could do to encourage warm feelings between the nations above the fray of day-to-day politics, especially as the imbalance in their global strength was becoming clear.

A few days later, on November 5, the US press observed Truman showing a telegram to Dwight D. Eisenhower, who was then supreme commander of the North Atlantic Treaty Organization (NATO). Eisenhower could be heard asking Truman how he liked the visit by Princess Elizabeth, and the president replied: "She was wonderful." He then handed the general a telegram, saying, "Here's something that will tickle you." This was probably the message sent by the King on November 4, now held in the Truman Presidential Library, which read: "The Queen and I would like you to know how touched we are to hear of the friendly welcome given to our daughter and son-in-law in Washington. Our thoughts go back to our own visit in 1939, of which we have such happy memories. We are so grateful to you Mr. President for your kindness and hospitality to our children. George R."

However, another British message had arrived at the same time. Churchill had seen the political opportunity created by the visit immediately. State Department records show that on November 5, Churchill had Sir Oliver Franks, the British ambassador in Washington, deliver a written request inviting himself over for a "renewal of our former comradeship" in the US capital, as "there are many things I need to talk over with you" and "also as Minister of Defence I should like sometime to meet your Military Chiefs. . . . Please let me know what would be convenient and agreeable to you." Before she had become the monarch, a pattern was set by Elizabeth's first meeting with a US president that not only could such encounters renew Anglo-US relations, but they could also be used to advance hard-nosed national goals—even in the era when kings and queens had been relieved of all real political power. Truman was in no position to refuse Churchill, and the talks in early January reset the basis for postwar military cooperation between the two nations, even if the seventy-seven-year-old prime minister did not get everything he wanted.

After almost five weeks of touring, the nervous princess who had flown across the Atlantic departed back to Britain by ship (with ninety-seven pieces of luggage) from Portugal Cove in Newfoundland "a laughing, relaxed figure," according to the Canadian author Pierre Berton. She left a lasting impression in the United States: in the annual Associated Press poll of female editors in December, Elizabeth was named runner-up as

"Woman of the Year" behind the intrepid war reporter Marguerite Higgins. That Christmas, Truman sent George VI a photograph of himself and the young royals, leading the King to send a thank-you note written on December 22, 1951, expressing his "glad" feelings that the president would soon be meeting Churchill.

"He is a wise man and understands the problems of this troubled world," the King wrote. "I have always felt that our two countries cannot progress one without the other, and I feel that this meeting will unite us even more closely." It was Truman's final missive from the King. His presidency outlasted the reign of George VI, who died at fifty-six from a coronary thrombosis just three months after Elizabeth returned from North America.

In his diary in the hours after the King's death became known, Truman wrote that George VI "was a grand man, worth a pair of his brother Ed," a reference to Edward VIII. Truman recalled how, when he met the King in August 1945 in Plymouth, George asked him for autographs on behalf of his daughters (then nineteen and fourteen).

His public admiration of Elizabeth was not merely for show, as shown when he wrote in his private diary entry: "Elizabeth, the King's daughter, will be a good and great Queen. She is a grand person—and so is her consort."

CHAPTER 2

We thoroughly believe that in the warmer, closer, stronger cooperation between your country and ours lies the best hope for the
security and peace of the world.

—Dwight D. Eisenhower, October 17, 1957

O ne legendary wartime leader returned to power in Britain shortly before Elizabeth's reign began, and another would soon be elected president of the United States.

Churchill and Dwight Eisenhower each had his own special relationship with the Queen, who knew them personally from an early age. Churchill took it upon himself to become a mentor to Elizabeth as she learned the political ropes, while Eisenhower had more intimate access to her family than any other American president she would know. He was the only one to be invited to stay at Balmoral Castle, the royal family's private summer retreat in Scotland—and the only one to receive a recipe from her.

"Seeing a picture of you in today's newspaper, standing in front of a barbecue grilling quail, reminded me that I had never sent you the recipe of the drop scones [also known as Scotch pancakes] which I promised you at Balmoral," the young Queen wrote in early 1960. "I now hasten to do so, and I do hope you will find them successful." One of Churchill's lessons for Elizabeth was to advise her to stay close to the Americans, and that was exactly what she ensured she and her family did.

Ike, as he was widely known, was instantly recognizable and beloved in Britain, where he had been showered with awards from a grateful nation for his wartime service as supreme commander of the Allied Expeditionary Force in Europe. Back in June 1945, on a visit to London, General Eisenhower (with Churchill at his elbow) had talked of the "bonds that must always remain" between the two countries and had praised his joint staff of Britons and Americans who proved "it can always be done by our two peoples, provided only both show the same goodwill, the same forbearance, and the same objective attitude that the British and Americans so amply demonstrated in nearly three years of bitter campaigning."

This was a proviso on the durability of the alliance that went largely unnoticed in the euphoria of the moment, but by the end of Eisenhower's first term in the Oval Office, he had become so furious with Britain that he effectively threatened to bankrupt the country. In a pattern that would repeat itself in the history of the Special Relationship, it would fall to the Queen to help patch up the wounds with her own brand of royal diplomacy.

Elizabeth's connection with Eisenhower predated her relationship with Truman. It was rooted in her formative war years, when she saw the commitment of America and its GIs to the existential battle for freedom against fascism. It gave her a life-long appreciation of the United States.

However, the King and his daughters inadvertently avoided an initial encounter soon after the rapidly rising general was appointed to his first command position in Britain in 1942. The Queen recounted years later how, as a teenager at Windsor Castle, she had taken refuge—along with her parents and sister!—under a covered table on a terrace of Windsor Castle so as not to be seen by a group of passing US servicemen.

"We all dived under the table and hid until this party had gone round," Elizabeth said in footage for a 1969 TV documentary. "We didn't know who they were, but we could tell they were Americans. We inquired afterwards . . . and somebody said it was General Eisenhower. It didn't mean anything in those days. Of course, afterwards my father told the story to Eisenhower, who was so staggered by the King of England hiding under his own dinner table when he had a general just walking around. It always amused him. He always referred to it whenever we met him. That was the sort of thing Papa enjoyed very much."

The war eventually brought the King close to the general. After the Allied victory in the North Africa campaign under Eisenhower's command in 1943, George VI went to Algiers to present him with the Knight Grand Cross of the Order of the Bath, making Ike an honorary member of an order of chivalry founded by George I in 1725. Shortly after the Normandy landings on June 6, 1944, the King visited the famous beaches and wrote to Eisenhower, the overall commander, expressing "intense admiration for all those who planned and organised so vast a project, and for the gallant and successful execution of it." In June 1945, Eisenhower added to his knighthood by becoming the first American to receive the exclusive Order of Merit, presented by the King at Buckingham Palace.

While on a holiday visit a year later, Ike, by then chief of staff of the US Army; his wife, Mamie; and their twenty-four-year-old son, John, were invited to spend the weekend at Balmoral as guests of the King and his family. The Eisenhowers were immersed in the Highland experience. George VI wore the distinctive gray, black, and red plaid Balmoral tartan designed by Queen Victoria's consort, Prince Albert, in 1853 and banned by royal decree from use by commoners, with one exception: the royal piper, who serenaded the dinner guests and played while John, in his US Army captain uniform, danced with the young princesses, Elizabeth and Margaret, dressed in tartan sashes. The following morning, the Eisenhowers accompanied the royal family to Crathie Kirk, the granite-walled Gothic Revival parish church for Balmoral, joining the congregation in hymns and kneeling together in the front pews in prayer.

The royals maintained regular correspondence with Eisenhower, himself an avid letter writer, up to and beyond King George's death. Eisenhower described the King in his letter of condolence to the Queen Mother as "a gentle human being" and "an inspirational force." He remained attentive to his relationship with the British royals. In March 1953, he sent a message via the US ambassador in London, asking the envoy to "please extend to Her Majesty and to all the members and peoples of the British Commonwealth my deep personal sympathy on the passing of Queen Mary," the widow of George V and Elizabeth's grandmother, who had just died aged eighty-five. "The hearts of all Americans go out to Her Majesty to-night as our prayers are extended to her, Princess Margaret and the members of the Royal Family for the great personal loss they have sustained."

Several of the royal horses stabled at the Royal Mews at Buckingham Palace were named after service chiefs, and a gelding named Eisenhower was one of the eight-strong team of Windsor Greys that pulled the Gold State Coach that took Elizabeth II to her coronation in June 1953. An estimated fifty-five million Americans saw the event on television—approximately one-third of the US population. This led *The New York Times* to proclaim that the ceremony to place the Imperial State Crown on the twenty-seven-year-old Queen's head was "the birth of international television."

Just as she had on her previous North American tour in 1951, Elizabeth arrived from Canada for her first state visit to the United States in October 1957 by air. Flying with the Royal Canadian Air Force to Patrick Henry Airport in Newport News, Virginia, she took part in celebrations for the 350th anniversary of the founding of the state (named after the virginal Queen Elizabeth I). This began with a tour of exhibits from the Jamestown Colony (named after Elizabeth I's successor, James I), where the English established their first permanent New World settlement in 1607. The American crowd that greeted her at the airport, estimated at fifty thousand, where they heard a booming twenty-one-gun salute, outdid Ottawa in "size, warmth and enthusiasm," according to reporters following the royal tour.

Against the backdrop of Britain's own unraveling empire, the Queen recast the colonization of the United States and its struggle for self-governance as a matter of shared pride and part of a common experiment in freedom.

"The great American nation was born at this historic place, 350 years ago," Elizabeth II said as she was welcomed by Governor Thomas Stanley at Jamestown Festival Park. "I cannot think of a more appropriate point for us to start our visit to the United States," she added. "The settlement in Jamestown was the beginning of a series of overseas settlements made throughout the world by British pioneers. Jamestown grew and became the United States. Those other settlements grew and became nations now united in our great Commonwealth. . . . In essence, they are both stories of experiments and adventures in freedom."

Perhaps it was simply the distance from Britain, perhaps there was something infectious about the pioneering American spirit, but the royal couple showed an informal side rarely seen back home. When Prince Philip spotted a young woman and two children waving a Union Jack flag "and 'hip-hip-hooraying' in British fashion," according to *The Philadelphia Inquirer*, he wandered over to chat with her. Learning that she was a British war bride and the two youngsters at her side were hers, the Prince remarked: "Well, you're well in now!"

The subject of a state visit to the US had been discussed in March between Eisenhower and British prime minister Harold Macmillan. The two nations, seemingly so close after their shared victory just a few years before in World War II, found themselves at a dramatic inflection point following the British invasion of Egypt in late 1956 to take control of the Suez Canal. Simply put: the US opposed the use of armed force to support Britain's ever-more-tenuous hold on its possessions around the world. As *Life* magazine had pointed out in an "Open Letter from the Editors of *Life* to the People of England" way back in 1942, "One thing we are sure we are not fighting for is to hold the British Empire together. We don't like to put the matter so bluntly, but we don't want you to have any illusions." Eisenhower furiously threatened to block the International Monetary Fund from providing Britain with a vital loan and to dump US holdings of pound-sterling bonds to force the British to end the conflict.

Britain's delusions of grandeur were thoroughly punctured by the episode, with Eisenhower's response showing where real clout lay in the postwar order: America was the undisputed western superpower. Sentimental concerns about any Special Relationship were not going to stop the president from taking what action he thought necessary to avoid a potential escalation into confrontation with the Soviet Union. With the Suez Crisis allayed, Eisenhower and Macmillan were keen to get ties back on track. It was left up to the Queen to complete the job.

The urgency of a full rapprochement between the two allies was driven home shortly before the royals left London, when Russia launched Sputnik 1, the world's first artificial satellite. The achievement dominated headlines and spurred an American effort to catch up in the space race. The day before she departed, Elizabeth wrote: "I do hope our visit will be of value between the two countries. There does seem to be a much closer feeling between the US and ourselves, especially since the Russian satellite has come to shake everyone about their views on Russian scientific progress." The flyover times for Sputnik were listed daily in the papers, but coverage of the royals would finally help knock the little metal ball out of the headlines.

Once in Washington, DC, Elizabeth and Philip traveled with the First Couple in Eisenhower's famous bubble-top limousine, a Lincoln Cosmopolitan convertible that he had fitted with a plexiglass top so he could see and be seen in all weather. Happily, the rain held off for the drive into the city, although drizzle had set in by the time of the formal wreath-laying at Arlington National Cemetery. Capitol police chief Robert V. Murray estimated the crowd lining the streets from the airport to the White House at one million people, which he proclaimed "one of the greatest in the history of Washington." The Queen would stay in the White House private quarters—a rare honor—appropriately enough in the Queen's Bedroom, formerly known as the Rose Room, which began to gain its new name after hosting her mother on the 1939 royal visit. The Queen Mother also stayed there on a solo visit with the Eisenhowers in 1954.

There were ardent declarations of friendship and admiration from the president. "Even more than the pleasure that your visit brings us, we are conscious of its importance, because of its effect on strengthening the ties of friendship that bind our two countries together," Eisenhower said at Washington National Airport. "Those ties have grown up in periods of tranquility and peace. They have been tested in the crucible of war when we have fought side by side to defend the values we hold dear. . . . We thoroughly believe that in the warmer, closer, stronger cooperation between your country and ours lies the best hope for the security and peace of the world."

It was as if the Suez debacle—when the US strongly believed it was British actions that posed a grave threat to the security and peace of the world—had never happened. In his toast at dinner that evening, Eisenhower dwelled at length on his personal relationship with the UK. "To me was given the great privilege of serving with the people of that nation for almost four years," he said. "From the royal family to the humblest citizen, they so conducted themselves that they enlisted the admiration, the liking, and the respect of every American who came in contact with them."

Sputnik was clearly on his mind too, and he echoed Churchill's expansive view of the Special Relationship by urging, "Our scientists must work together. NATO should not be thought of merely as a military alliance."

The five-course white-tie state dinner at the White House was a glittering occasion, with the thirty-one-year-old Queen wearing her favorite diamond-studded tiara, a wedding gift from Queen Mary, and the kingfisher blue Order of the Garter sash over a pale green satin dress featuring Canadian maple leaf designs, along with diamond-and-pearl earrings and necklace. The president sported his British Order of Merit medal on its red-and-blue-striped ribbon. Guests, including the prime minister of Canada, John Diefenbaker, were served chilled Hawaiian pineapple followed by cream of almond soup, broiled fillet of English sole, roast Long Island duckling, and frozen Nesselrode cream—a Victorian dessert of cream-enriched custard mixed with chestnut puree and candied fruits—with brandied sauce. All was eaten with gold cutlery from gold-rimmed white crockery on tables adorned with pink carnations and candelabra.

Jacqueline Cochran, a pioneering aviator and active Republican, was among the guests seated not far down the table from the Queen and the president. "That was the gayest, prettiest dinner that I've ever seen at the White House, and I've been to eleven," she recalled. "All the pink and white, just marvelous." She found herself next to Senate leader Lyndon Johnson, a Democrat. "We were seated so tightly that we literally almost couldn't eat because there were 92 people. Well, I guess they wanted as many of the family and important people as they could and I don't blame them and I sure felt important that night," Cochran said. Elizabeth II was "like a little girl talking . . . so charming and so pretty," she said.

But not everyone was enthralled, Cochran observed. "The Queen got up to make her toast and Prince Philip stifled a yawn and looked exceedingly bored. This was the funniest thing I've ever watched at such a dinner." Jet lag cannot really be used as an excuse for the Queen's consort—they had already spent five days in North America—but these had been jam-packed with events, speeches, and photo-calls.

In his speech, Eisenhower concluded: "The respect we have for Britain is epitomized in the affection we have for the royal family, who have honored us so much by making this visit to our shores. . . . I want again to say that my faith in the future of these two great countries and the whole Commonwealth of the British nations—indeed of the whole free world—is absolutely unimpeachable."

Elizabeth II wished the president health and happiness. "I pray that the ancient ties of friendship between the people of the United States and of my peoples may long endure," she said.

The Special Relationship was back on.

Britain's prime minister wasted no time in capitalizing on the positive vibes to arrange a meeting of his own with his US counterpart. Macmillan announced that very day that he would be in Washington for intensive talks the following week, with senior cabinet members attending, covering the combustible situation in the Middle East as well as the Soviet satellite. Meanwhile, the young royal couple still had a lot more of America to drink in.

The highlights of the trip included visits to two American institutions: a football game and a supermarket in Maryland, not far from the capital. For the outing, the Queen donned a $15,000 full-length mink coat gifted to her by the Mutation Mink Breeders Association of the United States, described as "deep bluish brown with slightly lighter under hair." On the way to the football game at College Park, Maryland, word was sent to the State Department escort that the Queen wanted to see "how American housewives shop for food." A security detail was dispatched to the nearest Giant supermarket, where the startled assistant manager had an hour to get ready for an unexpected royal visit.

Back at the game, the Queen was seated near the University of North Carolina coach, "Big Jim" Tatum, "a man who hates to lose football games," according to the Scripps-Howard agency. As Maryland progressed to a comfortable 21–7 victory, "Tatum's choice of phrases grew saltier . . . and his clarion tones could be heard a good three rows beyond the Queen's box." Elizabeth II "mostly wore a poker face." The physicality of the sport made an impression on the Queen, who asked Maryland's governor Theodore McKeldin: "How can they hit each other that hard without injury?" McKeldin replied: "Because they are in good condition and trained for it—and they wear fourteen pounds of equipment."

Afterward the royals dropped into the Giant supermarket in West Hyattsville, chatting to bemused afternoon shoppers "and studying the food packaging and mass sales operation." Large-scale supermarkets were virtually unknown in Britain at the time. The Queen admired the grocery carts. ("How nice that they can bring their children along," she exclaimed.)

Philip, meanwhile, was offered a sample of fresh cheese on a cracker, which he munched thoughtfully. "Good for mice," he said. He then stood "almost in awe before a rack filled with boxes of aluminum foil until a woman came up to him and explained that it is used for cooking food in ovens." The mink-coated Queen, who struck quite a contrast with "kerchiefed housewives in pincurls," thanked Donald D'Avanzo, the assistant manager, saying: "I enjoyed it very much." The store manager had been called to come in and escort the visitors but, thinking it was a practical joke, stayed at home.

D'Avanzo said, "It was the greatest thing that ever happened to me."

The next day Elizabeth made a private visit to an equine training center in Middleburg, Virginia, run by Paul Mellon, one of America's richest men and a fellow breeder of Thoroughbreds. She flew back in a British embassy aircraft to Washington, where, according to the Associated Press, she "stepped off the plane chewing gum." This was definitely *not* a part of normal royal behavior and, again, suggested a freedom she felt in America that would never have been seen back home.

The couple's farewell to the Eisenhowers at the conclusion of a "triumphant four-day visit to the nation's capital by the demure queen and her dashing husband" was "an easy-going exchange, much in the manner of suburban couples taking leave," the AP reported. The Windsors were getting along famously with their hosts.

"Please come back—it was nice to have you," the sixty-seven-year-old president told a smiling Queen as they shook hands at the White House North Portico. She was heard to say, "I do hope you'll come."

The British press voiced indignation that North Americans were treated to a more relaxed and spontaneous Queen than in the UK: "Why did she have to cross the Atlantic to become REAL?" wondered the *Daily Herald*. "People here have been reading of the Queen going about freely among ordinary people, behaving like a natural person. Canada loved it. America was bowled over by it. Why is it not allowed to happen here?"

The Queen rounded off her trip with two huge evening events in New York City, where she also added to her roster of presidential encounters by sitting next to eighty-three-year-old Herbert Hoover, who served from 1929 to 1933, during lunch at the Waldorf-Astoria. Later, at a dinner there for 4,500 guests thrown by the English-Speaking Union and the Pilgrims of the United States, closed-circuit television filmed her eating, usually a no-no. Dressed in a multicolored lace gown in iridescent shades of pale pink, blue, and green, she was then on to a glittering ball for another 4,500 guests at the Seventh Regiment Armory, a short trip along Park Avenue.

According to *The Philadelphia Inquirer*, the "petite monarch . . . held all of New York in the palm of her majestic hand." The royals then made a late-night drive to Idlewild Airport (later named after John F. Kennedy), where New Yorkers, including some women in bathrobes and curlers, lined the streets to catch a glimpse. The US chief of protocol overheard the Queen remark to her husband: "Philip, look at all those people in their nightclothes! I certainly wouldn't come out in my nightclothes to see anyone drive by, no matter who it was!"

The hectic day only whetted the royal appetite for more. "One day in New York is really just a teaser," she said, before boarding her Royal Air Force DC-7C for the propeller plane's fourteen-hour flight to London. The New York Sanitation Department recorded that two hundred tons of ticker tape and shredded telephone directories were deposited on the streets during the royal parade that day.

It would be just under two years before the Queen returned to North America for a joint US-Canada celebration on June 26, 1959, to mark the opening of the Saint Lawrence Seaway, a seven-lock, four-canal, 370-mile waterway for oceangoing liners linking the five Great Lakes to the Atlantic. At the launch ceremony, Eisenhower stood alongside Elizabeth II in her role as Queen of Canada as he proclaimed the huge project "a magnificent symbol to the entire world of the achievements possible to democratic nations peacefully working together for the common good." It was an occasion for emphasizing the bonds between friendly nations, in this case neighbors America and Canada, who "have grown up together" and share a common border with "neither gun nor fortress" dividing them.

With tens of thousands of Quebecois in the crowd, both the monarch and the president delivered part of their address in French, although in Eisenhower's case this amounted to a single sentence in his Kansas accent, which translated as "I am very happy to be with you in Canada again, where a year ago I had such a pleasant visit." *The Victoria Daily Times* observed contentedly that the Queen's "royal upbringing gave her an edge over the President in the French tongue," with nearly one-third of her speech in the language.

The formal launch occurred when the Queen, the president, and Prime Minister Diefenbaker of Canada boarded the royal yacht *Britannia* and sailed through the ceremonial gates a few minutes after midday. The sun burst through following a foggy start, and although this later gave way to an overcast afternoon, spirits were not dampened. As *Britannia* was slightly behind schedule, the vessels in the Port of Montreal began sounding their horns and whistles prematurely on the dot of twelve as they had been briefed, but the fireworks were held back for the yacht's big moment at 12:03 p.m.

Ike and the Queen waved from the bridge to the throngs lining the shore before entering the first of three locks on a thirty-one-mile cruise upstream, which included an onboard luncheon. The Buckingham Palace chef served up soft-boiled eggs on mousse of foie gras jellied with port wine sauce, chicken garnished with asparagus tips, and cauliflower served with

Madeira wine gravy followed by strawberry ice bombe fruit salad.

Five hours later, when the time came for Eisenhower to disembark and board a helicopter to his plane, the Queen bid him goodbye, saying, "It's been quite a day."

Ike replied: "Yes, but an enjoyable one." It had indeed been eventful: the final lock of the day proved too tricky for *Britannia*. Elizabeth joined sailors at the rail of the 412-foot vessel to try to push it away from the wall, but it took a hefty scrape as the water rose, depositing a streak of gold paint on the stonework. It was not the first mishap of the week. Prince Philip, who held the highest Royal Navy rank of admiral of the fleet, was at the helm two days earlier when he banged the royal craft into a pier while docking, leaving a twenty-five-foot graze along the hull.

Throughout this forty-five-day North America tour, mainly through Canada but also including a later stop by *Britannia* in Chicago—where Elizabeth lost a filling and made an emergency visit to a dentist—the Queen kept a closely guarded secret. She was pregnant. It was a struggle to keep it quiet, however, and speculation mounted when she took a couple of days off due to an "upset stomach," sending Philip to the Yukon without her. A royal press officer issued a statement denying pregnancy claims in the French media as "absolute nonsense."

By the end of the tour the British press were reporting how tired the Queen looked after a schedule that covered fifteen thousand miles by plane, train, and yacht, involving up to a dozen public appearances a day. She called off plans to return leisurely to Britain aboard *Britannia* and flew instead. The formal pregnancy announcement followed five days later, exciting much debate as to whether child number three was planned, given the gap after Charles, ten, and Anne, eight. It was the first baby for a reigning monarch since Queen Victoria's ninth, Beatrice, in 1857.

The pregnancy did not disrupt plans for Eisenhower's trip to the UK three weeks later for political talks with Macmillan ahead of a critical Camp David meeting with Soviet president Nikita Khrushchev. Macmillan had his own reasons for the invitation—he was up for reelection six weeks later and believed that cozying up with the popular president would play well with voters. The Queen did not hesitate to invite Ike up to Balmoral for an overnight stay, his second private sojourn with the royal family in Scotland and a mark of true acceptance. Just as he had done thirteen years earlier when a guest of her father, he landed at Dyce Airport (now Aberdeen International) and was driven the final fifty miles to the castle, this time accompanied by Prince Philip. His flight from London was the first by a US president in the plane of a foreign nation, a gleaming silver RAF Comet, attesting to the strength of the two nations' ties.

Breaking her vow not to make any more public appearances until the birth of her child, Elizabeth II greeted the fedora-wearing president at the gates of the Balmoral estate, accompanied by her sister and mother, for inspection of a Guard of Honor of Royal Highland Fusiliers watched by a crowd of excited locals.

"How nice of you to let me come," Ike said as he shook the Queen's hand. As the spectators burst into cheering and applause, he removed his hat and raised it aloft. This visit was all about relaxation; the talk was of "peace, babies, and absent friends"—a classic example of the "soft diplomacy" practiced by the Queen on behalf of her country not merely to make visiting statesmen feel at ease but to deepen their attachment to Britain. Not that that was really necessary in Eisenhower's case.

Elizabeth drove her guest herself for an afternoon picnic on the Balmoral grounds—she loved to drive after training as a teenage mechanic during World War II. In his thank-you letter Eisenhower could not resist a reference to the big news. "My wife and I are delighted about the coming 'event,' as is everyone in your Kingdom," he wrote. Macmillan was delighted with the president's visit—and he won his reelection.

While confined in the later stages of her pregnancy with Prince Andrew, the thirty-three-year-old monarch wrote a chatty letter, dated January 24, 1960, enclosing her recipe and a photograph from the visit. The "drop scones," very similar to American pancakes but with more sugar in the batter, came by their name in reference to the method of dropping the mixture onto a hot cooking surface. She was reminded to send the recipe by seeing a press photo of Eisenhower at the hunting estate of his friend W. Alton Jones, an oil millionaire, in Albany, Georgia, during a weekend's shooting.

"Though the quantities are for 16 people, when there are fewer, I generally put in less flour and milk, but use the other ingredients as stated," she wrote. "I have also tried using golden syrup or treacle instead of only sugar and that can be very good, too. I think the mixture needs a great deal of beating while making, and shouldn't stand about too long before cooking."

Elizabeth added that she had followed "with intense interest and much admiration your tremendous journey to so many countries but feel we shall never again be able to claim that <u>we</u>

are being made to do too much on our future tours! We remember with such pleasure your visit to Balmoral, and I hope the photograph will be a reminder of the very happy day you spent with us." She signed off: "With all good wishes to you and Mrs. Eisenhower. Yours sincerely, Elizabeth R."

The recipe called for four teacups flour, four tablespoons caster sugar, two teacups milk, two whole eggs, two teaspoons bicarbonate of soda, three teaspoons cream of tartar, and two tablespoons melted butter. It instructed: "Beat eggs, sugar, and about half the milk together, add flour, and mix well together, adding remainder of milk as required, also bicarbonate and cream of tartar, fold in the melted butter."

The president responded politely, writing: "I hope we may soon use it. You will understand my rather woeful ignorance of culinary practices when I tell you that I did not recognize the term 'caster' as a type of sugar. But when I called the British embassy for help, the problem was promptly solved for me."

Susan Eisenhower, Ike's granddaughter, remarked: "The key to know here is that my grandfather was the cook" in his marriage. "He enjoyed cooking so much that he had a kitchen installed on the third floor of the White House." She also recalled that her grandfather, much like Churchill, took up painting while in office as a form of relaxation. "It's very touching that he painted both Princess Anne and Prince Charles" while they were children, she said.

Eisenhower remained in correspondence with the Queen Mother for many years after his presidency ended in 1961, and he and

Mamie lunched privately at Buckingham Palace in August 1962 at the invitation of the Queen, when he also called on his old friend Churchill. He was back in January 1965 for the great man's state funeral. He was asked by the BBC to deliver a eulogy during live coverage of Churchill's casket making its way out of St. Paul's Cathedral to Tower Pier on the river Thames, where it was loaded onto a barge for a final two-mile journey through the heart of the capital.

"At this moment, as our hearts stand at attention, we say our affectionate, though sad, goodbye to the leader to whom the entire body of free men owes so much," Ike said. "May we carry on his work until no nation lies in captivity; no man is denied opportunity for fulfilment. And now, to you, Sir Winston—my old friend—farewell."

This closeness to Churchill was another reason why Eisenhower had a unique place among US presidents in the Queen's affections. She was drawn to him by his personal relationship with both her political mentor and her beloved father, while his association with the war reminded Elizabeth of her formative years. As a result, Eisenhower was treated with a closeness like no president before or since. Describing his 1959 visit in his book *Waging Peace*, Eisenhower wrote: "One quality of the royal family that has always intrigued me is the informality which prevails when its members are at home among themselves, particularly at Balmoral." He saw like no other US leader the way the Queen "acted as hostess and simple housewife" in private. Elizabeth II, who insisted on donning rubber gloves and washing the dishes after Balmoral picnics, loved the way Eisenhower fit right in.

Ike returned this intimacy with his own thoughtful hospitality. Jack Woodward, Eisenhower's personal steward on his Columbine planes, recalled a deep level of affinity. "We made two trips with Queen Elizabeth. . . . One time she came to visit with the President, we flew her around the United States, kind of a goodwill tour," he said. "After the second tour with Queen Elizabeth, we had gotten to know each other real well. . . . It got to the point on our second trip where . . . I was giving her Eisenhower matches and Columbine matches, she was giving me matches from her yacht and so forth. We were talking about our children and her children."

At Balmoral, Woodward said, "I went along as the valet to the President and he introduced his staff . . . He introduced John [Eisenhower] and Barbara [John's wife], he introduced General Snyder, his physician. Then he went to introduce me, and he said: 'Your Majesty, I would like to have you meet, ah'—couple of 'ah's' came out, every time he said 'ah' his face got a little redder. He finally says: 'Damn it, his name is Woody.'

"The Queen very graciously says, 'Yes, Mr. President. Sergeant Woodward and I have met before' and smoothed it all over." It was this type of familiarity that was so important in repairing the bonds between their countries after the Suez calamity and making sure that the transatlantic alliance remained not just strong but special.

CHAPTER 3

We shall always cherish the memory of that delightful evening.
—John F. Kennedy, June 9, 1961

John F. Kennedy's note of thanks after his rather awkward first and only black-tie dinner at Buckingham Palace was unfailingly polite.

The youngest elected US president arrived in London shattered from a bruising two-day summit with Soviet leader Nikita Khrushchev in Vienna and, ahead of his rendezvous with the Queen, unburdened himself to a close friend, the British aristocrat David Ormsby-Gore, and to Prime Minister Harold Macmillan during several hours of private talks. Kennedy relied on both Brits as invaluable confidants throughout his presidency.

However, at the table that night Elizabeth struggled to get to know a commander in chief who preferred the counsel of men—there were no women in his cabinet nor among the close circle of buddies he turned to for support. It did not help that there was tension between the thirty-five-year-old monarch and First Lady Jacqueline Kennedy, three years her junior, that spilled over into the evening. Jackie later gossiped that she thought her hostess "resented" her, leading to a dramatized portrayal in *The Crown*, the Netflix royal family saga. This was exaggerated, as was the melodramatic depiction of the Queen consumed with envy at the outburst of public enthusiasm for the glamorous Kennedys, especially the way that Jackie was feted in France on the first leg of their European tour.

However awkward that first dinner was, the strains were quickly forgotten and Elizabeth II would welcome Jackie on future occasions—although there would never, tragically, be time for the state visit envisaged for her husband. Nor did the relationship between the countries suffer. To a greater extent than any other American president of her reign, Kennedy was a lifelong Anglophile who respected Britain's indomitable resistance to fascism, its democratic traditions, and its influential, if waning, global role. While Jackie upstaged Elizabeth in the pages of *Vogue* and was dubbed "America's Queen" by her biographer, JFK leaned heavily on British advice throughout his presidency—sometimes to the frustration of his own cabinet members—and modernized the Special Relationship to ensure that both countries remained firm allies ready for the challenges of the nuclear age.

The dynamic between Britain's young monarch and America's powerful presidency changed dramatically with Kennedy's election in 1960. Part of the fascination with Elizabeth when she came to the throne was her youthful contrast to other world leaders, including the first two presidents of her reign—father figures who had children older than the fresh-faced new queen.

But as much as she featured on magazine covers throughout the 1950s, no one could accuse her of being fashionable—in fact, a good deal of the public interest was with her youthful embodiment of tradition, formality, and continuity. If she wore the occasional strapless dress, it was invariably a ball gown rather than anything more casual or risqué. Her husband looked his best in full naval uniform. The royal approach was summed up by one of her favorite designers, Sir Hardy Amies, who helped to style the Queen from 1950 to 1990. Asked by the New York stylist Simon Doonan why he never dressed Elizabeth according to trends, Amies replied: "Young man, you know that Her Majesty must never appear to be chic. There is an unkindness to chic, and she can never appear to be unkind."

JFK was nine years older than the Queen, and yet here was a more modern head of state with a First Lady who was fast becoming a fashion icon in her own right. This was also a First Family that resembled a royal dynasty as the Kennedys set about building a brand and promoting themselves under the influence of their powerful and ambitious patriarch, Joseph Sr., a prominent Democrat who considered running for the party's presidential nomination in 1940. They used wealth and political influence to stay close to the levers of power and in the public eye, where, just like the British royals, they would experience dazzling benefits but also devastating repercussions as a result of their prominence and celebrity status.

As with Truman and Eisenhower, the Queen's initial meeting with her next US president went back to her days as a young princess. In fact, she first met Kennedy as a result of his father's appointment as US ambassador in London by President Franklin D. Roosevelt in March 1938. This opened up the glamorous world of prewar London society to the older Kennedy children—notably Joe Jr., John (known as Jack), and Kathleen (known as Kick)—each of whom had an entrée into the "Season" of glitzy dinner parties, balls, and polo matches running through spring and summer, where royalty was often present. Kick was a debutante at Queen Charlotte's Ball, an annual party dating back to 1780, named after George III's consort, where young ladies were "introduced" into high society by being formally presented to the monarch. In Kick's case, the monarch in question was George VI, Elizabeth's father, who by tradition stood next to a large birthday cake as one by one the young women stepped forward and curtsied. Kick was such a triumph that she was named 1938's Debutante of the Year.

In March 1939, at the age of twenty-one, Jack Kennedy took the spring semester off from his studies at Harvard and began a job assisting his father at the embassy. The position involved some light administrative duties, but really it was a jumping-off point for extensive partying in London and travel throughout Europe. He donned white tie and tails for his own presentation to the King at a St. James's Palace levee (a courtly ceremony that entailed officials, diplomats, and military officers stepping forward in the Throne Room when their names were called to approach the monarch, who was seated on a dais).

"Met the king this morning at a Court Levee," Kennedy wrote to Lem Billings, his close friend from prep school. "The king stands and you go up and bow." Afterward he had tea with a group that included twelve-year-old Princess Elizabeth, "with whom I made a great deal of time," he told Billings.

Nothing more is recorded of that first prewar meeting between two youngsters who would go on to become heads of state and at one time or other the most famous people in the world. JFK was more interested in older girls—and in his own appearance.

On the evening of March 9, he attended a palace event "in my new silk breeches, which are cut to my crotch tightly and in which I look mightily attractive," he playfully informed Billings. Kennedy's travels to various countries preparing for conflict gave him an extraordinary firsthand insight into the precarious balance of power in Europe, and that summer he found himself with Ormsby-Gore in Berlin, the German capital, on August 23, the day that Germany and Russia surprised the world by announcing a nonaggression pact despite their previous animosity. He was given a secret message by the diplomat in charge of the US embassy for his father in London to pass on to FDR: German dictator Adolf Hitler would invade Poland within a week, making war inevitable.

Ambassador Joseph Kennedy and his wife, Rose, saw much more of Princess Elizabeth during frequent audiences with her parents as talks between the British and the Americans became more urgent. The young princess was increasingly invited to gatherings of international dignitaries as part of her training for her future role as Queen. At one Sunday lunch in April 1939 with Neville Chamberlain, the Conservative prime minister whose strenuous efforts to find accommodation with Hitler to avoid war the US ambassador admired and supported, Joe was seated between Queen Elizabeth and the future queen, still just twelve. Joe recorded that the princess "handles herself beautifully." She talked about a major American export: Walt Disney's hit film *Snow White and the Seven Dwarfs* and her favorite dwarf, Dopey.

Elizabeth discovered a ladybug on the table and—amid discussion of Britain's attempts to reach agreements with Balkan nations to side with the Western allies rather than the fascist powers—offered it to Chamberlain as a good luck charm. The bug was passed from spoon to spoon down the table to the Queen, who placed it on the seventy-year-old prime minister's suit, where it crawled onto his shoulder.

"It will probably go down my neck," he complained, looking uncomfortable. The Queen carefully removed it and passed it back to her daughter. It did not augur well.

Chamberlain's policy of appeasement was already faltering and would prove a devastating failure, as he himself was forced to admit in Parliament on September 3, 1939, the day he declared war on Germany following Hitler's refusal to answer a British ultimatum to withdraw from Poland. Joe and Rose took Joe Jr., Kick, and Jack—by now safely back from Berlin—to the public Strangers' Gallery above the House of Commons chamber that afternoon, where, after scurrying into a bomb shelter underneath Parliament when an air-raid siren sounded, they watched as the crushed prime minister told MPs: "Everything that I have worked for, everything that I have hoped for, everything that I have believed in during my public life, has crashed into ruins."

Joseph Kennedy's tenure did not end well either. His bluntly expressed defeatist and isolationist views angered his London contacts and the British media. Joe made no secret of his pessimism over Britain's chances of prevailing against Germany and constantly cautioned the US against becoming militarily involved. This stance greatly upset both the King and Churchill, Chamberlain's successor as prime minister. George VI wrote an angry letter to Joe Kennedy, described by his private secretary Alan Lascelles as "a stinker."

It was clear on both sides of the Atlantic that the ambassador could not continue, and he flew back to the US in October 1940 amid Hitler's relentless bombing of London, having been cut out of the real Anglo-American negotiations. He formally offered his resignation the day after Roosevelt's third election victory in November, further damaging his reputation by incautiously telling a journalist his view that "democracy is finished in England. It may be here." He meant that the war powers being taken by the British government were squashing democracy, as they could in the United States if it entered the conflict.

He also expressed his admiration for Queen Elizabeth, George VI's consort, in unfortunate terms that drove another nail into the coffin of his political career: "Now I tell you when this thing is finally settled and it comes to a question of saving what's left for England, it will be the Queen and not any of the politicians who will do it," Kennedy said. "She's got more brains than the Cabinet."

JFK struck a different note to his father in his Harvard thesis that became a best-selling book, *Why England Slept*, published in 1940. Jack was critical of the British political system for failing to prepare adequately for war. His title consciously echoed Churchill's own critique of the appeasement years, published in the US under the title *While England Slept*, which helped his case to become prime minister.

Where Joe had scorned Churchill and his warnings about Hitler, Jack Kennedy deeply admired the new prime minister's foresight and would go on to describe Britain's wartime leader as "the most honored and honorable man to walk the stage of human history in the time in which we live." As president, JFK gave Churchill the highest award America could give, proclaiming him the very first honorary US citizen, in words that contained a rebuke of his own father: "In the dark days and darker nights when Britain stood alone—and most men save Englishmen despaired of England's life—he mobilized the English language and sent it into battle."

The war significantly changed the young Kennedy's destiny: while serving behind enemy lines in the British Solomon Islands, he became a hero for leading his surviving men to safety after their boat was rammed by a Japanese vessel. The war had another dramatic effect on the Kennedy family: his older brother, Joe Jr., died tragically in 1944 when a bomber plane laden with explosives detonated prematurely before he and his copilot could bail out.

In the years that followed, Joseph Sr. refocused all his ambitions to groom his second son into the first Catholic president. On his first visit as president to Britain years later, President Kennedy raised a laugh when he dropped into the Grosvenor Square offices of the US embassy for a brief pep talk with staff, who numbered both Americans and Brits. "I worked at the American embassy—not too hard!—but I worked here for a few months before the outbreak of World War II, and therefore

I know this square on which this new building is ranged as well as I do my own street at home," he began. He went on to exhibit his heartfelt attachment to "this great country" he admired.

"Our friendship with Great Britain goes back to our earliest beginnings," he said. "This country, while no longer a far-ranging empire, is a great commonwealth composed of independent nations who are associated with this country. This country is an island which in the standards, physically, of the United States is not large. But nevertheless it has influence, it is persuasive throughout much of the world. . . . Its diplomats speak with a long tradition of over a thousand years behind them." The British believed in the same principles and stood for the same things as America, he said, "a people of courage and energy, whose judgment is respected."

The Kennedys were ostensibly on a private visit to take part in the christening of Jackie's niece, Anna Christina Radziwill, the daughter of her sister, Lee, who was married to the Polish prince Stanisław Albrecht "Stas" Radziwill. The main purpose for JFK, however, was to hold discussions with Prime Minister Macmillan about his crucial Cold War meeting in Vienna, at which the issue of Berlin's future was top of the agenda. Macmillan had already met Kennedy twice since his inauguration in 1961, a frequency that was testament to the precarious state of the Cold War.

The prime minister had briefed the Queen on the new president, writing that he had "surrounded himself with a large retinue of highly intelligent men." One of these was Ormsby-Gore, who had become a mid-level British foreign minister and was appointed British ambassador in Washington by Macmillan at Kennedy's request. Ormsby-Gore recorded later that, during Kennedy's London visit, he found the president in "great pain" after his encounter with the Russian leader.

"There is no doubt that Khrushchev made a very unpleasant impression on him. That's what he said to me. . . . That Khrushchev obviously tried to browbeat him and frighten him. He had displayed the naked power of the Soviet Union." Macmillan too was brought into Kennedy's confidence and told the Queen that Kennedy was "completely overwhelmed by the ruthlessness and barbarity of the Russian premier." In his briefing, Macmillan added: "Apart from his intelligence, [Kennedy] has great charm. He is gay and has a light touch. Since so many Americans are so ponderous, this is a welcome change."

The sixty-seven-year-old prime minister, born in the previous century, used "gay" in the sense of fun or lively, but was perhaps also hinting at an old-fashioned British meaning— womanizer. Macmillan was learning quickly about Kennedy's personality, although it was not until later that year when JFK, increasingly at ease with the older man, made his much-quoted remark, "I wonder how it is with you, Harold? If I don't have a woman for three days, I get terrible headaches." The contrast between the two men was vast: monogamous Macmillan was trapped in a loveless marriage that he maintained for the sake of appearances, fearing that divorce would wreck his career in prudish Britain. His wife's long affair with a parliamentary colleague of her husband's was common knowledge among the British Conservative establishment but—just as in the US with Kennedy's sexual adventures—kept out of the papers.

There was tremendous excitement in London at the arrival of the American First Couple. Half a million people lined the streets to see the Kennedys drive into the capital, and the next day crowds gathered to catch a glimpse of them at Westminster Cathedral for the christening. That evening, 2,500 swarmed Buckingham Palace, shepherded by mounted police, for the arrival of the presidential Rolls-Royce. Many stayed for two and a half hours to see them depart.

Jackie Kennedy's catty gossip about the Queen, recorded by two confidantes, was fueled by a clash of traditional British and modern American sensibilities, which made for a strained atmosphere even before the guests arrived. On the face of it, the Kennedys were receiving a rare compliment—no US president had dined at Buckingham Palace since the state banquet for Woodrow Wilson in 1918. However, in the still-hidebound world of early 1960s Britain, there was controversy behind the scenes over the guest list.

Asked by the palace whom she would like invited, Jackie asked for Princess Margaret, while her husband wanted to see Princess Marina, who was the Duchess of Kent and the Queen's aunt. Margaret was notoriously more fun at parties than her elder sister, while Marina, the daughter of a grand duchess of Russia and a prince of Greece and Denmark, was such a trendsetter that she had a color named after her—Marina blue. Jackie also wanted her sister and her brother-in-law to attend, but Lee was on her second marriage and Stas his third—and royal protocol dictated that divorce was a disqualifier when it came to dinner guests.

Back and forth the diplomats went as the palace objected to Jackie's guests and Jackie objected to the objection. According to Gore Vidal's account of what he was told by Jackie, it was the president who made the final ultimatum, telling the palace "not to bother about us, we're here unofficially."

Alarm bells rang in the British government, which was extremely keen for Kennedy to receive the royal treatment, so the palace relented on the Radziwills—although the final guest list for the fifty-seat dinner came as a nasty surprise to the thirty-one-year-old First Lady. There was no place for the two royals the Kennedys most wanted to meet.

"The queen had her revenge. . . . No Margaret, no Marina, no one except every Commonwealth minister of agriculture that they could find," Jackie told Vidal. Although likely embellished by the great American storyteller, Jackie's displeasure was evident. Vidal recorded Jackie saying: "I think the queen resented me. Philip was nice, but nervous. One felt absolutely no relationship between them. The queen was human only once."

This was when Elizabeth II asked about the Kennedys' recent state visit to Canada and the First Lady shared feelings of exasperation about the trials of being on public view at all hours. "The queen looked rather conspiratorial and said: 'One gets crafty after a while and learns how to save oneself.'" After dinner, the Queen asked, "You like pictures?" and led Jackie down a long gallery, stopping at a Van Dyck painting to say, "That's a good horse." Jackie found Elizabeth "pretty heavy-going," according to Vidal, a comment he repeated to Princess Margaret years later, who told him: "But that's what she's there for."

Vidal later relayed to Margaret how she was excluded as part of the power play and noted that she "nodded thoughtfully," saying: "That could've been true—I know I rang my sister, furious at not being invited, and she said, 'Ah, I thought since you were pregnant you wouldn't want to bother!' Too maddening!"

Macmillan, who was seated on Jackie's left, recorded the evening in his diary as "very pleasant." Jackie, who stayed on in

London for a couple of days while her husband returned to Washington that night, clearly thought otherwise.

Cecil Beaton, the society photographer, wrote in his diaries published in 1976 that she told him: "They were all tremendously kind and nice, but she was not impressed by the flowers, or the furnishings of the apartments at Buckingham Palace, or by the Queen's dark-blue tulle dress and shoulder straps, or her flat hair." The official photograph of the two couples that evening shows the men in black tie, as was required for an "informal" royal dinner, and Jackie in an ice blue sleeveless shantung silk evening dress with a boat neckline, from New York boutique Chez Ninon, looking a whole generation more modern than her hostess. London's *Evening Standard* declared: "Jacqueline Kennedy has given the American people one thing they had always lacked—majesty."

The Queen also played her part in the Cold War effort being waged around the globe by the US and Britain to push back Soviet influence. There was alarm in London and Washington at the move toward socialism in Ghana, the first British colony in Africa to win majority-rule independence, under President Kwame Nkrumah. Vice President Richard Nixon attended the 1957 independence celebrations in Accra, the capital, along with Marina, the Duchess of Kent, who was representing the Queen. (Nixon reportedly asked a Black guest at the party how it felt to be free, to which the man replied, "I wouldn't know, sir. I'm from Alabama.")

Nkrumah, a charismatic figure with influence across the African continent, dropped the Queen as head of state when Ghana became a republic in 1960, although it remained a member of the Commonwealth. However, he became increasingly authoritarian, sacking judges and locking up more than two hundred political opponents without trial. When questioned by the American press corps, during a two-day US visit in April 1961, about whether Ghana was now a satellite of the Soviet bloc, he defended his country as "neutral" but later went on a six-day visit to China and a ten-day state visit to Russia, agreeing to development loans and the purchase of Soviet planes for Ghana Airways.

All the more reason, then, for Elizabeth II to reschedule her long-planned visit to Ghana, which was called off in 1959 when she fell pregnant with Prince Andrew. The trip was viewed by the Queen as extremely important for maintaining good Commonwealth relations but also by Macmillan as the key to unlocking American funding for the Upper Volta Dam, a huge hydroelectric project to power most of Ghana and two neighboring countries, Togo and Benin. Kennedy was hesitating amid Nkrumah's promotion of "African socialism."

Five days before Elizabeth was due to depart for Accra, there were two bombings, causing some British officials to fear that her life might be in danger. She felt strongly about going, fearing that if she pulled out a second time Ghana would exit the Commonwealth and fully embrace Russia, giving a lead to other African nations. She told Macmillan: "How silly I should look if I was scared to visit Ghana and then Khrushchev went and had a good reception. . . . I am not a film star. I am the head of the Commonwealth—and I am paid to face any risks that may be involved. Nor do I say this lightly. Do not forget that I have three children."

Her ten-day visit was a triumph, with many Ghanaians attending one of several durbars—gatherings of tribal leaders with ceremonial music and dancing. Elizabeth II was photographed dancing the foxtrot at a state ball with Nkrumah, winning positive headlines around the world apart from in white-ruled South Africa. Ghana's government-controlled press proclaimed her "the greatest Socialist Monarch in the world." Macmillan enthused about the sovereign's determination, telling his press secretary: "What a splendid girl she is."

Upon her return, he wasted no time in telephoning Kennedy, saying: "I have risked my Queen, you must risk your money!" JFK praised Elizabeth's "brave contribution" and agreed to funding for the dam. She had shown her value not merely as a figurehead but as a player in the Cold War chess game.

Jackie returned to Buckingham Palace in March 1962, on the way back to the US from visits to India and Pakistan. The Queen laid out lunch for her, inviting her sister, Lee, and brother-in-law Stas showing there was no ill will from the previous year's dinner. Also present were Harold and Dorothy Macmillan and eight other guests in a small state dining room. There was still no place for Princess Margaret or Marina, but conversation was helped along by Jackie's news on a topic close to the royal heart—horses. She had been gifted a bay gelding named Sardar by President Mohammad Ayub Khan of Pakistan, which was being transported back to the Kennedy estate in Virginia, where their two children were learning to ride.

Elizabeth wrote to JFK: "It was a great pleasure to meet Mrs. Kennedy again. I hope her Pakistan horse will be a success—please tell her that mine became very excited by jumping with the children's ponies in the holidays, so I hope hers will be calmer!"

Jackie was on her best behavior afterward, telling the media: "I don't think I should say anything about it except how grateful I am and how charming she was."

Elizabeth had a role to play in ensuring smooth relations but was well aware that she was nothing like as central at this time as her prime minister and ambassador, a point that came across in a letter she wrote to Kennedy after consulting with Macmillan upon his return from another visit to Washington: "It is a great comfort to me to know that you and he are so close and that you have confidence in each other's judgement and advice," the Queen wrote. "I am sure that these meetings and this personal trust and understanding are of the greatest importance to both our peoples. I was also glad to hear from Mr. Macmillan that my Ambassador and his wife are getting on so well, and that you are finding them useful."

Even allowing for the British tendency toward understatement, this was downplaying things. When Kennedy had to deal with the Cuban Missile Crisis later that year, he had daily phone calls with Macmillan and also turned to Ormsby-Gore. One evening Jackie walked in on the two men "squatting on the floor" in the White House, looking over an array of spy photos of missile sites to decide which images to release to the public.

JFK made what would be his last visit to Britain in June 1963 for an informal overnight stay at the prime minister's country home, Birch Grove in West Sussex. This was the final leg of a European trip that first took him to West Berlin, where he memorably declared his solidarity with a city closed off from the communist east by a ninety-six-mile-long wall, saying: "Ich bin ein Berliner."

Kennedy then had a four-day tour of Ireland before landing in England and traveling by helicopter to the Peak District to visit the grave of his sister Kathleen. The lively Kick, who had taken British society by storm a decade before, had died aged twenty-eight in a plane crash in France in 1948 and was buried in a churchyard close to Chatsworth House, a stately home and seat since 1549 of the Cavendish family that she married into.

Five months later, JFK's life was also cruelly cut short at the age of forty-six.

The Queen shared the utter shock and grief felt around the world at Kennedy's assassination. She placed the royal court into mourning for a week and commanded that the great tenor bell at Westminster Abbey be rung every minute from 11:00 a.m. to noon on the day after the killing, a token of respect usually reserved for deceased senior members of the royal family.

Elizabeth, pregnant with Prince Edward, sent Philip to represent her at the funeral service in Washington. Unable to travel on doctor's orders to attend the British national service of memorial at St. Paul's Cathedral with three thousand guests,

Elizabeth arranged for her own service at Windsor Castle's St. George's Chapel with a delegation of 350 American service personnel she afterward invited to tour the state apartments.

Jackie was again the guest of the Queen in May 1965 for the dedication of the John F. Kennedy Memorial at Runnymede in Surrey, just a few miles south of Windsor Castle. A stepped pathway, made up of sixty thousand granite paving stones, winds up through woodland to a glade where a seven-ton block of Portland stone stands on a plinth, inscribed with words taken from Kennedy's inaugural address: "Let every Nation know, whether it wishes us well or ill, that we shall pay any price, bear any burden, meet any hardship, support any friend or oppose any foe, in order to assure the survival and success of liberty."

There is a view over Runnymede, a site made famous for its connection to democracy and freedom by the settlement there of the Magna Carta by King John of England in 1215. The royal party and a large contingent of the Kennedy family walked up to the memorial, led by the Queen and Ormsby-Gore, who had returned at the end of his service as ambassador, followed by Jackie with her seven-year-old daughter, Caroline, and son John Jr., aged four. JFK's little boy, known as John John, who became famous the world over for saluting his father's flag-draped coffin, walked up to the memorial sweetly holding Prince Philip by the hand.

Jackie, who took tea afterward at Windsor Castle with the royals, did not speak at the ceremony but issued a statement. "For free men everywhere, Runnymede is indeed sacred soil," she said. "It is the birthplace of our ideals of human freedom and individual dignity in which my husband passionately believed. My husband . . . had the greatest affection for the British people for what you have accomplished down through the ages in this land and for what you represent around the world. Your literature and the lives of your great men shaped him as did no other part of his education. In a sense he returns today to the tradition from which he sprang."

It was a fitting memorial for a president whose reputation as a beacon of hope for a better world, or at least more optimistic politics, was encouraged by a romanticized link with ancient royalty. It was Jackie who first used the image of Camelot—the fabled castle and court of legendary British King Arthur—in an interview with *Life* magazine shortly after her husband's death. She referred to the Broadway musical *Camelot*, with lyrics written by Alan Jay Lerner, a school friend of Kennedy's who was also at Harvard with him. Jackie said that Kennedy was a fan of the production and would listen to the recording before bed. She quoted the closing lines of the final song: "Don't let it be forgot, that once there was a spot, for one brief, shining moment that was known as Camelot." Jackie added: "There'll be great presidents again . . . but there will never be another Camelot." It was conscious mythmaking in action, and the term "Camelot" became synonymous with the Kennedy White House, evoking feelings of idealism and unfulfilled promise.

These were themes that Elizabeth herself touched on at Runnymede. "The unprecedented intensity of that wave of grief, mixed with something akin to despair, which swept over our people at the news of President Kennedy's assassination, was a measure of the extent to which we recognized what he had already accomplished, and of the high hopes that rode with him in a future that was not to be," she said, in memorable words reported around the world. Although she did not have a close personal relationship with JFK, she shared in the sense of loss as a fellow head of state and deeply valued his respect for Britain. It was a tragedy made even more poignant by the difficult period that lay ahead for the US-UK relationship during his successor's presidency.

CHAPTER 4

I am told by my protocol people that this visit of yours is an "unofficial" visit. I can only wish that "official" visits, of which I am something of a veteran, would have such favorable results.

—Lyndon B. Johnson to Princess Margaret,
November 17, 1965

It took something special to coax the workaholic thirty-sixth president away from the day-to-day concerns of office and onto the dance floor.

Lyndon Johnson was not known for levity, and his preferred leisure pursuit was golf because he could talk politics with fellow players. But after six weeks out of the public eye (during which time he was recuperating from a painful gallbladder operation) he was ready to return in style—by dancing with a British princess at the most sought-after White House event of the year.

The hubbub surrounding the visit of Margaret, the Queen's more risqué younger sister, along with her husband, the Earl of Snowdon, showed that royalty still held a magical allure in Washington, even under a president who did not attend too much to the Special Relationship and cared even less for revelry. The president's wife, Claudia Alta "Lady Bird" Johnson, who *did* enjoy the social side of the presidency, observed, "Lyndon was anti-party." Nevertheless the Johnsons put together a guest list that, in addition to senior politicians, included actors Kirk Douglas and George Hamilton (in keeping with Margaret's well-known fondness for A-list company). Evenings with Margaret were never drab affairs, and this night of royal jollity at the Johnson White House went on into the small hours—with the president giving a rare display of his foxtrot and waltzing skills, momentarily setting aside the cares of the Vietnam War.

The British government wanted Margaret's first US tour to include a date with the president—whom she already knew—partly to allay concerns that her trip spent mainly with friends in the western United States would otherwise seem too frivolous. As was usually the case with royal visits, British officials hoped it would bolster diplomatic relations—in this case, amid increasing strain over Prime Minister Harold Wilson's refusal to send troops to join the anti-communist war as Johnson dearly wished.

Despite Margaret's best efforts, those tensions only worsened as the tide of the conflict turned against the US; Wilson fell further out of favor when, in 1967, he announced the withdrawal of all British forces stationed in Southeast Asia and the Persian Gulf, adding to the pressure on American resources. On at least six occasions as president, including during several formal meals with Wilson, Johnson found himself making toasts to "Her Majesty the Queen," even though Elizabeth II was not actually present—and once, as vice president, he'd had to sit through an entire Queen's Speech in the Jamaican

Parliament delivered by her sister. He was, however, the only sitting American president Elizabeth did not meet during her reign. The LBJ Presidential Library in Austin, Texas, believes that they may well have met in October 1957, when then Senator Johnson attended Eisenhower's state dinner and was "likely" to have been introduced to the Queen, although no photograph exists of any encounter.

There were a host of reasons why there was little appetite on the US side for a formal meeting between the British monarch and President Johnson: he did not want to spare time for ceremonial occasions like a state visit in either direction; he rarely traveled to Europe, preferring to focus on foreign allies providing the most practical support in Vietnam, and he did not want to draw unnecessary attention to political difficulties in the Special Relationship. Wilson pressed incessantly for his own meetings, but Johnson was suspicious of him, believing that he wanted them to benefit his own standing back home or to seek US help to prop up the faltering pound.

Another important explanation for the failure of Johnson and Queen Elizabeth II to meet, especially during the earlier stages of his five years and two months in the White House, was simply bad luck. Elizabeth II's fourth pregnancy ruled her out from flying to attend Kennedy's funeral, while an infection prevented Johnson from traveling the other way for Churchill's state send-off fourteen months later. The Queen and the US president would certainly have met at the solemnities for either statesman in more favorable circumstances.

Elizabeth II's October 1964 tour of Canada, timed for her reemergence into public life after the birth of Prince Edward, came just a few weeks before the US presidential election, an inappropriate time politically to make a detour to Washington, as she had done to see Truman during her 1951 Canadian tour. In December 1964, when Wilson was the first foreign leader to visit the newly elected Johnson in the White House, the British premier attempted to invite LBJ to Britain using the Queen as a lure during his after-dinner toast, saying, "I hope you will, Mr. President, come to Buckingham Palace to visit London." He was ignored.

Johnson did not travel abroad for the whole of 1965 and visited Europe only twice during his entire presidency: in 1967 for Chancellor Konrad Adenauer's funeral in West Germany and later for a brief stopover in Italy on the way back from the memorial service for Prime Minister Harold Holt in Australia. Wilson visited him in Washington no fewer than six times, but his enthusiasm for the Special Relationship was not reciprocated, and Wilson came to be seen as something of a nuisance by the president. Ormsby-Gore, now Lord Harlech, the British ambassador to Washington from 1961 to 1965, observed that Johnson "basically has no feeling for world affairs and no great interest in them except in so far as they come to disturb the domestic scene."

Not that Wilson's denial of troops for Vietnam necessarily excluded Elizabeth II, who as Queen of both Australia and New Zealand supplied almost sixty-five thousand soldiers over the course of the conflict, which was a good deal nearer to those countries than to the United States or the United Kingdom. Australia lost 521 troops and New Zealand 37. Johnson paid homage to the Queen in this role when he made the most extensive overseas journey of his presidency in October 1966, taking in seven countries all closely connected to the Vietnam

War, including the first-ever US presidential visits to Australia and New Zealand. He toasted Her Majesty in Wellington at lunch with senior politicians as a band struck up "God Save the Queen," the national anthem New Zealand shared with Britain.

It was as vice president, when Johnson was sent by Kennedy to attend Jamaica's independence celebrations in August 1962, that he first met Princess Margaret. Elizabeth II deputized her thirty-one-year-old sister, who went with her husband of two years, Antony Armstrong-Jones, given the title Earl of Snowdon by the Queen, to represent the Crown. Johnson, along with Lady Bird, met the royal couple at a reception at King's House, the Kingston residence of Lord Blackburne, last British governor of Jamaica, before heading to the National Stadium to watch the final lowering of the Union Jack in a midnight ceremony attended by twenty-five thousand spectators.

Margaret, dressed in a "dazzling icy white gown and tiara," wore a "solemn" expression as "another one of the Empire's colonies broke away" after 307 years of British rule, the Associated Press reported.

As part of the secret advance preparations for Churchill's funeral, code-named Operation Hope Not, the US delegation was expected to be led by its president. Churchill, after all, was not only the greatest statesman of America's strongest international ally; he was also half-American, thanks to his Brooklyn-born mother, Jennie Jerome. The British planning had begun two presidents previously, in 1958, when Churchill nearly died from pneumonia—such was the organization required for the first state funeral for a commoner since the Duke of Wellington in 1852.

As the ninety-year-old former prime minister neared the end, after suffering a serious stroke on January 12, 1965, Johnson was home in Texas at LBJ Ranch preparing for his inauguration. He and his advisor Myer Feldman went "over temporary plans for trip to Great Britain in the event of Sir Winston Churchill's death," his appointment diary recorded. Three days later Johnson was sworn into office in a chilly Washington winter, standing for several hours outside reviewing a parade without an overcoat or hat. In the evening he toured five inauguration dances. Not surprisingly, he came down with a cold.

By January 23, headlines about Johnson's respiratory illness eclipsed the daily updates on Churchill's final struggle, even in the British press. This was because, alarmingly, the president was now suffering from chest pains, so he was whisked in an ambulance at 2:26 a.m. that day from the White House to Bethesda Military Hospital. Doctors diagnosed tracheitis, an inflammation of the windpipe, and prescribed antibiotics. At the back of everyone's mind was the heart attack that Johnson had suffered ten years earlier at the age of forty-six, but an electrocardiogram proved reassuringly normal. Johnson invited a small group of journalists into his room during the day to tell them that he "felt a little better" and "wouldn't hesitate right now to put on my britches and go back to the office if there was something that needed to be done." It was the standard bravado of every American president struck down by illness.

However, what his doctor described on January 24 as "in the category of the common cold" only got worse, and that night the White House diary recorded: "The President was awake much of the night with heavy coughing." At 3:35 a.m. he was brought the news that Churchill had died. A statement in Johnson's name proclaimed: "When there was darkness in the world, and hope was low in the hearts of men, a generous Providence gave us Winston Churchill. . . . The people of the United States—his cousins and his fellow citizens—will pray with his British countrymen for God's eternal blessing on this man, and for comfort to his family."

Churchill's funeral was set for January 30, six days' hence, and LBJ remained keen to go, dispatching Lloyd Hand, his chief of protocol, to London to liaise with Buckingham Palace and the American embassy. Johnson had an assurance of an audience with the Queen and told reporters on January 26 that he wanted to make the trip to England "very, very much." Hand recalled: "The president was just coming out of the hospital, and he called me in his office and said, 'I'd like for you to go over and talk to the royal family, to the prime minister, to our ambassador David Bruce, and ask each of them if they believe that I should come to Churchill's funeral, given the circumstances, and call me every night. And I did that . . . I called him every night and told him that everybody said he shouldn't come to St. Paul's. It was already twenty-five degrees Fahrenheit, and when they opened those great doors it dropped another ten degrees. They fully understood and would be opposed to him coming, having just come out of the hospital."

There has been much debate as to why Johnson did not send Vice President Hubert Humphrey, another Churchill admirer, in his place. This was probably down to a mixture of ego—Johnson did not want to be outshone by his deputy—and the fear of chaos if he suffered a debilitating relapse or even died so soon after his inauguration with his successor out of the country.

But the British press was unforgiving. With no president or vice president in attendance, and Secretary of State Dean Rusk forced to pull out at the last moment while in London because of influenza, it felt like a snub that the official American delegation was reduced to Earl Warren, the chief justice of the Supreme Court, and Bruce, the ambassador, accompanied by Hand, even though bad luck had once again played a big part.

"The funeral guest whose absence caused most perplexity was, sadly, President Johnson," the UK's *Observer* commented. "His final decision not to make the trip was a surprise only because he was initially over-optimistic about his power to recover from his feverish cough . . . so a diminished delegation was the best gesture that the United States was able to make to the memory of Winston Churchill."

Churchill invented the phrase "Special Relationship" and did more than anyone of his generation to popularize the idea. His Atlanticism was reflected during his funeral service, with the singing of "Battle Hymn of the Republic," also known in Britain as "Mine Eyes Have Seen the Glory," one of his favorite hymns. The cathedral had resonated to the same rousing verses just over a year earlier at its JFK memorial service. Johnson not only missed one of the most spectacular British public events of the century; it was also a chance to mingle with dignitaries from 111 countries, including four kings, one queen, one sultan, five other heads of state, and sixteen prime ministers.

Elizabeth II hosted a buffet luncheon afterward at Buckingham Palace for the Churchill family and chief foreign visitors. Its informality was marked by the presence of her young children, Charles, Anne, and Andrew, who wandered around the room, while there was also a brief appearance by ten-month-old baby Edward.

By the mid-1960s, in a dramatic reversal of the Kennedy-Macmillan years, diplomacy between the leaders of the US and the UK was all one-way traffic. Johnson always maintained that he regarded Britain as a special ally, but he felt let down by successive events. For one thing, he was enraged by the sale of 450 buses made by Britain's Leyland Motor Corporation to Cuba under Wilson's predecessor, Sir Alec Douglas-Home, against the spirit of the US trade embargo. In addition, Britain had committed troops to help defend the newly independent former colony of Malaysia from Indonesian attacks but began to run out of the cash needed to play the role of a world power, eventually leading Wilson to announce that all British forces "East of Suez" would be withdrawn, putting more strain on US resources.

As the connection between the two countries frayed, the British PM continually pressed for face-to-face meetings in Washington but drew an angry response from Johnson. In a late-night phone call in February 1965, after a particularly bad news day in Vietnam, Wilson told the president he "would like to come to Washington" to help deal with the "high level of concern in London" about a North Vietnamese Vietcong attack he feared might trigger a heavy US response. Johnson responded testily that it would be "a very serious mistake" for Wilson to come—seemingly to lecture him on US foreign policy—and that there was "nothing to be gained by flapping around the Atlantic with our coattails out." LBJ added that "the US did not have the company of many allies" in Vietnam and if Wilson had "any men to spare, he would be glad to have them." Finally Johnson snapped: "Why don't you run Malaysia and let me run Vietnam?"

Wilson tried to smooth things over when he secured a visit two months later for a private lunch in the White House, but even his gift to LBJ missed the mark. "When the visit was over, the prime minister gave the president a Burberry raincoat," Lloyd Hand recalled. "Well, the president opened the box, took out the Burberry raincoat, put it on, and the sleeves came halfway up his arms. He said, 'Lloyd, take this, catch him, tell him it doesn't fit me, could he send me another one.' I raced down the steps and out the diplomatic entrance. By this time, [Wilson's] limousine was pulling away. So I ran down alongside him—I'm sure his security guard wondered what on earth was going on—and I knocked on the window and they stopped. I told the prime minister what the president said and gave him the box back."

Nothing seemed to be going right.

It was during this rocky period that the British government saw a chance to sprinkle some royal stardust in Washington and remind America that the relationship was still special. Princess Margaret and Tony Snowdon were invited on their first trip together to the US in November 1965 by her lifelong friend Sharman Douglas, an American socialite and movie publicist. The first stop was California, and when the White House was informed of her visit, LBJ invited her for a dinner.

Douglas, thirty-seven, was the daughter of chemicals heiress Peggy Zinsser and politician Lewis W. Douglas, who was ambassador in London under Truman when "Charmin' Shar-man" burst onto the social scene. Now reunited in Hollywood, Sharman was eager to show Margaret and her husband all the glitz and glamour that Los Angeles had to offer. The couple met Paul Newman and British star Julie Andrews on the set of Alfred Hitchcock's thriller *Torn Curtain*, followed by a star-studded party hosted by Douglas. American papers breath-lessly recounted how Elizabeth Taylor and Richard Burton were among the first to arrive and the last to leave the Holly-wood bash, which went on until 2:00 a.m., while Andrews, Gregory Peck, and Warren Beatty sat at Margaret's table for dinner. The princess danced the night away with partners who included Fred Astaire, Gene Kelly, and Danny Kaye.

It all sounded dazzling and oh so exciting, but British dip-lomats were privately annoyed that carefully planned daytime visits to places like the Lawrence Radiation Laboratory at Berkeley did not garner nearly as many column inches. Later there would be questions in Parliament about the high public cost of funding what appeared from the media coverage to be mainly a nonstop three-week party, while details emerged of some typically rude behavior by Margaret that recast the initial starstruck reports in a less flattering light. At the Douglas party, she had sent a message over to Judy Garland that she would like to hear her sing. Garland left the messenger in little doubt that she did not regard herself at the beck and call of British royalty. She responded: "Go and tell that nasty, rude little princess that we've known each other for long enough and gabbed in enough ladies' rooms that she should skip the ho-hum royal routine and just pop over here and ask me herself. Tell her I'll sing if she christens a ship first."

After a few days' relaxation at the Douglas home in Arizona, the couple flew to Washington for the solemn task of laying a wreath on JFK's grave in Arlington National Cemetery ahead of the second anniversary of the assassination. Then there was another late-night bash, described by the London *Times* as "a discotheque party given by Mrs. Nicholas Katzenbach, the wife of the Attorney-General" at their home, where "the Princess danced late into the night" once again.

All this was a prelude to the main event: a black-tie dinner with Johnson the following evening, seen as the premier event of the Washington social season. This was officially just a party, not a formal "state occasion"—although the Queen's sister drew the Washington A-list, including Vice President Humphrey and his wife, Muriel; several cabinet members and their wives; and Johnson's favorite associate justice of the US Supreme Court, Abe Fortas, and his wife, Carolyn. Also attending were two senators and three governors, including the liberal Republican Nelson Rockefeller of New York, who would become vice president under Gerald Ford. Just 140 guests made the cut.

Johnson returned to the capital from his recuperation in Texas after an operation to remove his gallbladder, a troublesome gallstone, and a kidney stone. Although regarded as fairly routine, it was a major procedure performed by four surgeons and two anesthesiologists. His official diary recorded that when Johnson came around and asked why he was in so much pain, he was told it was because "they had to probe all over the abdominal region and go through 34 feet of intestine . . . to find [the kidney stone]."

The dinner on a cold Wednesday night in Washington was eagerly anticipated not only for the royal visitors and LBJ's reappearance but also because it was the first outing of his eighteen-year-old daughter, Luci, with her beau, Pat Nugent. The president's elder daughter, Lynda, twenty-one, was also among the select group of invitees, accompanied by twenty-six-year-old Hollywood heartthrob George Hamilton. While the White House insisted that he was merely an escort for the evening and not a date, arranged after the Johnson family enjoyed his performance in the movie *Your Cheatin' Heart*, just days later the pair were off to Acapulco together and a brief romance ensued.

"In spite of the fact that we rebelled against the Brits, there has always been a fascination with the country and especially with royalty by a very sizable number of our people," Luci Baines Johnson said. "My mother was a really magical hostess and she wanted to represent our country well and wanted everything about this to be the best that we could make it." Lady Bird was at the ranch in Texas with her husband in the days before the visit, however, leaving Luci in the White House. Disaster almost struck.

"I had two hamsters, Boris and Natasha. Somehow they found a way to escape their cage. So now we have two hamsters loose in the White House and Princess Margaret is coming. I just know that my father is going to ask for the first dance, and as he does, she's going to look down and two hamsters are going to run across her feet."

Luci and various White House staff spent hours searching for the rodents on the third floor where the family lived. Eventually she decided to go down to a kitchen to find food. "Lo and behold, Boris and Natasha had had the exact same idea. . . .

I found Boris and Natasha in the pantry before my mother and father came home. It was a disaster avoided."

Johnson chose evening gowns for both his daughters on a pre-operation visit to New York, while Margaret's shocking-pink silk gauze ball gown, with matching low-necked jacket with long sleeves, was by Belinda Bellville, a British designer who would go on to be a favorite of Princess Diana's. Lady Bird struck a stunning contrast in an emerald green strapless gown. A further fifty guests made it onto the list for the post-dinner dance starting at 10:00 p.m., with music from bandleader Peter Duchin and his orchestra. There was a guest appearance from folk group the Brothers Four.

The East Room had been laid out like a nightclub, cabaret-style, with numerous small tables covered in white cloths. It was certainly a more exuberant—and much longer—night than the kind of straitlaced state occasion usually associated with the Queen: during the evening Margaret smoked (something her sister never did), declined to wear a tiara because it would inhibit her dancing, and partied until 1:35 a.m. She certainly worked her magic on the recuperating president, and they opened the dancing with a foxtrot to "Everything's Coming Up Roses" inspired by her full name, Margaret Rose. The night seemed to have been just the kind of tonic that LBJ needed, for he stayed on even after his royal guests had departed to the British embassy.

Johnson used most of his short speech that night to praise, thank, and flatter his British guests, adding a couple of lines about the importance of the bond between the two nations that the visit reminded Americans about.

"Mark Twain once said: 'I have traveled more than anyone else, and I have noticed that even the angels speak English with an accent,'" Johnson said. "Tonight I know that is true."

 ⌒℘⌒

Princess Margaret's royal tour was a hit with the celebrity-hungry US press and captured the popular imagination at a time of bleak headlines from Vietnam. Bob Hope joked: "Everyone is conscious of the royal couple's visit. I waved at a traffic cop, and he curtsied back."

Despite his frustrations with Wilson, LBJ was generous in his praise of the transatlantic relationship: "A bond of friendship and common purpose has existed between our two great nations for more than 140 years. In a world of change, that bond is constant. In a world of uncertainty, that bond is unfailing. In a world of strife, that bond is our security. In the name of that bond—and in the hope and belief that it will never weaken—I would now like to propose a toast to Her Majesty the Queen."

The scripted praise of the US-UK "bond"—repeated five times—and the "hope and belief" this would never weaken may have been part of Johnson's pressure campaign on the UK government to send the troops Johnson wanted to Vietnam. Johnson himself was under pressure from his officials to make US support for the pound—which was once again in trouble, with a disruptive devaluation looming—contingent upon boots on the ground. One senior advisor, McGeorge Bundy, asked him to do just that in July 1965, in a private memo, requesting permission to tell Wilson's cabinet secretary, Burke Trend, that "a British Brigade in Vietnam would be worth a billion dollars at the moment of truth for Sterling." Johnson knew that this would be seen as tantamount to blackmail of America's supposed top ally.

By the time Margaret visited, the Vietnam situation was dire. The highest weekly toll of American troops since the war started was revealed on the day of the royal dinner: 86 killed in action and 230 wounded, with South Vietnamese deaths even higher, at 165 killed and 56 missing or captured, while the Vietcong were reported to have suffered 981 killed and 192 captured.

Yet Margaret's brief response to the president made not a single reference to affairs of state, international relations, war, or politics, dwelling solely on the pleasure and gratitude she felt from the evening and the company. After thanking Johnson for his welcome and congratulating him on his wedding anniversary and on overcoming his operation, she offered him a toast: "We are having the most wonderful time in the United States. The hospitality and kindness that we have received everywhere has touched us greatly, and it will make us take home superlatively happy memories of all we have done and seen. And we only wish we could have stayed longer."

Guests told Princess Margaret that it was the first party of its kind in the White House since the Kennedys. There is no doubt that the Johnson family found it a night to remember— although not for a kiss on the mouth for the president from Margaret after they sang a duet as depicted in *The Crown*, which was fictional. He didn't leave until 2:00 a.m., but despite the late night Johnson was back at work at 8:10 a.m. for a telephone briefing on Vietnam.

By 1966, opposition to the war was growing in Britain. In early June an antiwar protester blocked the Queen's car by sitting in the road during a visit to Yeovil in southwestern England. Later that month, there was the incongruous spectacle for the Queen of her Australian prime minister, Harold Holt, appearing on the White House lawn to pledge military support in Vietnam and declare: "You have an admiring friend, a staunch friend that will be all the way with LBJ." It was an echo of Johnson's campaign slogan, just a day after her British prime minister, Harold Wilson, freshly reelected with a larger cadre of left-wing MPs to placate, "disassociated" his government from US bombing of industrial facilities in Hanoi, the North Vietnamese capital. Wilson's act was seen as a betrayal in the White House.

The Queen did her best to maintain cordial head-of-state relations during this difficult period. On July 4, 1967, she found herself on the US border again during a nine-week visit to Canada for the centenary of its confederation. She took the opportunity to write to Johnson: "As we sail through the international waters of the St. Lawrence Seaway I send you my warmest greetings on this Fourth of July. While I am with my Canadian people to celebrate the centenary of confederation, it gives me great pleasure at the same time to pay tribute to the close relations between the two great countries that share this waterway. Long may our common history of peace and friendship serve as an example for all. Long may the United States prosper."

She received an effusive reply from Johnson: "Your Majesty, my countrymen join me in sending you our warmest thanks for your thoughtful and moving message. An eloquent expression of friendship, it means a great deal to us. We wish you, your government and the British nation every good fortune." This appeared to be a heartfelt personal expression of presidential warmth, but the phrasing was exactly as drafted for Johnson's approval by Francis Bator, his deputy national security advisor, whose job it was to help maintain good diplomatic relations with allies.

Johnson's decision not to run for reelection in 1968 meant the clock ran out on a meeting with Elizabeth II. But eighteen years after his untimely death from a heart attack at sixty-four, she became the first British monarch to set foot in his home state of Texas.

Arriving by Concorde at Bergstrom Air Force Base near Austin in May 1991, on a trip that also took in Dallas, San Antonio, and Houston, she delighted her hosts by declaring, "No state commands such fierce pride and loyalty. Lesser mortals are pitied for their misfortune in not being born Texans." She also made time for a private meeting with Johnson's widow and their daughters at the LBJ Presidential Library on the University of Texas campus.

"Queen Elizabeth's ability to come to my country and take the time to look people like me in the eye, and ask about what matters most to me, was an indication of why she won the hearts of her fellow citizens as well as people around the world," Luci Baines Johnson said. Her father's failure to meet the Queen was certainly not intentional, she added.

"Sometimes the opportunity that we all know would be meaningful and valued just doesn't happen," she said. "Life gets in the way."

CHAPTER 5

The Queen takes a great interest in international problems and has a great desire to discuss them. . . . We have not been chatting about home, the family, and the pictures on the wall.

—Richard M. Nixon, November 27, 1958

Richard Nixon had met Queen Elizabeth II several times prior to becoming president. In fact, he was the host of her first-ever Thanksgiving dinner back in 1958, when he was vice president. But despite sharing such a festive, family-oriented holiday, Nixon insisted that urgent world affairs allowed no time for engaging in mere domestic trivia. These two had more important things to talk about over roast turkey and pumpkin pie.

However, by the time he was president himself a decade later, Nixon's thoughts did turn more to private family affairs when Prince Charles, the Queen's twenty-one-year-old son, made his first visit to Washington, DC, along with his sister, Anne, who was then nineteen. Charles, billed by some of the media as the world's most eligible bachelor, found himself paired off much of the time with Tricia, the president's eldest daughter—twenty-four and romantically unattached.

It was not just media gossips who detected something more

than the usual diplomatic niceties at play. Charles recalled the visit in a 2015 interview: "That was quite amusing, I must say. That was the time when they were trying to marry me off to Tricia Nixon."

While wedding bells never did ring between the prince and the First Daughter, Nixon's presidency did signify a return to more frequent encounters between the British royals and the White House after the lean LBJ years.

Not only was Nixon fascinated by British royalty, he was named after it. His parents gave four of their five boys the names of medieval or mythical kings, with the future president's inspired by Richard the Lionheart, who reigned as Richard I from 1189 to 1199. Genealogists from the New England Historic Genealogical Society worked out that, through his maternal grandfather, Nixon was descended from King Edward III, who reigned from 1327 to 1377.

The friendly relations he nurtured with his fellow head of state Elizabeth II were again in contrast, however, to the lukewarm feelings at the highest political level. Edward Heath, the new Conservative prime minister elected a few weeks before the young royals' headline-winning tour, was far less interested in the United States than any of his postwar predecessors, and the Special Relationship was to spend another few years in the doldrums. The awkward atmosphere gave fresh impetus to the Queen's role, and she was deployed to help ensure that Nixon's visit to the prime minister's countryside retreat went smoothly.

Nixon, as vice president, met the Queen Mother when she

visited Washington as Eisenhower's guest in 1954, and he first encountered the Queen herself in 1957 during her first state visit, when, along with Second Lady Thelma Catherine "Pat" Nixon, they attended Eisenhower's lavish state dinner at the White House. The following day, Nixon hosted a lunch for the royal couple in the Old Senate Chamber, which was decorated with palms and orchids for the occasion. Nixon, in a dark blue suit, greeted the Queen, who wore a beaded cocoa brown satin dress with a fur stole draped over her shoulders, on the steps of the US Capitol before escorting her into the present-day Senate chamber, where, despite a legislative recess, they received "enthusiastic applause from the galleries packed with Senate employees," according to news reports.

But it was Nixon's trip to the UK as vice president a year later, in November 1958, that really opened his eyes to the power of the monarchy for an ambitious American politician. He was there on behalf of the US government to open the American Memorial Chapel in St. Paul's Cathedral, a shrine to US service members stationed in Britain who died during the Second World War. The chapel featured an honor roll book listing the names of the twenty-eight thousand who gave their lives in that conflict. (To this day, a page of the memorial book, kept on display under glass, is turned each morning.)

At the launch ceremony, a solitary Scots Guard bugler played "Taps," the American version of the British "Last Post" call, sounded in commemoration of war sacrifice. More than two thousand people present joined in the singing of "Battle Hymn of the Republic" in "a solemn reminder that regardless of revolutionary bygones and present differences the free world's two best friends are Britain and America," according to the UPI agency report, while millions more watched the television broadcast. The Queen and Nixon greeted a dozen Americans flown in whose sons, daughters, sisters, or brothers died in the air, sea, or land battles during the liberation of Europe.

Afterward the Nixons had lunch at Buckingham Palace with the Queen and Prince Philip before Nixon made a private visit to see the eighty-three-year-old Churchill, who was recovering from an illness that had prevented him from visiting the US at Eisenhower's invitation. That evening Nixon addressed the English-Speaking Union alongside its president, Prince Philip, telling seven hundred guests at London's Guildhall that military and scientific cooperation were vital to preserve freedom.

In words that find their echo in the speeches of American and British leaders today, Nixon concluded: "What must be made clear for all the world to see is that free peoples can compete with and surpass totalitarian nations in producing economic progress. No people in the world today should be forced to choose between bread and freedom."

Since this trip fell on the final Thursday in November, the US embassy in London hosted a Thanksgiving celebration, and an invitation was extended to Queen Elizabeth. She experienced—almost—the full menu on offer, declining only the oyster stew (in line with her rule against eating shellfish while on duty in case of food poisoning). She was served chicken soup instead.

There was some consternation among the American visitors shortly before her arrival when they realized that the vice president's tuxedo had been left behind in Washington. All the men in Nixon's party were lined up to be measured. "Someone would have to yield his tuxedo to the Vice President," the Associated Press recounted. "The frantic measuring was still in full gallop when Prime Minister Macmillan, Admiral Lord Mountbatten and other British notables arrived. Only 15 minutes before the Queen herself showed up the search ended with Jim Bassett of Los Angeles, a newspaper friend of Nixon."

Bassett's jacket was not a great fit, however. "Nixon appeared at the embassy door to meet the Queen in a tuxedo that sagged in front. The sleeves were too long. Nixon looked uncomfortable."

Pat Nixon was not best pleased. "I'll never let anybody else pack Richard's clothes again," she vowed.

Nixon learned a significant lesson about British royalty on his 1958 visit—and it wasn't sartorial. Rather, the trip impressed upon him how the magic of the monarchy could translate into positive newsprint.

"In the three days he has spent in London, Vice President Nixon has scored a great personal success wiping out most or all of the deep-seated prejudice which existed against him because of his ruthless political methods," wrote William H. Stoneman, a syndicated columnist for the *Chicago Daily News*, under the headline "Favorable Impression Made by Nixon on England Visit."

Despite being written off after losing the 1960 election to Kennedy and then the 1962 California governor race to the incumbent Democrat, Nixon claimed the White House in the three-way 1968 contest against Hubert Humphrey and George

Wallace. Just a month after his inauguration—and in stark contrast to the president he succeeded—he was on a plane to Europe, first for NATO meetings in Brussels and then on to England for talks with Prime Minister Wilson and the Queen.

Nixon was keen to renew his relationship with Elizabeth, who hosted him for lunch at Buckingham Palace on February 25, 1969, after he arrived at London's Heathrow Airport in light rain on another misty day. His first handshake after descending the steps of Air Force One was with the Queen's representative Lord Cobbold, the lord chamberlain, the most senior officer of the royal household. He was also greeted by Wilson, who was delighted to see an American president on British soil after Johnson's failure to cross the Atlantic.

"Winston Churchill called ours a Special Relationship," Nixon said at the airport. "Because we are partners in the quest for peace, we know that our relationship, that Special Relationship that we have, is not exclusive. Because that peace that we seek, the two of us, will be secured only when all nations enjoy the relationship of trust and confidence that unite us." He spent the evening in talks over dinner with Wilson at Chequers, the prime minister's country residence, a forty-minute drive from the airport, before traveling into central London to stay at Claridge's hotel.

Nixon's arrival at Buckingham Palace with Wilson after more talks that morning in 10 Downing Street marked a watershed in broadcasting—it was the first time that live color film was shot inside the Queen's London residence. Cameras recorded the president being met at his car by Brigadier Geoffrey Hardy-Roberts, master of the household, and led into the building as a fanfare of trumpets sounded. Crossing the Grand

Entrance Hall, Nixon climbed a short flight of steps to the Marble Hall to shake hands with the Queen, who was dressed in a fuchsia pink satin dress, and then Prince Philip, in a dark suit and tie, before walking down the hall, making small talk just out of earshot of the microphones. They were followed by a smartly tailored Prince Charles, fiddling with his shirt cuff, and Princess Anne wearing a jaunty red scarf. The Queen showed Nixon some of the paintings, including one of George III, before a lunch of poached salmon, lamb cutlets, and loganberry ice cream in the 1844 Room.

As the royal family strove to modernize, Nixon was part of another groundbreaking move: the cameras kept rolling as part of the first behind-the-scenes documentary about the Queen's everyday life. It caused a sensation when it was broadcast in the UK in June 1969 and later in the US. There were scenes of senior royals in their offices or private rooms in palaces, the royal yacht, and the royal train, relaxing together, having a barbecue at Balmoral, and indulging in leisure pursuits—such as Prince Philip keeping up his personal flying hours by piloting a plane and a helicopter.

One scene captured the moment when Nixon was led into a small receiving room by the Queen, Philip, Charles, and Anne to exchange gifts of silver-framed photographs. Nixon shook hands with Charles, saying: "I was just saying to Her Majesty, I've seen you on television." Then he greeted Anne, who replied: "I don't think you've seen me on television." There was some awkward laughter.

The president dropped in a word about his own offspring while speaking to Charles, saying: "Both of my daughters follow you both very closely." Philip, picking up on the president's drift straightaway, said: "I'm sure one no longer." It was clearly a reference to Julie Nixon, who had married David Eisenhower, grandson of Ike, in December 1968.

"Julie . . ." Nixon can be heard saying, as the group moved out of earshot down a corridor to lunch. After all, why would Julie be following the bachelor prince "very closely" now that she was married? Tricia, on the other hand, was still unattached. Philip appeared well-briefed on what Nixon had on his mind.

Nixon's palace lunch led to two royal return invitations from the president—one for Prince Philip, and another for Charles and Anne to make their first stateside visit. Before Philip's solo visit to Washington, Britain, along with the rest of the world, was mesmerized by TV coverage of the moon landing by astronauts from the US Apollo 11 mission on July 20, 1969. The Queen contributed a message, along with leaders from seventy-two other nations, engraved onto a tiny disc to be left behind by Neil Armstrong and Edwin "Buzz" Aldrin, the first men to walk on the surface.

"On behalf of the British people, I salute the skills and courage which have brought man to the moon. May this endeavour increase the knowledge and well-being of mankind," her message read. Documents released fifty years later showed initial royal reluctance to take part in this gesture of global support. Michael Adeane, the Queen's private secretary, wrote that the Queen approved the suggested text of the message but that "Her Majesty agrees that this idea is a gimmick and it is not the sort of thing she much enjoys doing but she certainly would not wish to appear churlish by refusing an invitation which is so obviously well intentioned." It was a sign of the palace's reflexive reluctance to indulge in populist activities that would periodically cause it problems in the years ahead.

Nixon hosted Philip at the White House for a stag—all male—dinner after the prince's solo tour of Canada in late 1969, where, in the new spirit of openness at the palace that emerged after some personnel changes among private staff, he spoke out in the forthright manner his family knew well but the world did not. In one particularly blunt comment on the question of monarchy's purpose in the modern world, he said: "The answer to this question of monarchy is very simple. If the people don't want it, they should change it. But let us end it on amicable terms and not have a row. The monarchy exists not for its own benefit but for that of the country. We don't come here for our health. We can think of other ways of enjoying ourselves."

The suggestion that Philip had better things to do than tour Canada ruffled a few feathers even as it reminded people that being a working member of the royal family was sometimes an arduous job as well as a privileged way of life. More typically candid statements were to come a few days later in the United States.

Philip's behavior confirmed that there was something about America that seemed to relax the royals. After the unprecedented sight of the Queen chewing gum and then mingling with supermarket shoppers on their memorable 1957 trip, Philip agreed to a live interview with Barbara Walters of NBC's *Today* show in 1969, a first for a senior royal. One biographer wrote that Walters spotted Philip at the White House and reprimanded Nixon for inviting only men to the dinner that night. Nixon, shamed, put in a word with Philip to do the interview, which the palace had already turned down.

Walters had covered Prince Charles's investiture as Prince of Wales a few weeks earlier and used that experience to work in a delicate question. "I'd heard when I was in Wales, and perhaps it was just one of those foolish rumors that go around, that there might be some possibility of the Queen abdicating at some future date for her son? She's still such a young woman [Elizabeth was then forty-three], and there might be some fears that His Royal Highness might be a very old man when he came to the throne. . . . Is it a rumor?"

Philip quickly responded: "As far as I know it's a rumor." Unwisely he kept talking. "I mean, it has its attractions," he said. "But no, I don't think it's been thought of very seriously. . . . The idea that he would only be capable of making any contribution if he was sovereign is really not true. There have been so many cases where the heir has in fact had a very particular ability to do things which you wouldn't have otherwise. But who knows, it's all in the future, anything may happen."

It was this final sentence that was picked up by some of the media—construing it as a sign that abdication was possible—although, as became abundantly clear as her reign went on, Elizabeth II was adamantly against the idea of abdicating. This was not just because she saw the upheaval after her uncle gave up the throne, but also because she feared it would weaken the monarchy by making it look like an option that could be abandoned on a whim.

The classic example of what Philip himself called dontopedalogy ("the science of opening your mouth and putting your foot in it, a science which I have practised for a good many years") came shortly afterward in a prerecorded interview with NBC's *Meet the Press*, when he was asked about royal finances.

"We go into the red next year," Prince Philip said, referring to the annual budget set when the Queen came to the throne that had not been changed since 1952 despite rising inflation. "Which is not bad housekeeping if you come to think of it. We've in fact kept the thing going on a budget which was based on costs of eighteen years ago. So there have been very considerable corners that have had to be cut, and it's beginning to have its effect . . . Now inevitably if nothing happens we shall either have to—I don't know—we may have to move into smaller premises. Who knows? . . . We had a small yacht which we've had to sell and I shall probably have to give up polo fairly soon, things like that."

This time the outcry was huge and sparked a public debate in the UK. It came against the backdrop of the 1960s social revolution, when attitudes toward traditional ways of doing things were changing dramatically, demands for egalitarianism were growing, and questions were raised about the legitimacy of hereditary monarchy. The royal finances *were* stretched—but Philip's examples of having to sell a small yacht and perhaps having to stop playing polo were widely ridiculed as out of touch.

Barbara Castle, a prominent left-wing Labour MP, said there was little sympathy for the husband of "one of the richest women in the world," while a group of dockworkers in East London wrote to Philip, sardonically offering to start a collection to buy him a polo pony. Wilson headed off a potential crisis by ordering a parliamentary review, always a good device for lowering the temperature of a hot issue because of the time it would inevitably take.

After the interview, Walters wrote to Philip to apologize for the fuss. He wrote back with customary British diffidence and politeness, saying that he did not mind being "the means of unlocking such a spectacular display of cheerfulness and goodwill . . . particularly in this day and age when most demonstrations seem to reflect nothing but anger and provocation."

Nor did Philip hold Nixon responsible for his NBC controversies, writing to him that "the weather in New York was horrible but otherwise all went well and I found Miss Walters particularly charming and intelligent. I hope we did a good piece." In his handwritten note, Philip was more concerned that he breached protocol at the White House dinner, which had a guest list that included Vice President Spiro Agnew, most cabinet members, and other notables like Ross Perot, the successful businessman who would later run for president, and British-born Bob Hope. "I was quite overwhelmed by the guests but delighted to meet such a distinguished company," he wrote, adding that he wanted to "humbly apologize."

"After the brilliance of the other speakers and yourself, I am afraid my contribution was very lame. That night I woke up in a cold sweat when I realized I had forgotten to propose your health!"

The dust had just about settled on Prince Philip's US adventure by the time Charles and Anne arrived in Washington, DC, from

Canada in July 1970. Nixon had sent Tricia to represent him at Charles's investiture as Prince of Wales, when she told reporters: "Our family are all great Anglophiles." However, despite taking tea with the Queen, there had not been time to meet Charles, who went off on tour after his big day. Nixon now set about remedying that. The prince found himself scheduled to attend several high-profile events in the company of the petite, blond Tricia, including the obligatory visit to Mount Vernon in the footsteps of two previous Princes of Wales, dinner and late-night dancing at a party for six hundred guests on the White House lawn, and a baseball game at the capital's RFK Stadium. The president seemed delighted at the chance to host the young royals, particularly the prince, even if Charles did show some discomfort in the ninety-one-degree heat at the baseball park. Rather than unbutton his immaculately tailored jacket, loosen his tie, or don a hat, he asked to be moved from the exposed presidential box to an area of covered seating.

Nixon's son-in-law, David Eisenhower, working the summer as a statistician for the Washington Senators, explained the differences between balls and strikes, walks and runs, to the bemused prince. *The New York Times* reported that "long before the end of the game in which the Senators defeated the California Angels, 4-0, the prince and princess had left to see the collection of mostly impressionist paintings at the gallery home of the late Duncan Phillips."

Charles was more in his element earlier in the day when he went with David to the Patuxent Wildlife Research Center in Maryland. The prince looked at barn owls, red-winged black-birds, peregrine falcons, and Andean condors, and put on a pair of protective boots to approach whooping cranes. "He conversed with the birds at length," reporters noted. "He's said more to that one crane than he's said to the press in all the time he's been here."

Apart from the birds, the highlight of the trip for Charles and the president turned out to be their private conversation in the Oval Office on the afternoon before the royals departed. Scheduled for half an hour, the encounter lasted eighty minutes and ranged over a wide spectrum of subjects, including world affairs, Anglo-American relations, the environment, youth attitudes, and world population, according to Gerald Warren, the deputy White House press secretary.

"The prince obviously made a very good impression on the president," he said. Nixon urged the prince to be a "presence," but Charles "pointed out one must not become controversial too often otherwise people don't take you seriously." Charles wrote in his diary later that "to be just a presence would be fatal. I know lots of Americans think one's main job is to go around saying meaningless niceties. . . . A presence alone can be swept away so easily." Nixon praised the prince in his own private diary, writing that he confounded expectations of "a rather callow, superficial youth with no particular interest or understanding of world affairs. His conduct completely dispelled that image." Tricia confided that, just before the prince left, he invited her to England. Pat Nixon whispered excitedly to reporters: "He'll be in touch."

There was to be no further meeting between the prince and the First Daughter, however. Tricia married Harvard Law student Edward Cox in a White House Rose Garden ceremony almost exactly a year after Charles's visit. The huge US media interest in the visit of the Queen's eldest children underlined the continuing American fascination with the royal family, even if Anne's unwillingness to live up to expectations of a fairy-tale princess—one headline called her the "un-fairy princess" for appearing "bored"—left some of the British media feeling defensive of a teenager still finding her feet on the global stage.

When Charles visited the White House thirty-five years later with his second wife, Camilla, he recalled the special attention he had received from President Nixon. Replying to a dinner toast from George W. Bush in November 2005, he said: "It brings back many fond and happy memories of my first visit here with my sister. I think it was in 1970, when we came to stay at the White House for the weekend with President and Mrs. Nixon, at the time when the media were busy trying to marry me off to Tricia Nixon."

By the time Nixon crossed the Atlantic for his next UK visit on October 3, 1970, there was a new man in Downing Street. Edward Heath's fixation with joining the European Economic Community meant that he was willing to downplay US relations to assuage French concerns that Britain looked westward to America too much to be considered a reliable member. Heath's biographer Philip Ziegler recounted Henry Kissinger's reported observation that Heath was the only British leader he had met who "not only failed to cultivate the special relationship with the United States but actively sought to downgrade it."

Nixon touched down at Heathrow at 11:13 a.m. and helicoptered to Chequers for talks with Heath and lunch with the
Queen. His entourage arrived in a fleet of four more US Air
Force helicopters. They were used as much for security as speed
during the tight timetable—by 4:29 p.m. he was back on Air
Force One—amid continuing anger among the British public
over the Vietnam War. Several hundred people gathered outside the entrance of the redbrick Tudor mansion, some waving
placards calling for peace in Vietnam.

When Nixon landed in the grounds of the thousand-acre
estate in the Chiltern Hills, he said he "looked down on a
beautiful forest. . . . It was just like *Shangri-La* [a mythical Ti-
betan valley immortalized by novelist James Hilton in his 1933
novel *Lost Horizon*]." Once again relations with the Soviet
Union were high on the US-UK agenda, as well as the highly
charged Middle East situation following the recent death of
Egyptian president Gamal Abdel Nasser and a brief conflict in
Jordan as King Hussein fought to expel hostile Palestinian
forces. Nixon told Heath that having a country retreat "clears
your thinking" and compared it to Camp David in Maryland,
which he visited frequently.

The Queen was on holiday with her family at Balmoral, but
in a sign of how much she wanted to nurture the Special Relationship and maintain personal contact with the US president,
she made the almost five-hundred-mile journey south to share
lunch. It was Elizabeth's first visit to Chequers, "and many
Britons considered the precedent a special salute to the Nixons," according to the Associated Press. The Queen also wanted
to thank the president and the First Lady for the hospitality
they showed her two eldest children just a few months earlier.

She had another mission: to ease the potentially awkward first encounter of an Anglophile president with Britain's least Atlanticist postwar prime minister.

Despite Heath's European focus—and Tricia's nuptials—Nixon remained very keen to see the Queen again and early in 1973 suggested a royal state visit to the US during bicentennial celebrations for the Declaration of Independence in three years' time. This was envisaged as a glorious tribute to the Special Relationship forged by nations that put war behind them to become one of the world's greatest democratic alliances, and would be a highlight of his second term.

But despite winning a reelection landslide, things did not go according to the script Nixon so fondly imagined.

CHAPTER 6

The United States has never forgotten its British heritage.

—Gerald R. Ford, July 7, 1976

The prospect of Queen Elizabeth II, a direct descendant of King George III, appearing in the United States during the giant national party for the two hundredth anniversary of the Declaration of Independence made some senior British officials nervous.

"One would wish to consider whether it was right for the Queen to be associated in this way with the celebration of a rebellion from the British Crown," wrote Robert Armstrong, Prime Minister Heath's principal private secretary, to Sir Martin Charteris, the Queen's private secretary, during behind-the-scenes discussions over Nixon's invitation. The British ambassador in Washington, Rowland Baring, husband of the Queen's lady-in-waiting Esme Cromer, "has some feeling that there may be a certain degree of uninhibited zest about the American celebrations of the Declaration of Independence with which it might not be entirely desirable that the Queen should be associated," Armstrong relayed. "A certain amount of ballyhoo is inseparable from this sort of celebration in America which would conspicuously lack dignity."

The Queen herself was, by all accounts, not worried. In the end, Downing Street, Buckingham Palace, and the White House found a compromise: Elizabeth II would arrive in Philadelphia, the city where the Thirteen Colonies committed themselves to split from the Crown, two days after July 4. Only then would she venture to Washington, DC, the capital named after the general who became the first president, for her first meeting with the thirty-eighth occupant of the White House. It proved to be one of the Queen's most memorable and successful US visits, showing just how wrong the men in suits were to be anxious.

In the delicate dance of protocol that always accompanies royal tours, George Springsteen, special assistant to Secretary of State Henry Kissinger, informed Brent Scowcroft, deputy national security advisor, on May 23, 1975, that "we have learned from the British Embassy that the dates July 7–11, 1976, have been suggested by Buckingham Palace as convenient for a State Visit by Her Majesty." This was the green light for the president to invite the Queen to America.

Springsteen attached a draft letter of invitation, which opened with a statement that "In a little more than a year it will be two centuries since it became necessary for our people 'to dissolve the political bonds' which connected them to yours." The White House rejected this reminder of past difficulties in favor of an approach focusing on present-day bonds: "On behalf of the people of the United States of America, it gives me great pleasure to extend to you and to the Duke of Edinburgh a cordial invitation to make a State Visit to the United States . . . on the occasion of our 200th anniversary celebrations. Your visit, I know, will serve to underscore the very close ties of friendship which unite our peoples."

The Queen replied formally to "gladly accept" the invitation for thirteen months hence, two years after she was originally invited by Nixon. Recalling her "happy memories of previous visits to the United States," she welcomed "the opportunity to see more of your country and the American people." The typewritten note from Windsor Castle was signed off with a handwritten flourish: "Your sincere friend, Elizabeth R."

The Queen was the first foreign head of state to receive a formal invitation to join America's bicentennial party. The next one went out to French president Valéry Giscard d'Estaing—France having been the main ally of the American revolutionaries.

Planning for the visits took a sinister turn in September 1975. Ford survived two assassination attempts within seventeen days, both in California by lone women who tried to shoot him. On September 5, Lynette Fromme, a follower of jailed cult leader Charles Manson, pointed a Colt .45 from just two feet away as Ford shook hands with a crowd in Sacramento after leaving his hotel. She did not have a bullet in the chamber, and a Secret Service agent grabbed the gun and forced her

to the ground without a shot being fired. In San Francisco on
September 22, would-be assassin Sara Jane Moore fired off two
rounds from a Smith & Wesson .38 revolver from a distance of
forty feet as the president emerged from a hotel in Union
Square, missing Ford's head by about five inches before a by-
stander intervened to grab her arm as she fired a second time,
wounding a taxi driver. Ford was bundled into his car, where
Donald Rumsfeld, his chief of staff, threw himself on top of
him as they sped away.

Ford's attitude toward the two assassination attempts was to
carry on as normal, as far as he could. "The most important
thing is that I don't think any person as president . . . ought to
cower in the face of a limited number of people, out of 214 million Americans, who want to take the law into their own
hands," he told reporters back at the White House on the evening of the second attempt. "If we can't have the opportunity of
talking with one another, seeing one another, shaking hands
with one another, something has gone wrong in our society."
He did make one concession to security, consenting to wear a
bulletproof overcoat for future public outings.

Across the pond, headline writers thought American society was already too dangerous. On September 25, Jack Marsh,
counselor to the president, wrote an urgent memo to his deputy, Russell Rourke, directing him to keep discussion of security for the Queen's visit strictly between a tight group of
officials and to send as few memos about it as possible: "I do not
want any public or even widespread knowledge internally of
our discussion of this," he wrote. "My guess is that the British
are somewhat concerned by the recent events from the stand-
point of the visit of the Royal Family."

As evidence of British sensibilities, he summed up press coverage of the assassination attempts: "Americans must expect their Presidents to be shot at until the Nation's 'gun-madness' is curbed by tougher laws, British newspapers said today."

Less existential concerns were causing consternation at another branch of the US government: the State Department Protocol Office. The subject of what to wear was on British and American minds. Buckingham Palace wanted to know the dress code so that the Queen's outfit could be custom-made. The big question: Was the state dinner to be white-tie or black-tie? White-tie meant tailcoats and ball gowns, jewels, tiaras, medals, and decorations; black-tie not so much ostentation. The Queen's previous state visit in 1957 had been a white-tie affair, but that was in mid-October, when Washington was much cooler than it would be in early July.

"It has been our policy to not have White Tie dinners from Memorial Day through Labor Day. The main reason for this is because White Tie would be too warm," wrote Maria Downs, the White House social secretary, to First Lady Betty Ford, seeking her thoughts in January 1976. The rigid traditions of previous years were ebbing away, she suggested. "The British Embassy has also informed the State Department that in Great Britain they have started wearing decorations with Black Tie during the summer months. . . . If our dinner is Black Tie, we will then be confronted with the question of do we copy the English once again and start wearing decorations with Black Tie for summer events of White Tie merit or do we stand by American social tradition?" Clearly the social revolution of the Swinging Sixties was beginning to have a pernicious impact on British high society. Betty Ford was not about to let standards slip in her White House. White-tie it would be—medals, tiaras, the works.

With the dress code settled, it was time for Henry Catto, the US chief of protocol, to set out other formalities of hosting British royals in a memo for the president and staff.

"The Queen is 'Your Majesty' at first greeting and 'Ma'am' thereafter; Prince Philip is 'Your (Royal) Highness' and afterwards 'Sir,'" he advised. With day dress, "the Queen and members of her party will wear hats. You may choose to do so but it is not obligatory," he wrote. "The Queen and members of her party will probably not wear black dresses. This is a personal preference of the Queen's and should in no way inhibit you from wearing black."

There was more information on greeting the monarch: "In large crowds, the Queen and Duke of Edinburgh usually do not shake hands. When being introduced, wait until they have extended their hands before extending yours." Unlike her subjects from Britain and the royal realms like Canada, "the Queen does not expect Americans to curtsy or bow, especially in an informal situation. You may, however, merely bow your head slightly when being introduced. If you wish to curtsy, it should be a short quick bob."

When escorting the Queen: "Walk beside her on her left. If it is necessary for one of you to go ahead of the other, you should allow the Queen to take the lead. She is always in the lead of a procession . . . please do not take hold of her arm or hand." Not every US president would follow the rules, but Ford appears to have taken close notice. For catering, there was the reminder that no uncooked seafood should be served, and for drinks: "The Queen and the Duke of Edinburgh drink sherry, gin and tonics. The Duke of Edinburgh drinks lager beer."

Prince Charles played no part in the bicentennial visit, making Ford the most recent American president the future king never met. In February 1976, at the age of twenty-seven and a lieutenant in the Royal Navy, he took charge of his first ship, the minesweeper HMS *Bronington*. As one of the world's most high-profile bachelors, he was attracting enormous media speculation about his romantic life, and in May of that year he gave an interview to *Good Housekeeping* that displayed his views of women and marriage.

"At the moment I don't feel like becoming domestic," he told the magazine, his words carried in newspapers across America. "I personally feel a good age for a man to get married is around thirty. After one has seen a great deal of life, met a large number of girls, fallen in love every now and then, one knows what it's all about." Charles eventually tied the knot with Diana Spencer at the age of thirty-two.

In a TV interview with journalist Alistair Cooke, the prince, who felt far less constrained by diplomatic niceties than his mother, came out in defense of George III. His ancestor, a byword for tyranny in the US, was a "complete idealist" who "only saw things in black and white," which led him to pursue the war against the thirteen colonies to the end, said Charles, who studied history at Cambridge University.

"I should hate what happened in a political and international sense should mask the king as a person, as a human being, someone who was a great patron, a great family man," he said.

It was not the most helpful preparation for his mother's visit.

Anne Armstrong, the first woman to act as US ambassador to Britain, presented her credentials to the Queen at Buckingham Palace in March 1976, and with them a note from President Ford stressing how much he was looking forward to the royal visit.

The monarch, about to celebrate her fiftieth birthday, was "a pretty woman, prettier than her pictures," Armstrong said afterward. Elizabeth's courteous reply to Ford thanked him for "the arrangements which are being made to enable us to participate in the American bicentennial in such an agreeable way." It was signed off once again with a handwritten "Your sincere friend, Elizabeth R."

Elizabeth II planned to arrive by sea at Penn's Landing, named for the first place that the English Quaker William Penn went ashore in 1682 (even if the actual landfall site was a little farther along the Delaware River) and founded the city he named after the Greek for "brotherly love" because of the religious tolerance he envisaged. On July 3, the royal party took a Royal Air Force Vickers VC10, a British-made plane, on the seven-hour flight from London's Heathrow Airport to Bermuda, a British overseas territory in the North Atlantic, where they boarded the royal yacht *Britannia* for the three-day, 780-mile voyage to Philadelphia.

Britannia was one high-profile asset of the royal family that was increasingly criticized by those who questioned the cost of the monarchy. It was also particularly beloved by the Queen, who made sure that it was pressed into action as often as possible to justify its expense. The yacht would host four US presidents before being decommissioned in 1979, making 696 foreign visits during twenty-five years in service. "The Royal Yacht's function is to ensure that Her Majesty has rest between some fairly merciless demands," wrote Baltimore-born Susan Crosland, the wife of the British foreign secretary Anthony Crosland, both of whom accompanied the royal party, in her account of an eventful voyage.

On the second night a force-nine (on a scale of twelve) gale blew up. "By evening *Britannia* rode the waves higher and higher, coming to rest for a moment at a 45° angle before lurching over a crest, resting once more with the deck pitched at the opposing 45°. When the passengers reassembled in the drawing-room for a drink before dinner, there was uncertainty as to who would be present," Crosland wrote.

Despite a belief that the Queen did not enjoy rough seas, she appeared "almost merry" in stark contrast to Philip, "his face less fresh than usual, ashen and drawn." Dinner did not last long. The Queen bade a memorable good night to her guests after coffee in the drawing room, holding on to the handle of a sliding door while *Britannia* pitched over a wave, her scarf flung out behind her. "Wheeeeeeee," said the Queen as she slid along with the door. She paused momentarily for the next wave to open the door so she could leave.

"Wheeeeeeeeee," said the Queen again, then "Good night" as she disappeared, with Prince Philip right behind her. Ewen Fergusson, Anthony Crosland's private secretary, informed his boss the next day that he managed to reach his cabin "with exactly two seconds to spare." At lunch, the Queen appeared in top form. "I have *never* seen so many grey and grim faces round a dinner table. Philip was not at all well," she said, giggling. "I'm glad to say."

On day three of the voyage, the Queen advised Susan Crosland how to cope when standing up for hours during the grueling official engagements that lay ahead on the six-day tour. "One plants one's feet apart like this," the monarch said. "Always keep them parallel. Make sure your weight is evenly distributed. That's all there is to it." Looking at the hour-by-hour plans for America, Crosland added: "Everyone agreed the schedule was murderous. . . . I have never experienced anything so arduous."

As *Britannia* entered Philadelphia harbor so the Queen could disembark at 10:00 a.m. sharp, the hot and humid July weather was as challenging as the high seas: "We were met by a wall of wet heat." Nevertheless, the welcome was spectacular, with city fireboats streaming columns of water into the air and a crowd of five thousand at the dockside waving mini Union Jacks and Stars and Stripes, bursting into applause at the sight of the Queen.

After a brief welcoming ceremony, the royal party headed into the city in a motorcade, with Elizabeth II riding in President Ford's own car, which he loaned for the day. The main event was the presentation of a Bicentennial Bell, forged at the Whitechapel Foundry in London, the same company that in 1751 made the famous cracked Liberty Bell. Weighing in at 12,446 pounds and five feet six inches in height, the 1976 bell was inscribed: "For the people of the United States of America from the people of Britain 4 July 1976" and "Let Freedom Ring."

This was not enough for a small band of protesters led by the Reverend Carl McIntire, a New Jersey fundamentalist, who objected through a bullhorn from half a block away that the new bell omitted the biblical inscription on the original (derived from Leviticus: "Proclaim LIBERTY Throughout all the

Land unto all the Inhabitants Thereof"). There was a more substantial protest from around four hundred members of Irish Northern Aid, who carried placards urging British withdrawal from Northern Ireland. They were dwarfed by an estimated throng of seventy-five thousand Philadelphians, who squeezed and pushed to catch a glimpse of the British monarch and drowned protests with cheers.

Unflappable amid the humid kerfuffle, the Queen delivered a short but heartfelt speech judged to have struck the right note with her American audience. "I speak to you as the direct descendant of King George III. He was the last crowned sovereign to rule in this country, and it is therefore with a particular personal interest that I view those events which took place two hundred years ago," she began, avoiding praise for her ancestor—unlike her son—but also sidestepping condemnation. This was the kind of studiously neutral approach that she employed to maintain her general popularity at home and overseas.

She then delivered an audacious take on the bicentennial that gave the newspapers their headlines: "It seems to me that Independence Day, the Fourth of July, should be celebrated as much in Britain as in America. Not in rejoicing in the separation of the American colonies from the British crown but in sincere gratitude to the Founding Fathers of this great Republic for having taught Britain a very valuable lesson. We lost the American colonies because we lacked that statesmanship to know the right time, and the manner of yielding, what is impossible to keep. But the lesson was well learned." She continued: "We learned to respect the right of others to govern themselves in their own ways. . . . Without that great act in the cause of liberty performed in Independence Hall two hundred years ago, we could never have transformed an empire into a commonwealth."

This was a twist on the story of Britain's—and her family's—lost empire and a rather generous reinterpretation of the fraught struggle for independence by numerous former colonies, many of which fought for decades to achieve what the patriots won in 1783. As evidenced by the years of bloodshed and suffering in neighboring Ireland and faraway India, to name just two former corners of the British Empire, Britain was much slower to learn the lessons of 1776 than Elizabeth suggested. But her words were taken in good spirit, as a tribute to the endeavor of the Americans and a recognition of the justice of their cause. *The New York Times'* front page carried the banner headline "Queen Calls 1776 a Lesson That Aided Britain."

Ahead of lunch with various dignitaries on *Britannia*, Hobie Cawood, the superintendent of Independence Park who showed the Queen the original bell, fell into discussion with Thomas Kleppe, the US secretary of the interior, and his wife, Glen, about one of the mysteries of royal behavior.

"I wonder what she has in her purse," Glen said. Cawood wondered too, saying: "You know she's got ladies-in-waiting. If she needs a dime or a Kleenex or something, all she's got to do is turn and look at somebody and they'll give it to her, but she carries the purse with her all the time."

After lunch, Thomas Kleppe had news and found Cawood: "He says, 'Hobie, Hobie, guess what—I know what's in the purse.' And I said, 'What?' And he said, 'Well, when we went into lunch, as the president's representative I sat on her left. And we were all gathered at the table and when she was seated, she opened up her purse and took out a C-clamp and screwed it into the table and closed her purse and hung her purse over the C-clamp. And when lunch was over, she picked up her purse, unscrewed the clamp, put the clamp back in the purse, and was ready to go.'"

What did the Queen keep in her purse? A clamp to hold her purse.

(According to Gerald Bodmer, chief executive of Launer, the British company that made the Queen's favorite purses, she always carried one because "she doesn't feel fully dressed without her handbag." Some were custom-made with longer handles to allow for easier handshaking. Over the years she was photographed removing a pair of glasses and a tube of lipstick from them and was also said to carry a makeup compact, mints, a penknife, and—at least while at home—treats for her corgis. The bag had another use: usually carried over the Queen's left arm, if she switched arms during conversation it was said to be a signal to a lady-in-waiting to intervene to help her move on. In the final photograph of Elizabeth II taken at Balmoral in front of a roaring fire and leaning on a cane, her trusty black handbag was right there on her arm.)

The Queen toured Independence Park and visited the nearby portrait gallery. "We came up on those steps, and looking east and west on Chestnut Street, almost as far as you could see, were people," Cawood said. "They all had handkerchiefs in their hands, and they were waving them and it reminded me of some of the things you saw in World War Two. But she was very touched by that."

Her host at that evening's black-tie dinner at the Philadelphia Museum of Art was Frank Rizzo, the larger-than-life city mayor and former police commissioner, who kept getting up from his plum seat next to the monarch to wander around and talk to other guests. The Queen's ladies-in-waiting were outraged and privately complained to Elizabeth that his behavior was rude. Maintaining the polite inscrutability for which she was known, but which nevertheless also managed to hint faintly at disapproval, Elizabeth simply said: "What a fascinating man he is."

At one point during the evening, Susan Crosland found two women engaged in a tussle outside the ladies' restroom. One was a lady-in-waiting, the other, it transpired, an FBI agent in a green satin evening gown who was under orders never to let the Queen out of her sight.

"You won't," said the lady-in-waiting, physically barring the agent's way to the facilities.

"I must," said the agent, grappling with her adversary.

"You won't," repeated the royal aide, resisting. The Queen reappeared, fanning herself with a menu, serenely unaware of the commotion.

"Frightfully hot in Philadelphia," she said. "Is it always like this in July?"

It was even hotter in Washington the next day—one hundred degrees in the shade. The interest stirred by the Queen's visit contributed to heavy city traffic, which delayed the arrival of the Kissingers and General George S. Brown, chairman of the

Joint Chiefs of Staff, who were supposed to be the main greet-
ers on the White House South Lawn for the Queen's formal
arrival with full military honors. Brown and his wife arrived
halfway through the ceremony, "wringing wet and crimson-
faced" after abandoning their trapped limousine. In his welcome speech, Ford found various ways to praise the British,
without whom there would not have been rebellious colonialists
in the first place.

"During the 169 years between the first settlement of Jamestown and our independence, thirteen colonies prospered, pro-
tected by the British Navy, enjoying the advantage of British
commerce, and adopting British concepts of representative
self-government," he said. "In declaring independence in 1776,
we looked for guidance to our British heritage of representative
government . . . as well as law."

Ford glossed over the next eight years of revolutionary
struggle and instead moved straight on to emphasize mutual
friendship. "Your Majesty's visit symbolizes our deep and continuing commitment to the common values of an Anglo-
American civilization," he said. "Your Majesty, for generations
our peoples have worked together and fought together side by
side. As democracies we continue our quest for peace and justice. . . . The principles of human dignity and individual rights
set forth in the Magna Carta and our own Declaration of Independence remain truly revolutionary landmarks. Your Majesty, the wounds of our parting in 1776 healed long ago.
Americans admire the United Kingdom as one of our truest
allies and best friends."

Ford also found room in his speech to deliver a domestic
message, talking up what he hoped was a big achievement of

his own presidency—the only administration born out of a predecessor's resignation, which followed a long period of turmoil that included the assassinations of JFK, Robert Kennedy, and Martin Luther King Jr.; the Vietnam War; and Watergate.

"As you travel throughout our land, I trust that you will find something else in the United States—a new sense of unity, of friendship, of purpose, and tranquility. Something wonderful happened to America this past weekend. A spirit of unity and togetherness deep within the American soul sprang to the surface in a way that we had almost forgotten," he said to Elizabeth II. This was the part of the message of national healing that Ford hoped would carry him to the Republican nomination and a presidential election victory of his own. While paying careful attention to his royal guests, he was also keeping a close eye on the Republican primary contest for that November's election. Although he had secured more pledged delegates in the state-by-state contest than his opponent, former California governor Ronald Reagan, the number was not enough to guarantee success at the party convention, scheduled for a few weeks away in August. It was the last time the nominee was not clear before the gathering, but Ford eventually prevailed.

The Queen, in her formal reply, name-checked the elephant in the garden—her great-great-great-great-grandfather—stressing how America's second president began the rapprochement.

"John Adams, America's first ambassador, said to my ancestor, King George III, that it was his desire to help with the restoration of 'the old good nature and the old good humor between our peoples,'" she said. "That restoration has long been made, and the links of language, tradition, and personal contact have maintained it. . . . Our countries have a great deal in common. The early British settlers created here a society that owes much to its origins across the ocean. For nearly 170 years there was a formal constitutional link between us. Your Declaration of Independence broke that link, but it did not for long break our friendship." Britain and the US now "are as close today as two peoples have ever been," she said. "We see you as our strong and trusted friend, and we believe that you, in turn, will find us as ready as ever to bear our full share in defending the values in which we both believe."

For the White House arrival Elizabeth wore a tailored powder blue coat with a matching large round hat with a bobble on it that did not please Richard Blackwell, a well-known and waspish fashion designer, who called it "a dreadful hat which bore no resemblance to what a queen should look like." Blackwell, founder of the annual "Ten Worst-Dressed Women" list, said the Queen looked "dull, dowdy, and ten years older than her age" and that her clothes failed "to give a good image of Britain."

The royals and the Fords had a private lunch at the White House, their first chance to get to know each other. This was the moment to exchange gifts. Betty Ford had put a lot of time and effort into this gesture, according to Downs, the social secretary.

"The official gift was a beautiful bronze equestrian statue," Downs recalled. It was a fifteen-and-a-half-inch-high sculpture by celebrated Western artist Harry Jackson called *Two Champs*, depicting cowboy Clayton Danks astride bucking rodeo horse Steamboat, on a Wyoming jade base. "When it arrived they had it on a turnstile going round and round. When we placed it upstairs for the presentation at the luncheon, we looked at it and felt it was kind of hokey going round and round while they are having lunch, so I asked the butler to unplug it." Mistake.

"Well, in the briefing that Mrs. Ford had, it was stated that it was supposed to rotate. So when the president and Philip looked at the gift, the president said, 'That's supposed to go around and around,' and they are standing there looking at it, and then the two of them got down on their hands and knees looking for the place to plug in the statue." A butler who witnessed the scene told Downs afterward: "They plugged it back in finally. But it took a while for them to find it." Ford and the Prince bonded over the search for an outlet.

Formalities that afternoon including laying a wreath at the Tomb of the Unknown Soldier at Arlington National Cemetery and visiting the Lincoln Memorial. The hot and humid weather in Washington broke shortly before the scheduled start of the white-tie dinner, due to be held in an air-conditioned, flower-bedecked marquee in the White House Rose Garden, causing no little panic among staff.

"There was a terrible storm . . . that caused the loss of four or five trees in the grounds," recalled Downs, whose job it was to ensure the smooth running of the evening. "Dick Cheney [then Ford's chief of staff] realized what was happening. He sent the troops down. He said, 'Go out and see if Maria needs some help out there in the tent.' So people came out from the West Wing and we literally battened down the hatches."

Fortunately, the storm subsided as the Fords were waiting to greet the Queen and Prince Philip at the North Portico, captured live for the American TV audience and beamed across the pond via satellite. Even more fortunately, the live camera coverage ended shortly before the Fords and the Windsors reached the elevator inside.

"They got into the elevator to go up to the Yellow Oval Room for an aperitif," Downs said. "The elevator door opened and there stood [the president's son] Jack Ford: bare feet, and bare chest in search of studs for his dress shirt. Mrs. Ford said to me later, 'I wanted to die. Here's the Queen with her tiara and Jerry and I and everybody, white tie, and here's Jack standing there big as life.' And she said, 'Your Majesty, I am so sorry, I'm so embarrassed.'"

Betty Ford recalled: "The Queen said, 'Oh, think nothing of it. I have one of those at home.' And obviously she does. In fact, a couple of them, from what I've read."

The two couples descended the Grand Staircase into the White House Entrance Hall to the strains of "Hail to the Chief." After a receiving line it was downstairs via another elevator to the Rose Garden and the air-conditioned marquee. Among the 224 guests were Lady Bird Johnson, widow of the thirty-sixth president, and Alice Roosevelt Longworth, the ninety-two-year-old daughter of the twenty-sixth, Theodore Roosevelt—as well as Paul Mellon, the Queen's horse-owning friend whom she visited on her 1957 visit and who was a regular at the Royal Ascot horse meet.

Several stars from the world of entertainment were present, including Bob Hope, singer Ella Fitzgerald, violinist Yehudi Menuhin, British leading lady Merle Oberon, and American actors Telly Savalas and Cary Grant. There were also a number of senior Republicans from uncommitted state delegations ahead of the all-important party convention, as Ford used the occasion to try to advance his reelection ambitions. This dinner was one of the hottest tickets of the Ford presidency, which meant there were many more people angling for an invitation than there were seats available. As Betty Ford admitted: "There were many months of lists, and probably a lot of bickering and arguing, but everybody had to be there for a reason." Just being nice was not enough. "A nice person had to come to some other dinner."

The Queen, wearing a full-length lemon yellow organza dress sparkling with sequins and the kingfisher blue Order of the Garter sash from her left shoulder to her right hip, was "resplendent in diamonds including a tiara, necklace, earrings and bracelet." Betty Ford was in green chiffon with a necklace of crystals and sequins. "Your Majesty, this evening we honor a very remarkable relationship between two sovereign nations," President Ford said in his toast, a speech which really went out of its way to stress the positive British contribution to the establishment of America. "During our two hundred years as an independent nation, the United States has never forgotten its British heritage. Nearly four centuries ago, the British came to a wilderness and built a new civilization on British custom, British fortitude, British law, and British government. Our Founding Fathers served in British colonial legislatures, fought in British military forces, and learned representative self-government from British books and practice."

Now for the tricky bit, which the president managed without mention of taxation, war, the French, or the Native Americans. "For all this, the colonists from England and other lands created in America a civilization different from that of the mother country. Inevitably, we dissolved the political bands that connected us. The United States won independence and established a nation that adapted the best of British traditions to the American climate and to the American character. Our reconciliation, our friendship and firm alliance seem, in retrospect, to have been natural for two nations that share the same fundamental devotion to human dignity."

All this was accompanied by a true American feast. Henry Haller, the White House chef, admitted that his first course of Maine lobsters, cooked, glazed, and decorated with truffles, had been "a lot of tedious work" but said it was "worthwhile" because he judged it a "queenly presentation." The saddle of veal for the main course cost the White House $800, he added.

After dinner, it was back up into the mansion for coffee and liqueurs before entertainment in the East Room from Bob Hope, followed by the husband-and-wife musical duo Captain & Tennille, who were egged on by Betty Ford to play their most suggestive songs. Not that the royal couple were fazed. Prince Philip clearly enjoyed the performance, but the Queen began to flag and appeared to doze off momentarily.

"We had two great hits, 'Love Will Keep Us Together' and 'The Way I Want to Touch You,'" Toni Tennille recalled. "I thought, 'I probably can't do "The Way I Want to Touch You." It might be a little too intimate for the White House.' But then when Mrs. Ford came in and said, 'Are you going to do "The Way I Want to Touch You"?' I said, 'We weren't planning to.' She said, 'Oh you must! It's Gerry and my favorite song.'"

Tennille then discussed the rest of the repertoire with Daryl "Captain" Dragon. "I said to Daryl, 'We really should do "Muskrat Love" too.' It was a huge hit and I thought everyone would get a kick out of it. I thought they seemed like a fun group!" "Muskrat Love" was notable for the way Daryl used squeaks from his synthesizer to re-create the sound of lovemaking rodents. However, the volume of the speakers in the East Room was rather high and not everyone seemed amused. Tennille recalled Henry Kissinger looking "miserable"—for years afterwards she would dedicate the song to him—while the Queen appeared to nod off. "So I started 'Muskrat, muskrat' and you know, here's Prince Philip, he's kind of tapping his foot and smiling. Queen Elizabeth . . . I think she had jetlag, bless her heart."

The evening was not yet over, and there was more mischief afoot. Having transferred again across the first floor of the White House to the State Dining Room for dancing, the crowd parted to allow Ford and the Queen to take to the floor as the US Marine Band struck up the next number on their playlist. Unfortunately, this was the Rodgers and Hart show tune "The Lady Is a Tramp." Not that many people seemed to notice at the time, but it was picked up by the press and portrayed as a big gaffe.

David Wright, who played bassoon and saxophone in the band, said that the choice of tune "was just accidental" because the songs were numbered, not named, and the band did not realize that any faux pas had occurred until the Associated Press report. "We didn't see the significance at the time," Wright said. "People were dancing. It was just a medley!"

Betty Ford was, however, slightly peeved but still tried to laugh the whole thing off. "If the Marine band, which plays for every occasion, doesn't have sense enough to come up with something appropriate . . . Boy, that's really bottle-feeding the band if you have to set it up," she said. "I thought it was a funny coincidence. It really didn't bother me." Laughing, she added: "Maybe it was referring to me."

Betty Ford gave herself high marks for the Queen's visit, writing in her memoirs: "If I hadn't kept mixing up Your Highness and Your Majesty (he's His Highness, she's Her Majesty) I'd give myself four stars for the way that visit went off." It came at a time of deep economic pain for both countries, and yet while the Ford administration was managing to get inflation under control, it spiraled to 25 percent under Prime Minister James Callaghan, who was forced to go to the International Monetary Fund for a loan of $3.9 billion, at that time the largest in the fund's history.

The deep cuts required in public spending contributed to criticism of the Queen's overseas visits, which brought a stout defense in the pages of *The Times* by Lord Chalfont, a Labour Party peer. He argued that state visits by the monarch were far from the useless, expensive junkets portrayed by British republicans.

"What, I think, is sometimes imperfectly understood is that the British monarchy still occupies a unique band in this spectrum of international diplomacy," he wrote. "It is true that the Queen, as a constitutional monarch in a representative democracy, has no executive power. She is the Head of State and does not treat or negotiate on behalf of the Government. On the other hand she has, for most people overseas, that indefinable quality sometimes described vividly (but inaccurately) as 'charisma' or more properly by the overworked and sadly de-based word 'glamour.' This derives partly from personality, partly from powerful historical and traditional associations, and not least from the collective love and affection of the great majority of the people of these islands."

Elizabeth herself drew deeply on her American visit five months later for her Christmas message theme of "reconcilia-tion after disagreements," broadcast on television—as was her tradition—at 3:00 p.m. on Christmas Day. "In 1976 I was re-minded of the good that can flow from a friendship that is mended," she told the nation and the Commonwealth. "Who would have thought two hundred years ago that a descendant of King George III could have taken part in these celebrations? Yet that same King was among the first to recognize that old scores must be settled and differences reconciled, and the first United States ambassador to Britain declared that he wanted 'the old good nature and the old good humor restored.'"

Elizabeth marveled at the welcome she received wherever she went, from New York, which the British occupied for seven years during the Revolutionary War, to Boston, where the first shots were fired. "The United States was born in bitter conflict with Britain, but we didn't remain enemies for long. From our reconciliation came incalculable benefits to mankind and a partnership which, together with many countries of the Com-monwealth, was proved in two World Wars and ensured that the light of liberty was not extinguished. . . . Reconciliation, like the one that followed the American War of Independence, is the product of reason, tolerance, and love, and I think that Christmas is a good time to reflect on it."

The bond forged with the Fords was real but short-lived—

despite President Ford's attempts to win over the American people after the turbulent Watergate crisis and exhausting Vietnam War, his controversial pardon of Nixon contributed to a narrow election defeat to Democratic opponent Jimmy Carter, who became the seventh president of the Queen's reign. Thanks to the triumphant state visit of 1976, the Special Relationship was back in good shape.

CHAPTER 7

We just talked about the need for world peace and how much it means to the other countries when she comes to visit.

—Jimmy Carter, May 7, 1977

There was no greater contrast in background, outlook, and personality between the Queen and the US presidents she had so far encountered than with Jimmy Carter, the Democratic peanut-farming former governor of Georgia.

Carter was the closest to her in age yet the furthest from her in his humble roots and limited experience of the worlds of high society, diplomacy, and international politics. This helps explain the awkwardness that remained between them despite Carter's elevation to the most powerful job in the world, their common deeply felt Christian beliefs, and their countries' reheated Special Relationship. The gulf between them was not helped by their first formal meeting. Carter surprised the Queen's seventy-six-year-old mother by, she claimed, planting an overfriendly kiss on her lips that she would talk about with indignation for years to come.

Carter was popular with Britons—who knew nothing of his

royal faux pas until several years after his departure from the White House—and he tried to maintain cordial relations with the royals, later hosting Princess Anne for her first solo visit to the United States. The Queen remained polite but wary.

Jimmy Carter's homespun style was evident from his inauguration at the start of Queen Elizabeth's Silver Jubilee year, which marked twenty-five years on the throne. "They are not our king and queen. There is nothing royal or imperial about them," *The Washington Post* wrote about the new president and his First Lady, Rosalynn Carter, after their swearing-in celebrations in January 1977. "They refuse to ride in a limousine, and rode instead to their own inaugural events in a mustard-colored Lincoln. She wears her unfashionable six-year-old evening dress from his gubernatorial inaugural ball for 'sentimental reasons.' He wears a clip-on bow tie. They walk from the Capitol to the White House. They pray openly and talk about Christ. He carries his own luggage."

Somewhat prophetically the article added: "They hold hands in public, touch each other often, even kiss a lot. Really kiss." The highly reserved Queen, whose consort usually kept himself at a distance of several paces when they were on duty in public, never seemed more buttoned-up than in comparison to the new US head of state. Carter would go on to burnish his man-of-the-people appeal when he made his first overseas visit as president to Britain, delighting crowds with his relaxed informality and folksy charm.

He flew to the UK with America gripped by a predecessor's

reappearance thanks to a British TV journalist. After a three-year absence from the public arena, the first episode of Nixon's paid interview with David Frost was broadcast by CBS on its *60 Minutes* show the day before Carter left, featuring the thirty-seventh president's refusal to admit criminal wrongdoing over Watergate but his admission that "I let the American people down and I have to carry that burden with me for the rest of my life."

This first installment of four programs drew forty-five million viewers, the largest-ever American television audience for a political interview, and served as a reminder of why many voters opted for the newcomer Carter over the incumbent Ford after his pardon for Nixon. Unlike Nixon, who came to office after a globe-trotting vice presidential role, Carter was a novice in international diplomacy, and Britain was his first test, after declaring in March that "Great Britain is still America's mother country" as he played host to Jim Callaghan, the prime minister. On that occasion he lauded the Special Relationship and Queen Elizabeth, "who has served so well for the last 25 years."

He was welcomed at the foot of the Air Force One steps at London's Heathrow Airport with a handshake from Callaghan, then launched into his first kiss of the tour. It was for a baroness in waiting, a Labour member of the House of Lords representing the Queen in the greeting party.

As the Associated Press put it: "Carter's first act on British soil was to kiss a lady—Phyllis Lady Stedman, a 60-year-old baroness." Unlike Callaghan, who was wearing a smart beige mackintosh, the besuited Carter was unprepared for the wet late-spring weather and had no raincoat. Approaching a platform set up with microphones for both leaders, he shook the hand of a saluting police officer who appeared "perplexed at his total lack of reserve." In his arrival speech, standing in the drizzle in the open with no umbrella, he declared that "it is not an accident that this is my first overseas trip because of the historical ties that have always bound the United States of America and the United Kingdom together in a special and very precious relationship. . . . We have a special mutual commitment to world peace, toward addressing in a courageous fashion the special problems that afflict human beings in the need for better health care and better education and jobs so that we won't be robbed by inflation."

The visit to Britain was an opportune addition to the Group of Seven (G7) meeting of leaders of the world's top economies in London, with Carter accompanied by W. Michael Blumenthal, his Treasury secretary, as well as Cyrus Vance, the secretary of state—but not the First Lady, who remained at the White House. During the Queen's reign, Rosalynn Carter was the only First Lady she did not meet. Touching down on Thursday night made time for extra talks with Callaghan and the chance to see a bit of the host country before the economic discussions to be held that weekend. US media was bemused by the lack of ceremony for Carter's first overseas appearance or protection from the light rain.

"Britain's only concession to the presidential visit was a damp red carpet," wrote North Carolina's *Herald-Sun*. "There were no blaring trumpets, no gun salutes, no rolling drums, nothing ostentatious. There was no shelter. . . . To say 'no frills' is an understatement." It all seemed indicative of budget-stricken Britain, where the economy was in bad shape due to high inflation, a slow recovery from the oil shocks of the early 1970s, and the decline of manufacturing and industry. After expressing the hope that the weather would improve, the president was whisked off in his five-ton, armor-plated Cadillac, flown in ahead of him, to spend the night at the US ambassador's residence.

Carter had hoped to visit the grave of Dylan Thomas, his favorite British poet, at his final resting place in southwest Wales, but, at Callaghan's suggestion, he flew instead by Air Force One to spend Friday in the northeast, a deprived area of England usually overlooked by visiting dignitaries. It had special significance for American tourists as the ancestral home of George Washington. The region was also supposed to symbolize both leaders' G7 goal of improving conditions for workers against a backdrop of global economic difficulties. From receiving the Freedom of the City of Newcastle upon Tyne—mercifully in sunny weather—to touring an American-owned Corning glassware factory in Sunderland, huge crowds turned out to catch a glimpse of the VIP visitor.

Addressing a throng of twenty thousand in front of the modern Newcastle Civic Centre, Carter immediately won cheers by hailing them with the local phrase "Howay the lads." On the drive in from the airport, he had spotted a newspaper sales poster stating "Howay Jimmy" and another referring to "The Lads." He asked Ernie Armstrong, a local member of Parliament accompanying him, what the references meant. Armstrong explained that, put together, "Howay the lads" was the traditional way of encouraging the beloved Newcastle United football team and a surefire way to win over the crowd. In his speech, Carter also adopted the local name for a native: "I'm very happy to be a Geordie now." One explanation for the name's origin was as a description for local supporters of King

George I, the father of the British king for whom Carter's home state of Georgia was named.

At the village green of Washington in County Durham, just ten miles to the southwest, the crowd chanted, "We want Jimmy!" as he planted a tulip poplar tree flown in from the first US president's Mount Vernon estate in Virginia. Callaghan planted a British oak but not as energetically as Carter. The British prime minister's nickname was "Sunny Jim" for his optimism, but it was clear he was being outshone on this occasion. Carter posed outside Old Hall, home of Washington's forebears, including the twelfth-century ancestor who changed the family name from Hertburn. He shook hundreds of "calloused, honest hands," as he called them, and cuddled a couple of babies as he made campaign-style forays into the crowd. Millions of Americans watched live TV coverage. Carter called it the most memorable trip of his life, adding: "I sense here a quiet determination and hope that is an inspiration for me."

The president continued to wow the international press and his fellow leaders the next day back in London, leading the other summiteers from 10 Downing Street in a seventeen-minute walk across St. James's Park to Lancaster House for lunch, causing a scrum of press and astonished public. The Buckingham Palace state dinner that evening after the first day of talks between the seven national leaders was in the main State Dining Room, seventy-four feet long and bedecked with mirrors, red silk damask, and crimson velvet curtain. Carter seemed taken aback by the opulence of his surroundings. "It's one of the most beautiful places I've ever seen," he said afterward.

Carter was afforded pride of place among the thirty-three guests, showing Britain's prioritization of its transatlantic relationship over the other nations represented: France, West Germany, Italy, Canada, and Japan. It was a dazzling occasion. The president "was openly awed by the pomp and splendor of the Queen of England in Buckingham Palace . . . [W]hen a pair of tall double doors swung open and Queen Elizabeth II entered, resplendent in a bejeweled formal gown, the President's famous smile was that of any mere peanut farmer in the presence of a royal woman," the *Chicago Tribune* wrote. "He approached her hesitantly and sat in awe by her side."

Carter later recalled telling the Queen "how much the American people appreciated her coming over last year to celebrate our two hundredth birthday. And she said that it was one of the warmest welcomes she'd ever received. I told her that I got a similar welcome in northern England yesterday."

For Carter, dressed in a black tuxedo and bow tie, it was "the first time I've ever been in Buckingham Palace. I was here as a tourist several years ago, my only previous visit to London. I saw it through the fence—it's beautiful." His first and only British royal dinner was also a networking opportunity, which Carter found "a very productive evening" mixing with his fellow leaders and "getting to know them even better on a personal basis." As for his royal interactions over dinner of salmon fillet St. Germain, mousse de volaille à la crème, and a pineapple sherbet, Carter said afterward that "the whole family was very gracious to us." In his own discussions with the Queen, "We just talked about the need for world peace and how much it means to the other countries when she comes to visit, and how close we are to England because of our historical background."

Photos showed Carter and the Queen Mother all smiles as

the president escorted her by her white-gloved hand to their places in a formal group portrait with the G7 leaders before dinner, where he stood on her left. Her distress at his overfamiliarity apparently arose at the end of the evening as a result of a parting kiss. It was only revealed to the general public almost six years later in a newspaper diary column, thanks to an unnamed dinner guest at Clarence House, the Queen Mother's London residence, who divulged that the royal matriarch was in the habit of giving an "anti-toast" during which "she raises her glass and utters the names of people she does not particularly like."

On this occasion, she was heard to mutter, "Tony Benn, Idi Amin, Jimmy Carter." The first of these three men was a prominent Labour MP and lifelong anti-royalist who wrote that "the existence of a hereditary monarchy helps to prop up all the privilege and patronage that corrupts our society"; the second was the brutal former military dictator of Uganda then in exile in Saudi Arabia. But why Carter?

A guest plucked up the courage to ask the Queen Mother. "Because he is the only man, since my dear husband died, to have had the effrontery to kiss me on the lips."

In a conversation recounted by William Shawcross in her official biography published in 2009, the Queen Mother complained that it was "one of the banes of my life" that she tended to remind some middle-aged men of their mothers. "I recognize the glazed look that comes over their faces," she said, in the moment just before they would tell her about the comparison. The Queen Mother told Shawcross that she saw Carter coming in for his kiss: "I took a sharp step backwards. Not quite far enough."

Carter's mother, known as Miss Lilian, was seventy-eight at

the time, just two years senior to the elder Elizabeth. He clearly felt that the incident had been blown all out of proportion when he reflected in 2015 upon "a beautiful banquet with the British royal family" that was a "very enjoyable event that caused me some pain a year or two later." Carter recalled his "delightful chat about serious matters and also personal things" at the dinner table with the Queen, who "complained about having seven different uniforms she had to wear on annual occasions and how difficult it was to fit into them when her weight tended to increase. We decided it might be good to shift to centimeters on everything except waistlines, which would continue to be measured in inches."

He then recounted that he was approached by the Queen Mother after the meal and they fell into conversation about how their families were affected by all the attention that went along with public life. Then he discussed the kiss, which from his point of view was a simple parting gesture nowhere near the royal lips, blaming the media even though it was recounted in the Queen Mother's own official biography: "As we said good night, I kissed her lightly on the cheek and she thanked me for coming to visit. More than two years later, there were reports in the British papers that grossly distorted this event, stating that I had deeply embarrassed her with excessive familiarity. I was distressed by these reports but couldn't change what had happened—nor did I regret it."

While relations with the royals took an awkward turn—unknown at the time to the public and media—the international talks in London, which included a NATO meeting on his final day before flying back to Washington, were heralded as a great success for Carter. His charisma convinced *The Times* to declare that "for the first time since President Kennedy died the western world can feel that it has a leader." It added: "His personality and optimism have stolen the show."

On the Sunday morning before the second day of G7 discussions, Carter attended an 8:00 a.m. communion service at Westminster Abbey given by the archdeacon, the Right Reverend Edward Knapp-Fisher, who prayed for God's blessing on the summit and especially on the president and all his people. Afterward he was given a tour and asked Knapp-Fisher whether Dylan Thomas could be commemorated in Poets' Corner along with William Shakespeare and Jane Austen. The archdeacon said that Thomas, who died at thirty-nine in 1953 after a drunken binge in New York, may in the fullness of time be included "whatever his morals."

Carter replied that quite a lot of time had already passed, adding: "I would like to recommend it. I will pray for his soul if you will commemorate him."

Reports of Carter's interest inspired a petition that was supported by Britain's greatest living poets, including Sir John Betjeman and Ted Hughes. Five years later, when a plaque commemorating the Welsh man of letters was finally installed next to those for Henry James and George Eliot in the abbey, Thomas's daughter Aeronwy Thomas-Ellis credited Carter for providing the impetus. Carter eventually fulfilled his wish to see Thomas's home, resting place, and writing shed in Laugharne, Wales, on a private post-presidential visit in 1986.

Jimmy Carter's handwritten note to the Queen dated May 10,

1977, said that "it has been a great honor and pleasure for me to visit your great country" and that he was "particularly grateful for the hospitality and friendship which was so evident on my visit to Buckingham Palace from you and all the Royal Family."

The main events celebrating Elizabeth II's Silver Jubilee took place a month later. Alongside various Commonwealth leaders, Carter was represented at a service at St. Paul's Cathedral in London by his twenty-seven-year-old middle son, James Earl "Chip" Carter III, and his wife, Caron. They were invited to have lunch at Buckingham Palace with Prince Charles the following day and to watch celebratory fireworks later that week with the Queen.

Robert Fellowes, her assistant private secretary, wrote a letter to President Carter dated June 9 thanking him for the gift of plates decorated with reproductions of paintings by the nineteenth-century American artist Winslow Homer, delivered by Chip, saying they "will be treasured not only for their design, which is exquisite, but also as a token of a friendship which is among Her Majesty's chief pleasures in this her Silver Jubilee year." Unfailingly polite, the letter went on: "The Queen particularly asked me to send her very best wishes to you, your wife and family for the future and hopes that it will not be long before she has a further opportunity of meeting you again."

The following week Carter repaid the royal hospitality he received in London by hosting Princess Anne, the Queen's twenty-six-year-old daughter, during a five-day trip to the US. Accompanied by her husband Mark Phillips, it was her first solo royal visit to America after the joint tour with her brother in 1970, when she had played second fiddle and at times appeared frustrated or even bored. This time she was center of attention and showed more of her character, which meant some of the type of wisecracks and sarcastic remarks more typical of her father as opposed to the polite reserve of her mother.

When Walter Washington, the mayor of the District of Columbia, told her that her mother was the "first reigning queen" to visit city hall a year earlier on her bicentennial tour, Anne remarked: "Really, you don't get too many of them then?" She quipped that not only had the Queen enjoyed her trip, but that "you kept her very busy." When she arrived at the White House to meet Chip and Caron, her hosts for lunch, the president's son told her that photographers wanted them to pause for pictures before they went upstairs. "They're very original, aren't they?" the princess said.

On that first day packed with events in the nation's capital, including a ten-minute meeting with President Carter in the Oval Office and with Rosalynn Carter in the Yellow Room of the White House, Anne, who was four months pregnant with her first child, wore a blue-and-white maternity dress, a blue straw hat with flowers around the crown, and white gloves with a white handbag. At the Smithsonian's Museum of History and Technology, Anne and her husband were applauded by their first crowd of the day. In the *We, the People* exhibit upstairs, Margaret Klapthor, a political history curator, gave her a quick lesson in the hardships faced by pioneers in wagon trains heading west.

"It was not very pleasant," the princess remarked. Sidney Dillon Ripley, secretary of the Smithsonian Institution, showed Anne a reproduction of a log cabin and explained its importance in the origins of American presidents.

"They have to be born in a log cabin," said Ripley.

The princess asked: "Even now?"

Ripley replied: "It helps."

That November, the Queen received a congratulatory telegram from President Carter. "I was delighted to learn of the birth of a son to Princess Anne and Captain Phillips," he wrote, as Peter Mark Andrew Phillips became Elizabeth's first grandchild. "Rosalynn and I enjoyed seeing them here at the White House this summer. Please convey our best wishes to them both on this happy occasion. Sincerely Jimmy Carter."

Telegrams would continue to be exchanged formally on the Queen's birthday and on July Fourth, but there would be no more meetings between Carter and royalty. He lost the 1980 presidential election, making way for a Republican president who found himself much more on the Queen's wavelength.

CHAPTER 8

I must admit, the Queen is quite an accomplished horsewoman.

—Ronald Reagan in his memoir, *An American Life*, 1990

The two most iconic photographs of the Queen with an American president are both with Ronald Reagan, the former California governor and Hollywood actor.

There was one thing Elizabeth appreciated that distinguished him from the other presidents—he shared her love of horses. The first of the two remarkable images shows the heads of state together on a ride through Windsor Home Park, an outing never repeated with another world leader, not least because of the logistical and security headaches it caused. It proved to be worth the many hours that went into arranging it from the point of view of cementing relations and garnering priceless yards of positive publicity.

The second of the two special photographs shows something completely different to the painstakingly prepared canter—a moment of spontaneous delight from Reagan at the deadpan delivery of a joke from Elizabeth that perfectly displayed their complementary but opposite public personas. A photographer's lens skillfully caught the moment when the president suddenly erupted in laughter at a very British quip and immortalized the poker-faced Queen and the affable president in a classic image of the Special Relationship.

The initial encounter between the British royal family and the Reagans came in March 1974, when twenty-five-year-old Prince Charles was invited for a long weekend at Sunnylands, the Palm Springs, California, estate of American ambassador to London Walter Annenberg and his wife, Lee. Annenberg, a publishing magnate and philanthropist appointed to the Court of St. James's by President Nixon in 1969, endeared himself to the British with donations to support the restoration of St. Paul's Cathedral and Winfield House, the US ambassador's residence in London, as well as funds for a swimming pool at Chequers. The Annenbergs became friends with the Queen and used their network of international contacts to turn Sunnylands into a retreat for leading figures to converse away from the lens of public attention.

During a star-studded stay, Charles found himself playing a round of golf on the estate's private course with the governor of California and then joining the Annenbergs and the Reagans for a cozy dinner. This marked the start of one of the closest relationships between any royal and American First Family member: the friendship between Charles and Nancy Reagan, which would last until her death in 2016.

"Rarely have I enjoyed myself so much or had such a marvelous opportunity to relax completely as I did with you," Prince Charles wrote in his thank-you letter to the Annenbergs. "I so enjoyed meeting the Reagans—they were full of charm and great warmth, and it was great fun to listen to Mr. Reagan, whether he was being serious or funny. Thank you for introducing him to me. And thank you for so many other things, like asking Bob Hope and Frank Sinatra to come 'round."

This friendship led Nancy Reagan to meet the Queen a year before her husband when she represented the White House at the wedding of Prince Charles and Diana Spencer in July 1981. Her decision not to curtsy but rather to shake hands with Elizabeth was announced two days before their first meeting and provoked a statement from Buckingham Palace that "normally there is a bow or a curtsy, but if Mrs. Reagan wants to shake hands that'll be fine." Cue a predictable storm in a teacup from the British tabloids. "I Won't Bow, Says Nancy" headlined *The Sun* above two pages devoted to the story. The day of the event, Mrs. Reagan not only shook the royal hand but gave a slight nod, bringing more confounded headlines. "Mystery of Phantom Curtsy," proclaimed the *Daily Mail*.

Sheila Tate, Mrs. Reagan's press secretary, explained that the First Lady "inclined her head slightly as you would when you meet someone. It was definitely not a curtsy." Linda Faulkner, the First Lady's social secretary, defended the republican position, saying: "We are not royal subjects, and this is not something we are obligated to do." Whatever the protocol debate, the First Lady got along famously with both the Queen and the Queen Mother as they watched a match at Guards Polo Club in Windsor Great Park. The elder Elizabeth sent Nancy a box of Bendicks Bittermints as a souvenir.

The First Lady was asked by the Queen to convey to President Reagan the idea of a UK sojourn. A formal invitation for the June 1982 visit came from Buckingham Palace in December 1981 but went unanswered for two months, causing alarm in London. Several European nations were vying to host Reagan on his first presidential tour of the continent after he barely ventured overseas in his first year, traveling only as far as Canada and Mexico. Sir Nicholas "Nico" Henderson, the British ambassador to Washington, reassured the Foreign Office that the absence of a response was due not to disdain but to dysfunction, writing in a classified memo released in 2012, "It is really for the president to respond to her invitation, which he has not done personally, something that I have pointed out several times here. As you know those surrounding the president are not deliberately rude: It is simply that they are not well-organized and do not have experience of this sort of thing."

Reagan was coming to Europe for a G7 summit in France, an audience with the pope, and a NATO meeting in West Germany. As Britain sought to muscle in, it had a trump card—the prospect of riding out with the Queen. "I need hardly say that the only absolutely stable and central item in any discussion of the President's visit is this riding event," Henderson wrote to London after discussions at the White House.

The British trip was confirmed. News of the two-night stay emerged on March 6 when Mike Deaver, Reagan's deputy chief of staff, told the *Los Angeles Times* that the president would be Elizabeth's personal houseguest at Windsor Castle, a royal privilege previously bestowed on an American leader only by her grandfather King George V for Woodrow Wilson's visit in 1918.

Reagan would also be the first US president to address a joint session of Parliament in Westminster Hall, Deaver announced prematurely, catching the British off guard. The news triggered an outcry from the opposition Labour Party, which would normally have been consulted before an invitation was extended to a foreign dignitary to speak in the oldest part of the Palace of Westminster, dating back to 1097. The last head-of-state address had been by President Charles de Gaulle of France in 1960. Many Labour MPs objected to Reagan being granted this rare honor, because they opposed the impending deployment of US nuclear-armed cruise missiles in Britain— first agreed on under President Carter—as well as his administration's support for the murderous right-wing regime in El Salvador. After a furious debate, Prime Minister Margaret Thatcher proposed a different venue in the Palace of Westminster: the Royal Gallery, an opulent chamber behind the House of Lords that was adorned with numerous portraits and statues of monarchs.

Classified papers released after thirty years reveal that behind the scenes, Deaver, having jumped the gun and caused the row, told the British on March 21 that Reagan would speak only in Westminster Hall or not at all. Henderson countered that the Royal Gallery recently hosted a French president and a Soviet premier. "It would look petty for the president to appear to be saying where he must speak and that he would not speak, say, in the Royal Chamber, which had been good enough for Kosygin and Giscard," Henderson told him. Deaver relented.

Memos were also frantically exchanged by officials behind the scenes to work out details of the horse ride by the president and the Queen. Deaver underlined its importance to the White

House, noting, "Carter couldn't have done a thing like that—think of the photo opportunity."

British officials were left in no doubt that American wishes should be fulfilled despite logistical and security objections when international affairs took an alarming turn during the preparations, which made it even more imperative that the visit go well. In the spring of 1982, Britain engaged in a military conflict with Argentina over the Falkland Islands, eight thousand miles away in the South Atlantic.

The military regime in Buenos Aires invaded on April 2 and raised the Argentine flag based on a claim to the Islas Malvinas dating back to 1493. Thatcher launched a large naval task force on April 5 for the two-week journey to recapture the British Overseas Territory, led by two aircraft carriers, eight destroyers, and two cruise liners acting as troopships. The monarch had an extra level of interest: her son Prince Andrew, who at the time was second in line to the throne after Charles, was serving as a Royal Navy helicopter pilot with HMS *Invincible*, one of the aircraft carriers.

The conflict put the US in a difficult position. While the Special Relationship with Great Britain was usually front of mind, Argentina was also important as a bulwark against communism in Central and South America—leading some American officials to push for neutrality in the conflict. Reagan asked Alexander Haig, his secretary of state, to act as intermediary, but his shuttle diplomacy was exhausted by April 30. Haig declared that because of Argentina's "failure to accept compromise" and its "use of unlawful force to resolve disputes," the US was abandoning mediation efforts and siding with Britain.

Reagan said that he was still hoping for a diplomatic settlement and that there would be no involvement militarily by the United States. In reality, invaluable help in the form of US supplies and intelligence was given all along to Britain. Its full extent was not revealed until classified CIA files were opened twenty years later, revealing how Haig secretly told British officials at the end of March that the US diplomatic effort "will of course have a greater chance of influencing Argentine behavior if we appear to them not to favor one side or the other."

In a secret cable sent to "Dear Margaret" Thatcher on April 1, the eve of the Argentine invasion, Reagan wrote: "I want you to know that we have valued your cooperation on the challenges we both face in many different parts of the world. We will do what we can to assist you here. Sincerely, Ron."

In practice, this meant use of the US military base on Ascension Island, a staging post for the British task force, as well as fuel, ammunition, and satellite photographs to help plan the British operation. The press and public were not aware of the full details of US assistance at the time, and perception of lukewarm American support increased hostility toward Reagan. Nevertheless, with the British days away from their offensive, Reagan's UK visit began on June 7, 1982. The royals pulled out all the stops to make sure he was memorably feted as a thank-you for his country's assistance—and to provide an extra reason to keep giving it.

In a pattern repeated over the years, the British press was quick to pounce on a slight protocol mishap and, once again, Nancy was in their sights at the Windsor Castle arrival ceremony.

Reagan motioned to his wife to accompany the Queen on the walk into position in front of the Band of the Grenadier Guards as he followed behind with Prince Philip. The president had to be ushered by the Queen into place beside her for the playing of the national anthems, while Nancy stood her ground on Elizabeth's left instead of taking a step back as convention decreed.

Larry Speakes, the acting White House press secretary, sought to calm excitable British scribes: "I think it is a question of 'ladies first,' a fine old Reagan family custom."

In his personal diary, Reagan described the experience of arriving to meet the Queen using an unconscious echo of Truman's "fairy princess" remark thirty-one years earlier. "Flew out for London & helicoptered to Windsor Castle. This was a fairy tale experience," he wrote. "Black tie dinner with the Queen & Prince Philip plus family—the Queen Mother et al." This first dinner was an informal one, to be followed by the full white-tie state dinner the next evening at the castle.

First, though, came the horse ride. Although it was devised for relaxation, the ride itself had been meticulously prepared during intense transatlantic consultations about the president's preferred horse, saddle, and riding style. Reagan rode Centennial, a black gelding given to the Queen by the Royal Canadian Mounted Police, while Elizabeth was on Burmese, a twenty-year-old mare also gifted by the Mounties. She rode the same horse for eighteen successive Trooping the Colour ceremonies, including the previous summer, when a teenage gunman had fired six blank shots from the crowd. Burmese had skittered briefly, but the Queen had her quickly under control and the ceremony went ahead as normal, confirming the bond between horse and rider.

The two leaders set off for an hour-long, eight-mile ride in a private section of the royal estate, followed by a security entourage and Philip driving Nancy in a four-in-hand (a carriage drawn by four horses). Classified documents show there were White House concerns over what Reagan should wear—"nothing too formal," came the reply. In the end both the Queen and the president donned tweed jackets, despite the summer heat, as well as jodhpurs and riding boots, while neither wore a riding hat.

Two styles of horsemanship were on display, according to *The Times*: "The Queen favoured that of a National Hunt diehard, as tidy, restrained, and proper as the familiar silk scarf on her head. President Reagan plumped for the Tom Mix school of equestrian discipline and jogged around in his unfamiliar English saddle with a rolling freedom more usual in Wyoming than Windsor." The route included the royal family's private golf course and the Royal Mausoleum, where Queen Victoria and Prince Albert are buried.

Reagan was whisked afterward into London for his joint address to Parliament, calling for action to spread democracy around the world and "leave Marxism-Leninism on the ash heap of history." He made a clear reference to events in the South Atlantic. Saying that voices had been raised in protest at the sacrifice of young lives for lumps of rock and earth so far away, he added: "Those young men are not fighting for mere real estate; they fight for a cause, for the belief that armed aggression must not be allowed to succeed, and that people must participate in the decisions of government under the rule of law." At Downing Street later for lunch with Thatcher, with whom he was slowly building his famous rapport, she described the speech as "magnificent."

The British did not call this a state visit, partly because there was not time for the full three days of events but also partly to avoid upsetting the French, who rolled out the red carpet on Reagan's first European stop. But the white-tie banquet in St. George's Hall at Windsor Castle was no different to such special occasions. Under a wooden ceiling featuring the coats of arms of every Knight of the Garter—the most senior British order of chivalry—and overlooked by suits of armor around the walls, 158 guests ate roast lamb off two-hundred-year-old hand-painted plates. The Queen, seated next to the president, wore a pearl-and-diamond tiara and a short-sleeved, gold-embroidered gown with her Order of the Garter sash. Nancy Reagan, seated opposite between Princes Philip and Charles, was in a white beaded gown with a boatneck design by James Galanos of California.

"I greatly enjoyed our ride together this morning, and I was much impressed by the way in which you coped so professionally with a strange horse and a saddle that must have seemed even stranger," toasted the Queen, to laughter. Before the serious business of the Falklands War, there was the usual reminder of the value of the Special Relationship, even though on this occasion British officials ruled that the phrase was not to be mentioned, perhaps to avoid appearing needy.

"Had King George III been able to foresee the long-term consequences of his actions, he might not have felt so grieved about the loss of his colonies," Elizabeth II said.

But the Queen, anxiously hanging on every update from the South Atlantic, where dozens of British sailors had been killed by Argentine attacks, gave her strongest public statement on the conflict during this dinner, her son's involvement lending extra weight to her words of gratitude to the United States: "Above all, our commitment to a common cause has led us to fight together in two World Wars and to continue to stand together today in the defense of freedom. These past weeks have been testing ones for this country, when, once again, we have had to stand up for the cause of freedom. The conflict in the Falkland Islands was thrust on us by naked aggression, and we are naturally proud of the way our fighting men are serving their country. But throughout the crisis, we have drawn comfort from the understanding of our position shown by the American people. We have admired the honesty, patience, and skill with which you have performed your dual role as ally and intermediary." She spoke from knowledge of the true extent of American support, as a figurehead and diplomat but also as a mother.

In his response, Reagan emphasized not only the historical links embodied by the storied setting but also the family bonds that brought an extra intimacy to the partnership of nations. "It's a rare privilege to be even a momentary part of the rich history of Windsor Castle," he said. "This place symbolizes both tradition and renewal, as generation after generation of your family makes it their home."

Reagan then referred to Diana, the Princess of Wales, who attended the more intimate black-tie dinner but, eight months pregnant, gave the state-style banquet a miss. "We in America share your excitement about the impending birth of a child to the Prince and the Princess of Wales. We pray that God will continue to bless your family with health, happiness, and wisdom." At least in the short term, his prayers were answered— Diana gave birth to a son, William, thirteen days later.

Unlike his parliamentary address, Reagan did not refer directly to the Anglo-Argentine war but delivered general words on his global freedom agenda. With a toast to "the continued unity of our two nations," he concluded, "Together, it is within our power to confront the threats to peace and freedom and to triumph over them." The following week, British troops recaptured Port Stanley, the Falkland Islands capital, to bring the war to the decisive end that Thatcher needed and the Reagan administration wanted in order to avoid a drawn-out conflict that could have led Buenos Aires to turn to the Soviet Union for assistance.

In *An American Life*, Reagan wrote, "There were many, many small moments that made my job fun. . . . Landing in a helicopter on the lawn of Windsor Castle for a fairy-tale visit with Queen Elizabeth and the royal family. The highlight of our stay there came when the Queen and I went horseback riding together, and Nancy and Prince Philip took a horse-drawn carriage ride. I must admit, the Queen is quite an accomplished horsewoman. We will always remember our visit to Windsor Castle because of the Queen's and Prince Philip's warmth and welcoming hospitality—they could not have been more gracious." While out on the canter, Reagan invited the Queen for a return visit to his California ranch the following year so he could reciprocate her hospitality, including a ride using his own Arabian horses.

Unfortunately, the weather would have other ideas.

The Queen was developing a fondness for the United States that would lead her to take the five private overseas holidays of her reign there, all linked to her love of horse racing.

First, fulfilling a long-held ambition to visit the West Coast, she took up Reagan's offer with a ten-day semiprivate tour early in 1983. As soon as he caught wind of it, Walter Annenberg offered Sunnylands.

"Lee and I wanted to make sure that should a desert visit to a rather unusual modern home be of interest for the agenda on the trip, we would be honored to entertain Her Majesty's party," the former ambassador wrote to the Queen's private secretary, Sir Philip Moore.

Following a Caribbean tour of Jamaica and the Cayman Islands, the Queen landed on February 26 from the royal yacht *Britannia* in San Diego, where her navy-and-white contrasting print outfit and matching "nautical cap" were described by one American commentator as "downright ugly," while another thought the hat "seemed inspired by the top of a salt shaker."

The president provided a plane to fly the royal party to Palm Springs for lunch at the private home where Charles had first met the Reagans nine years earlier. The Annenbergs entertained eight members of the royal entourage and ten other guests, including former president Gerald Ford and his wife, Betty; British ambassador Sir Oliver Wright; and Selwa Roosevelt, who was married to a grandson of President Theodore Roosevelt and had succeeded Lee Annenberg as US chief of protocol.

"Your Majesty, your presence brightly rekindles our five and a half years in Britain, certainly the proudest years for Lee and me," Annenberg said in his toast. The menu of salmon mousse, followed by rack of lamb served with string beans, glazed carrots, and potatoes Parisienne paired with a 1966 Château Lafite Rothschild, with maple soufflé for dessert, was served on Royal Copenhagen Flora Danica porcelain. The Queen noted that she also collected it, "but Walter has more than I do." The weather was anything but sunny at Sunnylands, but despite heavy rain, the group used golf carts to tour some of the 208-acre grounds as planned.

"It looks like I brought the British climate to California," the Queen quipped from under her umbrella. It was just the start, and the ten-day visit would be dominated by atrocious weather.

That evening Air Force Two brought the royals to Los Angeles for a dinner hosted by Nancy Reagan at Stage 9 of 20th Century Fox Television Studios, the recently vacated set of *M*A*S*H*, transformed into a garden scene with fake green turf and hung with large white Japanese lanterns. It was the night before the final episode of the long-running Korean War comedy-drama aired on CBS. Hollywood's stars came out in force. Entertainment for the five hundred guests was provided by Frank Sinatra, Dionne Warwick, Bob Hope, Perry Como, and eighty-seven-year-old George Burns, who tried a mildly risqué joke that appeared to amuse the Queen.

"Acting is easy," Burns said. "If the director wants me to cry, I think of my sex life. If the director wants me to laugh, I think of my sex life."

The next day the Queen used the first speech of her West Coast tour at Los Angeles City Hall to thank the US for backing Britain over the Falkland Islands. She suggested that the outcome was very much in line with Reagan's rhetoric of spreading democracy.

"The support of your government and the American people touched us deeply and demonstrated to the world that our close relationship is based in our shared commitment to the same values," she said.

These harmonious relations were not matched by the weather, and by the next morning the seas were so rough that *Britannia* could not rule the waves. Plans were abandoned to sail up the coast from Long Beach to dock in Santa Barbara for the visit to the Reagans' secluded Rancho del Cielo (Heavenly Ranch) in the Santa Ynez Mountains, so officials hastily commandeered a US Navy bus to drive the royal couple to the Long Beach airport instead. It was believed to be the first time Elizabeth II had ever been on a bus.

The elevated ranch was shrouded in cloud, with the winding six-and-a-half-mile approach road dangerously slippery in driving rain and near-zero visibility. "The queen was a wonderful sport and refused to cancel their plans," Nancy wrote. "The road to the ranch was so muddy that she and Philip drove up the mountain in a Land Rover through a fog that was so thick you couldn't see a thing." Elizabeth changed into knee-high rubber boots and her Burberry mackintosh in the four-wheel-drive vehicle from the Santa Barbara airport, all the while wearing the same turquoise hat with feather trim. Another plan was reluctantly scrapped—the horse ride.

"The queen was dying to go riding with Ronnie," the First Lady added. "That plan of course went right out the window."

Reagan was criticized by US media for making the treacherous drive to greet the Queen at the airport. "The royal visit chewed up most of Reagan's day at a time his administration faces a host of serious foreign and domestic policy problems," one paper editorialized. It underlined the importance of the royal visit to the president and the responsibility he felt not only to return Elizabeth's hospitality but also to be seen to match her determination to keep calm and carry on.

The Reagans provided a lunch of enchiladas, chiles rellenos, refried beans, tacos, rice, and guacamole. The Queen appeared to enjoy this first taste of Mexican food, memorably telling Deaver, "That was so enjoyable, especially the used beans."

After accompanying the royals on the flight back, the First Lady stayed on board *Britannia* on Tuesday night, insisting that she slept "wonderfully" despite the storm still raging in Long Beach Harbor. This was an opportunity for true bonding.

"It was not the Queen and First Lady but two mothers and wives talking about their lives, mostly our children. She was beginning to be concerned about Diana," Nancy said. Just a couple of years after the excitement of the royal wedding and the birth of Prince William, some of the press had turned on the Princess of Wales, still only twenty-one, amid reports of rows with Charles and rumors she was suffering from the eating disorder anorexia nervosa (she was in fact afflicted with bulimia nervosa). The Waleses had just endured a miserable ski holiday in Europe, where Diana was hounded by photographers, and she was criticized for hiding her face behind her hands in exasperation at their persistence.

The royals could not sail into San Francisco on *Britannia*, and Reagan again provided a plane, which flew low over the harbor so the Queen could catch her first view of the Golden Gate Bridge through the rain. Last-minute accommodation was found for the night in the presidential suite at the St. Francis Hotel, while Nancy commandeered works of art from local museums to adorn the walls. On short notice the White House emptied Trader Vic's for a memorable night out for Elizabeth, who had not eaten in a restaurant in fifteen years and took delight in sampling the rum punch. She was given a fortune cookie at the end, which she cracked open to read before popping the message into her ever-present purse.

Protesters were mostly kept at a distance, but at a reception the following day at San Francisco's Civic Center, Seamus Gibney, of Irish Northern Aid, infiltrated the gathering. Just as singer Mary Martin was about to perform, he stood up and shouted, "Stop the torture," referring to the British treatment of Irish Republican Army (IRA) prisoners. He had evaded security and entered the Davies Symphony Hall with a photograph of IRA hunger striker Francis Hughes, who had died two years earlier, on his lapel.

"I was so excited when I came onstage and then that man was hollering and I lost all my nerve," Martin recounted. Gibney was ejected by police as the crowd roared approval for Martin. "When they all stood up, my nerve came back," she said.

During a visit that day to Silicon Valley, the head of the Hewlett-Packard electronics company, David Packard, presented a computer to the Queen on behalf of the president, saying she could keep track of her racehorses on it. Packard said the royals were so intrigued by the computer demonstrated for them that "we had a hard time getting them away from it." Visitors to Buckingham Palace later confirmed that it was installed and indeed used by the Queen to log the progress of her Thoroughbred breeding and racing.

That night Elizabeth II took center stage. She was described as "every bit the queen her American cousins had been hoping to see" when she arrived at the official dinner in San Francisco's de Young Museum in Golden Gate Park in her pearl-and-diamond tiara and matching jewels. The Queen told her hosts that her visit had been "spectacular and has fulfilled a long-standing ambition on my part to visit California and the West Coast. What better time than when the president is a Californian?"

Her enthusiasm was not feigned—she had been disappointed back in 1957 when California could not be included on her schedule. The San Francisco dinner was the invitation of the year, and there was frantic lobbying behind the scenes for places. The guest list included California governor George Deukmejian and his wife, Gloria; Shirley Temple Black, the former child star and ex–chief of protocol for Presidents Ford and Carter; Gordon Getty, director of Getty Oil; the Reverend Billy Graham; and Steve Jobs, chairman of Apple. Joe DiMaggio, the baseball legend, cut short a visit to New York to attend.

"I wouldn't have missed it for the world," DiMaggio said. "I didn't know that we were going to actually be introduced to the Queen."

It was here that the iconic photograph of Reagan roaring with laughter was taken, as, without the merest flicker of a face muscle, the bespectacled and bejeweled Queen delivered the line "I knew before we came that we had exported many of our traditions to the United States. I had not realized before that weather was one of them." In an era when it was never clear that the moment had been captured on film until it was processed later in the darkroom, Diana Walker, a *Time* photographer who caught it perfectly, explained that she was ready for the punch line.

"Often the toasts . . . are given to the press before they happen so they can meet their own deadlines. So, I read what the Queen was going to say, and I saw where the laugh line was. . . . I got all set up for this picture. And then it happened."

The evening was rounded off with an intimate champagne party on *Britannia* for thirty guests to celebrate the Reagans' thirty-first wedding anniversary. *Britannia*'s crew presented them with a cartoon depicting a horse being brought on board for Reagan while Nancy sang "Our Love Is Here to Stay" as an aide played the piano. The president, making a toast, said: "I know I promised Nancy a lot when we were married, but how can I ever top this?"

For all the effort that had gone into buttressing personal ties between the heads of state, and Reagan's relationship with Thatcher, for whom he developed a deep admiration for her no-nonsense handling of the Falklands conflict, there was a serious but brief rift in October 1983. The president gave the green light for US troops to invade the Caribbean island of Grenada, a small Commonwealth realm, after a Marxist-Leninist coup and the summary execution of its prime minister Maurice Bishop. Thatcher said she was "deeply disturbed" by a warning from Reagan that the US was considering a military response due to concerns over the safety of the two hundred American students who were on the island, the growing Cuban presence, and the construction of an airstrip that could accommodate large Soviet planes. He did not inform Thatcher until the invasion was irreversibly under way, although the US force was joined by several Caribbean nations, including the Commonwealth realms of Barbados and Jamaica, where the Queen was also head of state.

Classified documents contain stern words from the prime minister but also show that the British relaxed fairly quickly following the swift arrest of the coup leaders, the end of hostilities, and the restoration of order. Proof that the Special Relationship was back on an even keel came the following summer when Reagan visited for a G7 meeting in London and to commemorate the fortieth anniversary of the D-Day landings in France. Ahead of the political and ceremonial meetings, the president and First Lady were hosted by the Queen and Prince Philip to "a quiet little lunch" in their private quarters at Buckingham Palace, according to Nancy, who added that "when the Queen and the president get together, they always talk about horses for a while."

Reagan arrived from a four-day tour of Ireland that quite literally helped to prove his ties to Elizabeth. Genealogists researched his Irish roots for a visit to Ballyporeen in County Tipperary, home of a great-grandfather, Michael Reagan, who emigrated to America. Reagan wrote delightedly, "I was presented the family tree. . . . Our family line going back to Brian Boru [an eleventh-century king of all Ireland] has us related by way of Mary Queen of Scots to every Royal family in Europe. I'm a 6th cousin of Queen Elizabeth of Eng[land]." The elected American king actually had royal blood. Harold Brooks-Baker of *Burke's Peerage* said: "This link makes Mr. Reagan the most royal of American Presidents with the exception of George Washington."

Reagan became the first sitting US president to visit the famous Normandy beaches for an anniversary ceremony, with the Queen and other European leaders joining him at Pointe du Hoc, the clifftop vantage point overlooking both Utah and Omaha landing beaches, which was taken at great cost to the Second US Ranger Battalion. Reagan's speech recalled that "the Allies stood and fought against tyranny in a giant undertaking unparalleled in human history" and "when one Ranger fell, another would take his place."

At the black-tie dinner at Buckingham Palace for the leaders of the world's advanced economies back in London later that week, Reagan was seated between the Queen and the Queen Mother, while Nancy was seated next to Prince Charles, with whom she was seen in deep conversation. Their relationship led to the most memorable night of the Reagan White House in November 1985, when Charles brought Diana for a star-studded dinner and the Princess of Wales famously danced with actor John Travolta to the soundtrack of *Saturday Night Fever* (to the delight of guests and the world's media). Travolta later revealed how Nancy Reagan instigated the moment by telling him it was Diana's "fantasy," so he went and tapped the princess on the shoulder.

"She looks at me, and she had that kind of bashful dip [of her chin] that she did . . . and I said, 'Would you care to dance with me?' It was a storybook moment," Travolta told PBS in 2021.

Schedules did not allow for a second riding attempt at

Rancho del Cielo, but Reagan closely followed the Queen's future visits to the US on her private horse-related holidays. His diary entry for October 14, 1984, recorded that he "called Queen Elizabeth in Wyoming to say goodbye. She's had a real vacation in our USA and is now heading home." (She had spent three days at the ranch of her racing manager, Lord Porchester, and his American wife, Jean.) In a letter to Reagan, she enthused about "looking at beautiful thoroughbreds" in Kentucky and "walking in the wide-open spaces" of Wyoming. On May 22, 1986, Reagan recorded another call "to the Queen of Eng. who is visiting her racing stable in Ky."

Their final meeting in office came in June 1988 when Reagan took tea at Buckingham Palace on a swing through London to brief Thatcher on his latest talks with Soviet leader Mikhail Gorbachev in Moscow. He would be back exactly a year later, after leaving the White House, to become the first president of the Queen's reign to receive an honorary knighthood from her—nominated by her government for services during the Falklands War. Reagan could not actually use the title "Sir" as royal subjects could, but he could use the initials "GCB" after his name. Nor was he "dubbed" by a sword but instead was handed a box containing the insignia by Elizabeth during a private lunch with Nancy at Buckingham Palace.

Emerging in front of the media to find that Reagan had already taken the lid off to show the gold badge on its crimson ribbon and accompanying star to the cameras, the Queen placed a wary hand on the precious box.

"Don't drop it!" she said, repeating herself when Reagan seemed not to hear her the first time.

"I can't say how proud I am," Reagan said.

The Associated Press noted that the honor may not have conveyed many actual benefits but that "at dinner parties Reagan can sit closer to the Queen than unknighted former presidents."

Sir William Heseltine, who joined the royal household in 1965 and became private secretary in 1986, confirmed the special relationship between the two of them: "I know that Her Majesty and Reagan had a happy time together, both during his visits, particularly the '82 one, and her later return visit to the States. . . . It was obvious to all that they occurred in an atmosphere quite different from the normal stiffness and formality."

CHAPTER 9

Rain or shine, your long walks have left even the Secret Service agents panting away.

—George H. W. Bush, May 14, 1991

On a sweltering May morning in Washington, DC, described as like being trapped inside a fresh-baked pound cake, Queen Elizabeth II looked calm and cool at the welcoming ceremony for her third state visit to the United States. She was wearing a royal purple linen jacket and a distinctive purple-black-and-white-striped boater hat. Quite unexpectedly, the hat was about to become famous.

The visit had been arranged to mark the two countries' joint triumph in another armed conflict in which the US and Great Britain fought together, this time in the small Gulf emirate of Kuwait, from where the invading forces of Iraqi dictator Saddam Hussein were rapidly ejected. From a lectern set up on a platform on the White House lawn, President George H. W. Bush, one of the taller commanders in chief at six feet two inches, paid fulsome tribute to the contribution of British troops to the American-led coalition's success.

"Years from now, men will speak of American and British heroism in the Gulf, as they do today of our cooperation in two World Wars and forty years of peacetime alliance," Bush told the Queen, who was waiting patiently for her turn to speak. "The past year has reaffirmed our alliance of shared principles, our fidelity to democracy and to basic human rights, the fact that there will always be a Britain and that Britain will always be our friend," Bush concluded.

The Queen took his place behind the lectern to respond. But it was not her very British play on words about the "warm welcome" (down on the grass, several guests fainted from the heat) nor her "particular pleasure that this visit comes so soon after a vivid and effective demonstration of the long-standing alliance between our two countries" that made the headlines.

"All I got is a talking hat!" NBC correspondent Jim Miklaszewski told viewers watching on TV.

Neither the president nor his staff had thought to pull out the special step that was tucked into the lectern to elevate the five-foot-four-inch monarch, leaving the royal face obscured by a clump of several large microphones. Only a glimpse of her reading glasses and a purple-black-and-white-striped boater were visible to the perspiring crowd below.

The papers jumped on the faux pas, with headlines like the *Miami Herald*'s "Blimey! Is That a Talking Hat?," but the Queen had the last laugh. After taking her place to address a joint meeting of Congress later in the week—the first ever by a British monarch—she opened with a line that earned a roar of laughter and a lengthy standing ovation: "I do hope you can see me today from where you are."

While Eisenhower and Reagan were probably the Queen's favorite presidents to date, George Herbert Walker Bush quickly became a close contender. The forty-first US president was born two years before her, the closest in age apart from Carter, and similarly had a large brood of children (five who survived to adulthood in his case, four in hers); his eldest, George Walker Bush, later the forty-third president, was a little over two years older than her eldest, Charles, the future king.

The Queen admired Bush's record of service as one of the youngest navy pilots in the Second World War, his death-defying heroism embodying that tumultuous era when her indelible view of the United States as her nation's greatest ally was formed. There were parallels with her husband, Philip, who served as one of the Royal Navy's youngest first lieutenants during the war and also saw action in the Pacific theater.

Bush was, like the Queen, a dog person and liked to ride horses occasionally but did not own them or claim to be as comfortable in the saddle as Reagan, although there was a strong equine connection with the Queen through mutual friends. The first time she privately visited Kentucky, in 1984, on the advice of her American Thoroughbred-breeder friend Paul Mellon, she stayed with William Stamps Farish III, an oil company heir and the wealthy owner of a Houston investment firm, and his wife, Sarah, on their vast Lane's End Farm estate near Lexington. Farish was close to Bush, having served on the board of Zapata Petroleum Company, which had been founded in 1953 by the future president. When Bush was Reagan's vice president, Farish oversaw the blind trust that looked after his assets. The Queen, who originally met Farish in 1973 watching a match at Guards Polo Club in Windsor, felt very much at home in his company. On her several Kentucky visits, Will and Sarah arranged small private dinners with horse folk for the monarch at which she relaxed to an extent rarely experienced in Britain, another reason why the United States felt like a special place.

The Queen's own relationship with the Bushes started on a slightly awkward note, however. When their limousine arrived at the Grand Entrance to Buckingham Palace for a lunch in June 1989, nobody stepped forward to let the First Lady out of the car. "Open it!" an exasperated Queen snapped in a raised voice, frowning and shaking her head, leading a US Secret Service agent to scurry to the vehicle.

Before lunch in the ivory-and-gold Music Room for thirty-four guests of duck with honey and brandy sauce, followed by mango ice cream and a 1955 vintage port, Elizabeth and Philip wandered with the First Couple along the palace's Picture Gallery—for the benefit of photographers as much as an appreciation of the priceless Poussin and Van Dyck oil paintings. Conversation was not yet flowing between the two heads of state.

"It's very quiet," the president was heard to remark. The Queen deployed the same conversational gambit she had used with Nixon two decades earlier, which was clearly part of her repertoire for uncomfortable silences: "You must be awfully busy." When the two couples lined up for their photo-call together, the US press noted how the Queen appeared to admonish the president by telling him, "Smile."

Barbara Bush was not sure they were really hitting it off.

She chatted with Elizabeth while their husbands inspected an honor guard of troops and learned that the Queen had recently visited Kentucky, staying with the Farishes.

"I asked her if she had seen my little puppy," the First Lady recalled. The Bush's family dog, Millie, was an English springer spaniel gifted to the Bushes years earlier by the Farishes, who had taken one of Millie's recent litter of puppies called Pickles. But the Queen seemed unmoved by the question.

"She said rather coolly that we'd talk about that later, and I thought, 'Oh my, you are not supposed to ask the Queen a direct question or something.'"

The exchange of gifts was the real icebreaker, much to Barbara Bush's relief. The Queen led the First Couple over to a table displaying pictures of the royal couple in silver frames, an idea she copied from the signed photo JFK gave her in 1961, which became her own signature gift to visiting dignitaries. "She presented them and then turned over a leather frame and gave it to me with the biggest smile," Barbara wrote in her memoir. "There was a signed picture of Her Majesty with 'Pickles.' I was so thrilled that I almost cried. There was our sweet little puppy. . . . Nothing could have made me happier."

Also on the table was a small silver bowl with three little feet. The president studied it momentarily and asked the Queen what it was. Elizabeth replied: "I don't know. *You* gave it to *me*!" Ice broken, the Buckingham Palace visit was a success, running thirty minutes over the time allotted in Bush's tight schedule.

Overall, the first of his three UK visits as president was regarded as a triumph, because he also slipped seamlessly into the same close relationship with Thatcher enjoyed by his predecessor. The Iron Lady found Bush Sr. "staunch and steadfast on everything which is of fundamental value to democracy, free-dom, and justice." Earlier in Brussels, Bush and Thatcher had won two significant concessions from their European allies at a NATO summit: the ability to keep short-range nuclear mis-siles in West Germany, and the go-ahead on Bush's proposal to negotiate a substantial reduction in conventional forces with the Warsaw Pact countries. Not known at the time, of course, was that the Soviet Union was just months away from crumbling—the Berlin Wall would fall that November.

Later that same month, Thatcher also fell after eleven and a half years as the British premier.

Like all the Queen's favorite presidents, Bush was attentive to the wider royal family: he hosted Prince Charles for dinner at Camp David in February 1989 and for lunch at the White House a year later; he invited Prince Philip for a meeting in May 1990 while the consort was on a solo tour as international president of the World Wildlife Fund; he met Princess Diana in October 1990 when she visited an inner-city HIV children's center; and he joined a tea hosted by the First Lady for Princess Margaret in March 1991.

The Queen, accompanied by around forty courtiers, flew on Concorde for her May 1991 state visit, her last supersonic trip on the pride of the British Airways fleet. Landing at Andrews Air Force Base at 10:10 a.m., the distinctive delta-winged jet cut several hours off the subsonic flight time, which meant that she could leave London in the morning and still attend the welcoming ceremony on the White House lawn beginning shortly after 11:00 a.m. It was the start of a thirteen-day visit, with official engagements in and around the capital, then in Florida and Texas, with the final three nights on a private holiday once again in Kentucky horse country.

Going straight to their personal wartime bond, Bush welcomed her as "freedom's friend . . . for as long as we remember—back to World War II when, at eighteen, you joined the war against fascism." The monarch—or, at least, her stripy talking hat—finished up her response to the president by combining the personal with the political in a way that summed up her own larger-than-life appeal: "Friendships need to be kept in good repair. Not just the personal friendships between heads of state, but the more diffused friendships between the governments and peoples of two nations. There is a symbolism in the events of such a visit that defies analysis, but which has a way of reaching the hearts of people far and wide." That, in a nutshell, was what the modern monarchy aimed to achieve: celebrating while at the same time adding to the store of shared experiences between two countries that tried their best to get along for the greater good but—as memorable moments like the "talking hat" episode suggested—did not always get it quite right.

"The next morning, instead of talking about how wonderful the state dinner was, it was all about the talking hat," recalled Laurie Firestone, Bush's White House social secretary. "It was a great story and a cute picture of the Queen."

Bush would later insist that he did not realize how the Queen looked to onlookers or he would have intervened mid-speech. Under questioning from the White House press corps the next day, he sought to pin the blame on his chief of protocol.

"How come you didn't take out the step for the Queen, Mr. President?" he was asked.

Bush replied, to laughter, "That's what we hired Joseph Reed for." The press corps gave a collective "Ooh" at this under-the-bus quip. Asked how he liked the Queen, Bush went on: "Very, very impressive; an engaging conversationalist and most impressive. I do feel badly I didn't [bring out the step]. I thought about it and—but she started to speak. And I didn't realize how it would look from a straight angle, or I would have interrupted her because it wasn't fair to her. And I'm just sorry that it was overlooked."

At the end of the briefing, which was on the South Lawn, the First Lady passed by. "He's apologizing for not pulling the step out for the Queen, Mrs. Bush," shouted a reporter.

Mrs. Bush, to laughter: "He doesn't need to apologize . . . It was someone else's job—come on."

The president: "See, we've got our line together."

There was another possible explanation for his lectern oversight—Bush was not feeling well. The sixty-six-year-old president had just begun treatment for Graves' disease, an immune system disorder that results in an overactive thyroid gland. Ten days before the Queen's visit he suffered shortness of breath while taking his customary two-mile jog at Camp David and spent the night in Bethesda Naval Hospital, where he was found to have atrial fibrillation. That led to the thyroid diagnosis, and five days before Elizabeth's arrival he started treatment—doses of radioactive iodine—which had left him feeling more tired than usual.

The Bushes hosted an intimate lunch of red snapper with ginger for the Queen inside the White House with a handful of guests, including William and Sarah Farish; British ambassador Antony Acland and his wife, Jenny; and the eldest Bush son—forty-four-year-old George and his wife, Laura.

"I jokingly told Her Majesty that I had put our Texas son as far away from her as possible at the table," Barbara Bush wrote, "and had told him that he was not allowed to say a word to her."

The Queen wondered why. "Was he the black sheep in the family?" she asked. She was about to find out. At this point, "Dubya," who at the time was managing general partner of the Texas Rangers baseball team, intervened to say that he guessed he probably was. The Queen, as deadpan as ever, remarked: "Well, I guess all families have one."

This only prompted the younger George to ask who the black sheep of the royal family was. It brought a laugh from the Queen, but Barbara Bush quickly said: "Don't answer that!" She explained that her son was in the habit of saying exactly what he felt and told Elizabeth that he had threatened to wear cowboy boots that evening to the state dinner either with Texas flags on them or GOD BLESS AMERICA.

When the Queen asked him directly which pair he was going to wear, George replied: "Neither. Tonight's pair will say GOD SAVE THE QUEEN."

When the president showed the Queen the Truman balcony after lunch, with its view to the south of the Washington Monument and the Jefferson Memorial, renovations were visible on parts of the White House where paintwork had been stripped back to reveal scorch marks from 1814, when British soldiers set the Presidential Mansion on fire. "I teased her that it was her folks who had done this," Bush recalled.

Knowing full well the Queen's love of all things equine,

Bush decided to induct Her Majesty into the mysteries of the White House horseshoe pit he had reinstalled after Eisenhower removed it. The monarch was puzzled. Horseshoe throwing?

As well as a copy of an essay written by George III entitled *America Is Lost*, she had presented Bush with a gift of silver-plated horseshoes inscribed with her insignia . . . but she had not figured they might be tossed around the garden. Fortunately, the president brought along some well-worn old horseshoes he kept for the purpose and proceeded to toss a few. Elizabeth declined to have a go herself.

"She was very happy to watch the president practice this very obviously difficult sport," said a Buckingham Palace spokesman tactfully. "This was the first time the Queen had seen a horseshoe thrown by anyone."

The Queen had some ceremonial business to perform at the White House before the customary trip to Arlington National Cemetery. In the Rose Garden, she presented Bush with the Winston Churchill Award "in recognition of the leadership you have shown to the world in recent months."

The president joked that he was so pleased he had prepared "a forty-five-minute speech—but if I gave it, we would all melt." He kept his remarks mercifully short, as the Washington, DC, pound cake was now well and truly baked. "I'm old enough to remember, from World War II, Winston Churchill's leadership. He inspired the United Kingdom, but he inspired everybody in this country as well. And I think it's a marvelous symbol of the lasting, special relationship between the United Kingdom and the United States of America," he said.

Then it was back to the South Lawn for a tree planting, which again had strong echoes of past glories: a replacement linden tree for one planted by President Franklin D. Roosevelt in honor of the Queen's father's coronation in 1937, which had blown down in a recent storm. Bush said: "It is my honor now to dedicate this tree to a truly great and good man, King George VI."

The increasingly humid weather finally broke at Arlington, where Elizabeth laid a wreath at the Tomb of the Unknown Soldier as the rain started to pour. Much to the relief of Joseph Reed, the protocol chief whose nerves were already frayed by the lectern incident, the Queen produced her own umbrella out of her trusty handbag, saving him from censure for a second gaffe of the day.

The star-studded lineup for dinner included the hero of the hour, General "Stormin' Norman" Schwarzkopf, leader of the victorious coalition forces. He had also been one of the commanders of the US invasion to restore order in Grenada, but all that was water under the bridge now. The Queen would award him an honorary knighthood later in the trip. In the receiving line for dinner guests, when she came face-to-face with George W. Bush, Elizabeth looked down at his ankles. Without a word he pulled up his trouser legs enough for her to see cowboy boots with the Stars and Stripes on them. Other guests, including chairman of the Joint Chiefs of Staff Colin Powell, actors Angela Lansbury and Morgan Freeman, and golfer Arnold Palmer, dined on medallions of Maine lobster with cucumber mousse, roast lamb with watercress and Belgian endive salad, and pistachio marquise with raspberries.

Amid the usual tributes to the "relationship between America and Great Britain which has perhaps never been more special," the president managed to add an American equine joke, which earned a hearty laugh from most of his guests: "We've got a lot of things in common. Americans share the Queen's love of horses. And I often wonder if I'd be standing here today if it weren't for a horse fancier named Paul Revere."

The lessons of 1976's musical goofs having been learned, there was no pop duo this time, nor an attempt at dancing to the band. Entertainment for the evening featured spirituals and a French love song from the American opera singer Jessye Norman, who had performed "God Save the Queen" at the "Fanfare for Elizabeth" concert for the Queen's sixtieth birthday at the Royal Albert Hall in London in 1986.

"This is now the fourth time I have had the honor of proposing a toast to the president of the United States in the very place where my father once proposed a toast to President Roosevelt," observed the Queen, dressed in a white silk dress and wearing a tiara studded with diamonds and sapphires. "No wonder I cannot feel a stranger here. The British have never felt America to be a foreign land. Here we feel comfortable and among friends."

There was an unusual first for the Queen during the next day's events when she was accompanied by Barbara Bush to Drake Place in Marshall Heights, one of Southeast Washington's grittiest neighborhoods, to visit a new affordable housing development. The historically impoverished Black area had become the epicenter of the city's crack cocaine crisis and associated violence but, according to Mrs. Bush, "The good people of the neighborhood started their own patrol and took back their streets."

After watching children demonstrate double Dutch jump roping, martial arts, and basketball, there was a stunning breach of royal protocol. The Queen was only ever to be touched on her gloved hand, if she offered it. But that day Her Majesty received the first ever public hug of her reign at the three-bedroom home of Alice Frazier, described by *The Baltimore Sun* as an exuberant sixty-seven-year-old great-grandmother. She greeted the Queen with a warm "How are ya doin'?" before wrapping her arms around her.

It had been Frazier's plan all along—she told journalists the day before that "I'm used to hugging people" and would treat the Queen no different to other houseguests: "After all, we are both mothers." While "exhibiting faint alarm," the Queen managed to smile broadly while keeping her arms stiffly by her sides. It was described as "one of those incredibly awkward moments the British are so good at." Elizabeth II ended up staying twenty minutes at Frazier's home, where she was surrounded by curious grandchildren and other family members in a room decorated with pictures of Jesus, Martin Luther King Jr., and John and Robert Kennedy.

"I told her this was my palace," Frazier said later, unfazed that her guest declined to sample any of the food she prepared (despite a briefing that the Queen would not be eating).

"Alice was so innocent and so proud of her new home," recalled District of Columbia mayor Sharon Pratt, who also joined the tour. "Of course, everyone had told us that the Queen can never eat in public. . . . Alice had prepared all this food and she kept insisting that Queen Elizabeth come in here and have some fried chicken and devilled eggs and potato salad. Queen Elizabeth was clearly amused by it. She was enjoying it in her restrained fashion." Pratt also said that the royal visitor took the breach of protocol in stride. "She knew that this woman was just so authentically excited about having her in her own home . . . and I just thought it spoke volumes about who she was as a person."

The housing project was followed by the more usual state visit fare of a luncheon at the Library of Congress with celebrities, politicians, and other worthies, ahead of a garden party at the British embassy for 1,800 guests. Prince Philip caused a minor panic when he asked for a beer with his roast turkey, sending a member of the catering team scurrying out for a six-pack from a nearby liquor store.

That evening there was another first—a baseball game. In the 1992 documentary *Elizabeth R*, the Queen's private secretary Robert Fellowes is shown briefing her about the distinctive American sporting occasion that baseball fanatic and former Yale first baseman President Bush was taking her to see. When Fellowes raised the possibility that Prince Philip might be asked to throw the ceremonial first pitch, Elizabeth responded with a withering "Oh, rilleh?" and, after a slight pause, "Are you sure?" in a way that made clear it would definitely not happen. Royal arms are for waving, not pitching.

Elizabeth did, however, overrule British security concerns by walking out on the field with Bush before the Oakland Athletics–Baltimore Orioles game. "All that independence-from-England stuff appeared to be forgotten as the Memorial Stadium crowd of 32,596 applauded Queen Elizabeth II when she emerged from the dugout," *The Baltimore Sun* reported. "The Queen seemed delighted—albeit reservedly—by the welcome." Hatless and wearing a dark red-and-black paisley dress, she greeted the players, coaches, and batboys before watching the action, or at least the first two innings, in the private box of O's team owner Eli Jacobs.

The Queen "asked a lot of questions about baseball," said Robin Winternitz, a waitress for the owner's box. She also asked for a martini.

The next day, in the moments before the Queen's big speech to Congress, Fellowes talked her through what she could expect. "You go straight to the podium . . . and it is going to be built for you and not for anyone else this time," he concluded mischievously, drawing a chuckle from Elizabeth. Once in position, the British sovereign waited patiently for the assembled senators and representatives to settle down before bringing everyone back to their feet with the joke about whether she was visible ("I do hope you can see me today from where you are"), delivered in her usual deadpan style with only the faintest glimmer of a smile.

She spoke "the old-fashioned way," observers noted, reading from paper instead of a teleprompter.

While it was standing room only, several Irish American members stayed away. Senator Edward Kennedy of Massachusetts was there, laughing and applauding, but his nephew Representative Joseph P. Kennedy II, the second of Bobby Kennedy's eleven children, missed it and came to the House later to condemn the "long and painful occupation" of Northern Ireland by British forces. Raymond McGrath, a Republican representative from New York and another absentee, said that his Irish bricklayer father "would roll over in his grave five times if I was alive in there." Instead, he spoke outside the Supreme Court at a small protest by a dozen or so demonstrators against British policy in Northern Ireland.

The Reverend Al Sharpton urged Black members to boycott the Queen to protest Britain easing sanctions on South Africa following the release of Nelson Mandela but against Mandela's wishes—he wanted to keep up pressure for reforms on the government. At least three Black representatives stayed away.

Elizabeth kept her speech short, just twelve minutes, including interruptions for half a dozen rounds of applause. Buckingham Palace said her remarks had been written by British officials. Americans watched as the unelected head of an ancient hereditary system rejected by their Founding Fathers extolled the merits of democracy. It was incongruous but at the same time meaningful, not unlike the modern monarchy itself.

"Your Congress and our Parliament are the twin pillars of our civilizations and the chief among the many treasures that we have inherited from our predecessors," she said. "Some people believe that power grows from the barrel of a gun. So it can, but history shows that it never grows well nor for very long. . . . We have gone a better way; our societies rest on mutual agreement, on contract and consensus. . . . The spirit behind both is precisely the same. It is the spirit of democracy."

It was a measure of the Queen's fondness for Bush that she prepared an unusual gift for him that evening in the form of a musical tribute at the return dinner at the British embassy. After a hundred guests, including Jane Fonda and her partner Ted Turner, the founder of CNN, dined on smoked salmon and caviar, roast duckling with cherry sauce, and poached pears doused with chocolate sauce and raspberry cream, four kilted bagpipers of the First Battalion Argyll and Sutherland Highlanders entered to serenade their colonel-in-chief, who was still a princess in 1947 when her father appointed her head of the regiment.

Pipe Sergeant Jim Motherwell stepped forward to play a solo march for the president dedicated to the Gulf War victory. Motherwell composed "Desert Storm" while recovering from injuries received on duty in Northern Ireland. At the end of the rendition, he presented a leather-bound copy of the musical score to Bush. Motherwell then saluted the president and offered an ancient Gaelic toast: *"Slainte do'n Bhanrich, Slainte Dhuibh Uile Gu Leier"* ("Health to the Queen, health to one and all"). The president, who had returned Motherwell's salute, shook his head in apparent bewilderment. He handed Motherwell a dram of brandy in a shallow two-handled silver cup known as a quaich, the piper's traditional reward.

"After I'd finished he handed me my quaich and I have to say that was one of the few occasions when I have really, really needed it," Motherwell recalled. The Queen never forgot—she made him her personal piper seven years later, a role that involved playing at 9:00 a.m. every day as a unique wake-up call.

Elizabeth II renewed her acquaintance with two former presidents the following evening, after leaving Washington, DC, and traveling south. Aboard *Britannia*, which crossed the Atlantic to serve as accommodation for several nights, she hosted a dinner for former presidents Reagan and Ford and their wives, among other guests mostly from Florida. A British embassy spokesman said that, of the four living former presidents, those two were invited because, unlike Carter and Nixon, both had hosted the Queen on US visits—an explanation that sounded more like an excuse to avoid awkward encounters.

Unlike the Queen, who was sixty-five and determined never to retire, her two ex-presidential guests were showing their age. Ford, then aged seventy-seven, had both knees replaced the previous year due to arthritis and told guests, "It's amazing how much metal they put in. I have to carry a card to get through the airport security." The Queen's post-dinner chat with Reagan, captured in *Elizabeth R*, included the eighty-year-old former president persistently asking for decaffeinated coffee from wandering stewards who were armed only with the caffeinated variety.

"If you take a cup we'll find some . . . I hope," the Queen reassured him. She signaled for a steward to come over.

"It's just coming through," the white-uniformed waiter said.

The Queen told Reagan: "We try our best."

Reagan spotted another steward with a large silver pot. "Is that decaffeinated?" he asked.

"No!" said Elizabeth and Nancy Reagan in unison.

Finally, a third steward emerged with the magic liquid.

Reagan: "Decaffeinated!"

Of most interest to a British audience was a very unusual glimpse of Elizabeth II discussing political views. Faultlessly discreet throughout her long reign, she was shown in the film agreeing with Reagan about the expense and bureaucracy of government services. She was heard saying, "All the democracies are bankrupt now because, you know, because of the way

that the services have been planned for the people to grab."
Reagan, whose administration was known for cutting back on
domestic spending, said, "We tried to get some of these things
changed and reduce them." The Queen added: "It's extraordinary, isn't it, how—I mean, I think the next generation are
going to have a very difficult time." It was an insight suggesting
another reason why she was fond of Reagan—they shared some
common ground on issues of the day.

As with Reagan, the Queen would later have the pleasant
responsibility of bestowing a knighthood on Bush over lunch at
Buckingham Palace. Out of office for almost a year, Bush,
along with his wife, was first presented with a glass of sherry
before Elizabeth declared, "Before we forget, we must do what
we are here to do." She produced two leather boxes, one containing the ornate gold chain "collar" and badge of the honorary Knight Grand Cross of the Most Honourable Order of the
Bath, the other containing an insignia on a sash.

Prominent subjects of conversation over lunch were the political careers of the Bushes' two elder sons: George was running for governor of Texas and Jeb for the same position in
Florida. Bush Sr. was later asked to sign an undertaking that,
should he leave the order or pass away, the ceremonial collar
would be returned—a requirement of all recipients. He was
just the eighth American in the postwar period to receive the
high British honor, after Reagan and six wartime generals.

CHAPTER 10

Her Majesty impressed me as someone who but for the circumstance of her birth, might have become a successful politician or
diplomat. As it was, she had to be both, without quite seeming to
be either.

—Bill Clinton in his memoir, *My Life*, 2004

Not many visitors to Great Britain are invited to tea with the
Queen. Even fewer turn it down. Yet when Bill Clinton
added a day in London onto a mini European tour in May 1997,
the White House sent word that "the President and Mrs. Clinton were very grateful for HM The Queen's invitation to tea at
the Palace, but would wish to decline politely."

Clinton primarily went to Britain to spend time with Tony
Blair, who had just been elected prime minister in a landslide
election victory and with whom the president hoped to re-
launch efforts to achieve a lasting peace in Northern Ireland.
Records of frantic last-minute behind-the-scenes negotiations
on Clinton's schedule for the day reveal that he "wanted to be a
tourist" with First Lady Hillary during the free time he had in
the afternoon after meeting with Blair's cabinet in Downing
Street and holding a joint press conference. The White House

had "no clear idea" exactly what the Clintons would do in London, according to notes made by Blair's private secretary before the hastily arranged trip, but they had expressed a desire to visit a garden and some shops and try some Indian food with the prime minister, US officials said.

The rejection of the Queen, whom Clinton had met twice already as president and would meet again a few years later for tea, was not intended as a snub but did suggest a change in attitude toward the British royals by a new generation of American politicians. Clinton, after all, was the first commander in chief born after the Second World War. For his part, Blair and his "New Labour" Party appeared to be more in tune with the turn-of-millennium zeitgeist than an eleven-centuries-old hereditary institution. Nevertheless there was a "good rapport" between Elizabeth II and this first baby boomer president (just over two years older than her son Charles), according to Dickie Arbiter, the Queen's press officer at the time. "She liked Clinton because he was a bit of an Anglophile, having been a Rhodes scholar at Oxford University," Arbiter said.

According to genealogists, there was another, more tenuous connection. Both Clinton and 1992 election rival Bush were supposedly descended from King John (of Magna Carta fame) via links to John's son, Henry III, and Clinton was also related via John's youngest legitimate child, Eleanor, who was married to Simon de Montfort, Earl of Leicester, *Burke's Peerage* said.

Although both Clinton and Bush supposedly inherited a little of Henry III's genes, it did not escape Clinton's notice that the longest-reigning medieval king took barbarous revenge against de Montfort, a political rival, after defeating his rebellion against the throne, sending parts of his mutilated body to different corners of England. Clinton joked: "Now that I knew the roots of my differences with the president went back seven hundred years, I suppose I couldn't blame his campaign for being faithful to the tactics of his ancestors."

Clinton's election year coincided with what the Queen described as her annus horribilis, when three of her four children's marriages collapsed: second son, Andrew, announced his split from Sarah Ferguson; daughter, Anne, completed her divorce from Mark Phillips; and in December, Charles and Diana announced their separation following that summer's bombshell account of Diana's emotional and matrimonial breakdown, *Diana: Her True Story*, written by Andrew Morton with her secret cooperation.

The tabloids had stories of Sarah on holiday topless in France that summer with her American financial advisor John Bryan, who was shown in one photo apparently kissing her toes, and a recording of an intimate conversation between Diana and a male friend she called "darling" and who called her "Squidgy." In January 1993 came publication of a deeply private call between Charles and his lover Camilla Parker-Bowles, in which the heir to the throne expressed a desire to "live inside your trousers." Charles's popularity plummeted, with the *Los Angeles Times* reporting that the leaked phone call "raised doubts in political and editorial circles . . . that he will ever be king."

Toward the end of 1992, there was an extensive fire at Windsor Castle that seemed to symbolize the wretched year. This difficult time for the Queen coincided with a chill in the

Special Relationship after two officials from Prime Minister John Major's Conservative Party went to the US to help Bush's campaign against Clinton. British Home Office archives were also searched in a vain effort to show that Clinton applied for UK citizenship while a graduate student at Oxford to avoid the Vietnam draft.

"After the election, the British press fretted that the special relationship between our two countries had been damaged by this unusual British involvement in American politics," Clinton wrote later. "I was determined that there would be no damage, but I wanted the Tories to worry about it for a while."

Several tense years ensued, with significant policy clashes on the handling of the war in Bosnia and the peace process in Northern Ireland, especially over Clinton's decision to grant a US visa to Gerry Adams, president of the Irish republican party Sinn Féin, for a much-publicized two-day visit to New York in January 1994. Major was so furious that he refused to speak on the phone with the president for a week, and *The Sunday Times* berated Clinton's "shameful decision" over "one of the world's leading terrorists," which meant "slighting America's closest ally and plunging the special relationship into its worst crisis since Suez."

Nevertheless, Clinton gradually warmed to the unpretentious prime minister, thanks to a bridge-building visit by Major the following month, when the president took him for the day to Pittsburgh, the Pennsylvania city where Major's father and grandfather worked for many years. The two leaders began to repair their relationship over glasses of Iron City Beer at the Tin Angel restaurant before Clinton flew Major back to Washington on Air Force One for a stay-over in the Lincoln Bedroom at the White House.

The Special Relationship was being patched up, and not for the first time, it was left to the Queen to finish the job. Her chance came with Clinton's first visit as president to Britain for the fiftieth anniversary of D-Day in June 1994.

The Clintons arrived at Royal Air Force Mildenhall air base in Suffolk from Rome, and after being greeted by Major, Clinton first went to the Cambridge American Cemetery and Memorial, the largest US military resting place in the British Isles. It has the graves of 3,811 Americans, with a further 5,127 names recorded on the Wall of the Missing, including Joseph Kennedy Jr., JFK's elder brother, who died in 1944.

"The victory of the generations we honor today came at a high cost," Clinton said. On the south coast, where a royal outdoor garden party for veterans had to be moved into tents, the lashing rain and thirty-five-mile-per-hour gusts of wind were reminiscent of weather conditions exactly fifty years earlier, when General Eisenhower postponed the invasion of France by twenty-four hours hoping for calmer seas.

"It would have been historically incorrect to have good weather," said General John Shalikashvili, chairman of the US Joint Chiefs of Staff.

Clinton was seated directly on the Queen's left that evening at the Guildhall in Portsmouth for the largest state dinner of her reign, hosting thirteen other heads of state from the Allied countries as well as five hundred further guests, including many veterans. In her dinner speech, the Queen quoted her father's radio address from June 6, 1944, in which he said: "We and our allies are sure that our fight is against evil and for a world in which goodness and honor may be the foundation of the life of men in every land."

Clinton had spent lunch at Chequers in talks with Major over the bloody war in Bosnia, which was also on the Queen's mind. Dressed in a blue gown and wearing her Belgian Sapphire Tiara, Elizabeth II told the black-tie gathering: "We have seen that the peace which victory brought is a fragile thing. Events around the world, some of them close to home in Europe, prove that to us day after day. It is up to us to make sure that the prayers of fifty years ago are truly answered by rededicating ourselves to the creation of a world at peace."

This was Clinton's first meeting with the Queen and, according to his memoir, he was "taken with her grace and intelligence and the clever manner in which she discussed public issues, probing me for information and insights without venturing too far into expressing her own political views," noting that this was "taboo for the British head of state." Clinton's own humble origins growing up in small-town Arkansas—notwithstanding his distant ancestral links to the British monarchy—were about as far removed from the privileged palace world of royal life as it was possible to be. Nevertheless he claimed to recognize innate qualities in the Queen who, "but for the circumstance of her birth, might have become a successful politician or diplomat. As it was, she had to be both, without quite seeming to be either."

The Clintons were given a rare invitation to stay overnight on *Britannia*, where they also found Princess Margaret and the

Queen Mother, who, as Queen in 1944, had addressed the nation by radio from Buckingham Palace on D-Day. The president thought the ninety-three-year-old "still lively and lovely, with luminous, piercing eyes." He described the royal yacht as "comfortable" with "a lot of kind of relaxed banter." Clinton added: "I loved it. I thought it was a kind thing for her to do, something she didn't have to do, to ask us to stay there that night. And I'm sure it was done in larger measure for symbolic reasons, because of what D-Day meant to both of our countries and how we did it together. But it meant a lot to me, both as president and as a person."

The First Lady recalled: "We were in close quarters. It was just like being with a family that was having a good time together despite the solemnity of the occasion. . . . I saw a more playful and somewhat, you know, funny and very incredibly warm side of [the Queen] as well. Sometimes there would be a wry exchange about, how as a woman leader, you always have to have your hair done—well, she always looked perfect, unlike some of us. She had a sense of style that really stayed with her."

As it happens, the New York *Daily News* was impressed with the way Hillary's hair stood up to the "howling winds" of the unpredictable English summer. "The wind was blowing with great gusto" when the Clintons were en route to the dinner, it reported. "While [President] Clinton's steel wool hair appeared to bounce around, Mrs. Clinton's unswept hairdo remained perfectly firm with not a hair out of place. A British sailor tried gamely to hold an umbrella in position to protect the Clintons from the elements, but the effort foundered and the umbrella was almost blown out of his hand."

The foul weather mainly blew itself out overnight. President

Clinton was up early in the sunshine to do his customary jog (accompanied by his security detail) through the Portsmouth Naval Base. After breakfast, he joined the Queen on nearby Southsea Common for a "drumhead" religious service of commemoration, with military band drums forming an altar. Then it was back onto *Britannia* for lunch with the dozen other heads of state before leading an armada of battleships, minesweepers, frigates, landing craft, tugboats, and hundreds of accompanying small vessels across the English Channel in tribute to the largest seaborne invasion in history.

Hundreds of US sailors lining the flight deck of the vast nuclear-powered aircraft carrier USS *George Washington* gave a traditional British welcome to the Queen and their president as *Britannia* approached to transfer Clinton. Following instructions from a British manual, the sailors practiced carefully for their big moment: after an officer shouted, "Hip, hip, hip," they all raised their hats and in unison shouted "Hooray!" and repeated this twice more.

Captain Chuck Connor, a navy spokesman, said: "The British are born planners. Nobody does ceremony like these guys." Elizabeth told the president about her own recollection of D-Day, when she was eighteen. "The Queen told me that on D-Day, 'I was at the dentist,'" Clinton said.

The drumhead service was notable for a rare public engagement alongside fellow royals for Diana, the Princess of Wales, who was dressed in a somber dark blue suit and wide-brimmed hat. Her estranged husband, commander in chief of the Parachute Regiment, spent the day in France at events recalling their heroism behind enemy lines.

Clinton observed: "During the little time I had spent with

Princess Elizabeth stepped onto American soil for the first time on October 31, 1951, followed by Prince Philip, to be greeted by President Truman, First Lady Bess Truman, and their daughter, Margaret, at Washington National Airport.

"When I was a little boy I read about a Fairy Princess—and there she is," President Truman said of Princess Elizabeth.

Queen Elizabeth II's recipe for drop scones, sent by her to President Eisenhower.

MENU

Date.................................

DROP SCONES

Ingredients

4 teacups flour

4 tablespoons caster sugar

2 teacups milk

2 whole eggs

2 teaspoons bi-carbonate soda

3 teaspoons cream of tartar

2 tablespoons melted butter

Beat eggs, sugar and about half the milk together, add flour, and mix well together adding remainder of milk as required, also bi-carbonate and cream of tartar, fold in the melted butter.

Enough for 16 people

Eisenhower *(center)* was the only president invited to stay at Balmoral Castle in Scotland with the royal family, seen here in August 1959, with *(left to right)* Prince Philip, Princess Anne, the Queen, and Prince Charles.

Prince Philip, First Lady Jacqueline Kennedy, Queen Elizabeth II, and President John F. Kennedy at Buckingham Palace in London for their informal dinner on June 5, 1961.

Lyndon B. Johnson was the only president of the Queen's reign she did not meet, but her sister, Princess Margaret, dined with him at the White House on November 17, 1965.

Elizabeth II helped smooth relations between Prime Minister Edward Heath *(left)* and President Nixon, seen here with First Lady Pat Nixon *(right)* at Chequers in Buckinghamshire on October 3, 1970.

The Queen's eldest son, Prince Charles, frequently found himself paired with President Nixon's daughter, Tricia, on his first US visit, including at a Washington Senators baseball game at RFK Stadium on July 18, 1970.

In celebration of America's bicentenary, President Ford danced with the Queen at a White House State Dinner on July 7, 1976. Unfortunately, the band struck up "The Lady Is a Tramp."

President Carter met Elizabeth II just once, at a dinner at Buckingham Palace for G7 leaders on May 13, 1977. In this pre-dinner photograph he held hands with the Queen Mother and surprised her later with a parting kiss.

President Reagan and Queen Elizabeth II rode out together in Windsor Home Park in an iconic image of the US-UK Special Relationship on June 8, 1982.

Bad weather forced the cancelation of a planned second horse ride at the Reagans' Rancho del Cielo home in California, where the Mackintosh-clad Queen and Prince Philip arrived on March 1, 1983.

Nobody adjusted the lectern for the Queen when she followed President George H. W. Bush at the White House arrival ceremony on May 14, 1991, and became the "talking hat" after disappearing behind the microphones.

President Clinton, First Lady Hillary Clinton, and daughter Chelsea Clinton visited Queen Elizabeth II at Buckingham Palace on December 14, 2000.

"She gave me a look that only a mother could give a child," President George W. Bush said when the Queen arrived at the White House on May 7, 2007.

When First Lady Michelle Obama broke with protocol and put her arm around the Queen, her gesture was reciprocated, much to the surprise of onlookers at a G20 reception at Buckingham Palace on April 1, 2009.

President and Mrs. Obama pose with the Queen and Prince Philip at Buckingham Palace on April 22, 2016.

The Queen and President Trump inspect the Guard of Honor at Windsor Castle on July 13, 2018.

President Biden and First Lady Jill Biden share a smile with Elizabeth II at the Eden Project in Cornwall during the G7 on June 11, 2021.

President Biden, watched by the First Lady, signed a book of condolence for Queen Elizabeth II on September 18, 2022.

Charles and Diana, I liked them both and wished that life had dealt them a different hand." Just a few weeks later Charles gave an interview to the BBC admitting his adultery after, he said, the marriage was "irretrievably broken down, us both having tried." That same night Diana appeared at a function in London in her famous shoulderless "revenge dress" as their relationship unraveled further. Her own revelatory TV interview, known for her comment "There were three of us in this marriage, so it was a bit crowded" followed in November 1995, prompting the Queen to issue a statement that "an early divorce" was now "desirable." It was finalized in August 1996.

Throughout this period Diana visited the United States regularly, utilizing her huge public profile to support fundraising events that brought in many more dollars thanks to her presence. She appeared to find America a welcome escape from the pressures and intrusive media attention on the other side of the Atlantic. In her first international appearance following her divorce, she helped to raise more than $1 million for breast cancer research at an evening auction in Washington, DC, after cochairing a White House breakfast with Hillary Clinton and designer Ralph Lauren and fashion editor Anna Wintour. It was a private visit, and Diana stayed at the Brazilian embassy as a guest of her friend Lucia Flecha de Lima, the wife of the Brazilian ambassador to the United States.

The Clintons had been back at Buckingham Palace for tea with the Queen in December 1995, ahead of the first visit by a US president to Northern Ireland to celebrate a fifteen-month cease-fire in paramilitary activity that had given real cause for optimism. Clinton wrote to Elizabeth II afterward, thanking her for her "warm welcome" and expressing the hope that American partnership with Britain would "continue to offer us opportunities for peace and progress." However, the violence resumed in February 1996 with a bomb planted by the Irish Republican Army in London's Docklands that killed two people, and in June a large bomb devastated the center of Manchester, injuring 212. Clinton believed that the election of Tony Blair in May 1997 was the chance to revive the peace process and added a day in London at the end of May after a NATO summit in Paris and an EU-US meeting in The Hague.

British officials scrambled to put together an itinerary that met Clinton's request for something "fun" and "photogenic" besides his talks with the new prime minister. During the planning stages, government papers made public in 2021 show that Philip Barton, Blair's private secretary, wrote to US officials, saying: "The Palace has been in touch with us to say that HM The Queen would be very pleased to invite the president (with or without the prime minister) and/or Mrs. Clinton and Mrs. Blair to tea next Thursday."

The timing of tea, however, did not fit in with Clinton's other plans for the day. "Tea at the Palace is at 5pm, which probably rules this out for the president and prime minister as I suspect they will be at the outside event then," Barton added. "But this might be a possibility for Mrs. Clinton and Mrs. Blair." After consultations, the following day he recorded: "The Americans said the president and Mrs. Clinton were very grateful for HM The Queen's invitation to tea at the Palace, but would wish to decline politely." The president said "he wanted to be a tourist," Barton recorded.

Both sides were keen to project a youthful image for the two leaders. Barton wrote: "All were agreed that we wanted something that would show the president and the prime minister to the wider world as young, dynamic, and serious leaders. We suggested that they might go for a stroll in Trafalgar Square before visiting the Sports Cafe at the end of the Haymarket, where the president and the prime minister could be shown how to play various sophisticated computer games by a group of children." The US embassy ruled that out because "it was not serious enough." An official from the British Foreign Office suggested that lunch at Downing Street would be "an opportunity for the president (saxophone) and the prime minister (guitar) to play together briefly (with or without other musicians who might be at the lunch)." That was also rejected.

On the day, Clinton attended a meeting of Blair's cabinet, with the First Couple lunching privately with Tony and his wife, Cherie. There was to be no Indian curry—instead, the Blairs hosted the Clintons that evening at the fashionable Le Pont de la Tour restaurant overlooking Tower Bridge, where they ordered seared tuna followed by roast wild salmon (Bill); salad, then grilled Dover sole (Hillary); foie gras followed by fillet of halibut (Cherie); and stuffed squid before roast leg of rabbit (Tony). Their £298.86 bill also included several glasses of wine and two bottles of beer, as well as water. The restaurant threw in a bottle of Bollinger 1989 vintage champagne on the house (menu price £91.50). Fellow diners clapped and cheered the two couples as they departed.

The day cemented relations between the Democratic president and the New Labour leader, but there was fury among
Clinton's security detail when some of them were split up from
the president by the raising of Tower Bridge just as the motorcade was crossing the Thames. A sailing barge had booked a
bridge opening, and river traffic had precedence by law, no
matter who was waiting to drive over. The Clintons were stuck
on the south side of the Thames and had to wait.

Hillary was back in London just over three months later for the
funeral of Diana, Princess of Wales, after her untimely death at
thirty-six in a car crash in Paris. The Clintons heard the news
while on holiday on Martha's Vineyard in Massachusetts, and
the president paid immediate tribute, saying: "We liked her
very much. We admired her work for children, for people with
AIDS, for the cause of ending the scourge of land mines in the
world and for her love for her children, William and Harry."
Nancy Reagan also attended the service in Westminster Abbey
and lamented that "magic doesn't last, and it always costs more
than you can imagine."

At the British embassy in Washington, visitors left cards,
candles, and bouquets of flowers at the front gate. Michael Mc-
Guire, the *Chicago Tribune* foreign editor, argued that "she was
America's Princess as much as she was Britain's Princess."
Much ink was spilled on both sides of the Atlantic analyzing
just why Americans were so affected by Diana's death and took
her to their hearts seemingly as much as the British.

Elaine Showalter—a feminist literary critic and writer on

American popular culture—pointed to Diana's "very American sensibility" compared to Prince Charles. "We have a sense here in America that anything is possible, that you are not a predetermined person; that if you are a woman from whom nothing is expected but you want to make your life count, you can do it. She shared that spirit and that's why she appealed so much to Americans."

The *Miami Herald* thought that "she was a superstar Cinderella with the polish of a natural-born socialite. . . . In a way she fulfilled the American dream. To emerge from obscurity and overcome adversity and make something of herself." (Although as the daughter of an earl who was a hereditary member of the House of Lords with a stately home in thirteen thousand acres of the English countryside, and one of the largest town houses in central London overlooking Green Park, she did have *some* advantages in life.)

Hillary Clinton received a letter of apology from the Queen after returning to Washington. "I am writing to say how deeply your presence at the funeral last Saturday was appreciated," the Queen wrote. "I don't believe anyone could have anticipated the public outpouring of grief. It was a moving tribute to Diana's humanitarian work in a violent and troubled world. My only regret is that we were unable to offer you any hospitality while you were in London. As you will appreciate, this is the holiday season, when most of the staff are away and advantage is taken of our absence to open Buckingham Palace to the public. I do hope you will understand the difficulties and accept my apologies."

President Clinton's engagement in the Northern Ireland peace process paid off in April 1998 when George Mitchell, the Democratic senator he appointed as the first US special envoy, announced that a settlement had been reached, which became known as the Good Friday Agreement. It was another triumph for the Special Relationship, which was firmly back on track thanks to the personal rapport between Blair and Clinton.

The president's relations with Queen Elizabeth II were cordial but not as intense as they had been with the previous two presidents. Records at the William J. Clinton Presidential Library & Museum show that there was the usual formal exchange of pleasantries between Buckingham Palace and the White House on occasions like July 4 and the Queen's birthday. On August 3, 2000, a special message arrived from the president for the Queen Mother to congratulate her on her one hundredth birthday: "On this special occasion, we cannot help but remember the inspiration of the example set by you and His Majesty the King George VI during the Second World War, when Britain stood alone in the face of tyranny." As well as signing the typewritten letter, Clinton added in his own hand: "You are an inspiration to people of goodwill everywhere."

The Queen would see Clinton once more, when he made a valedictory visit to Ireland and the UK in December 2000 in the last weeks of his second term. He arrived in Britain after being feted in Dublin by Bertie Ahern, the taoiseach (prime minister), as "the best American president Ireland has ever had." After spending the night at Chequers with the Blairs, the Clintons helicoptered aboard Marine One into Hyde Park in central London, where the president took a Jimmy Carter–style impromptu stroll, greeting Londoners and tourists, to the consternation of his security team.

Then the First Couple were driven to Buckingham Palace for tea, coffee, and biscuits (cookies) with the Queen. It was not actually *tea*, which takes place in the late afternoon, but an audience held—appropriately—in the Queen's Audience Room. The website of the royal household explains: "Audiences generally last approximately twenty minutes, and the conversations which take place are entirely private. No written transcript or recording is made." This was a standard format for meeting a head of state not on a full state visit. The Clintons' audience extended to half an hour, while their twenty-year-old daughter, Chelsea, was given a private tour of palace state rooms by Christopher Lloyd, an art historian who, as surveyor of the Queen's pictures, was in charge of the royal collection of paintings. After the visit, the Clintons departed for a shopping expedition in Notting Hill.

The president told fellow drinkers in the Portobello Gold pub that he regretted not taking more time to relax more during the past eight years. "I haven't got long to go, so I can afford to be a bit more relaxed, I only wish I did this kind of thing more often," he said. He said that he was tired after watching the denouement of the 2000 election the previous night, when Al Gore finally conceded to George W. Bush. Clinton also approached a vagrant sitting quietly drinking beer in the corner of the pub and told him: "It is every citizen's right to meet at least one US president once in their life, so hello!" The man did not respond.

On Air Force One on the way back to Washington, Clinton was asked if he discussed politics with the Queen. He said that they talked about Zimbabwe, the southern African Commonwealth nation, where Elizabeth II was concerned about

growing unrest surrounding that year's parliamentary elec-
tions. "She's very careful, you know," Clinton told reporters on
the plane. "She observes strictly the British tradition of not
making policy statements." Zimbabwe would leave the Commonwealth in 2003.

Clinton added: "She's a highly intelligent woman who knows
a lot about the world. She has traveled a lot. She has fulfilled
her responsibilities, I think, enormously well and I'm always—
I always marvel when we meet at what a keen judge she is of
human events. I think she's a very impressive person. I like her
very much." He told the Queen that he enjoyed playing a round
of golf with her second son, Prince Andrew, one summer on
Martha's Vineyard. "He beat the living daylights out of me."

Clinton observed how the seventy-four-year-old Queen's
hair had turned all white but that she still had "youthful" eyes.
"She has these baby blue eyes—just piercing," he said, in an
echo of his remarks about the Queen Mother.

After Elizabeth's death in September 2022, Clinton praised
her as "a smart person" who "knew what she was doing." He
added: "And she believed that the life she had devoted to pre-
serving the British monarchy was not a wasted life."

Asked why American presidents carved out time again and
again to meet with "someone who really didn't have any actual
power," he replied: "You do it the first time because it's a show
of respect to the country. You do it the second or third time—
as I did—either because she wants to do it and invites you, or
because you got something out of it. And I gained a much
keener insight into the whole culture of the country."

Clinton continued: "She was an amazing woman. When her
own marriage had problems, she felt pain. When her children

were troubled, it bothered her, as a mother and as the representative of the country in terms of what it would do to the crown. I'm telling you, she knew that her job was to keep the United Kingdom united, to keep the United Kingdom on track with America."

He concluded: "There's something to be said for someone who wants to keep the show on the road, and Queen Elizabeth did. And by and large, she succeeded, often against all the odds."

CHAPTER 11

She gave me a look that only a mother could give a child.

—George W. Bush, May 7, 2007

Tony Blair wasted no time in rushing to Washington for his first meeting with George W. Bush just a month after the new president's inauguration. Blair's office played down concerns that the prime minister would not be able to forge as close a relationship with the Republican as he had with his ideological soulmate, Bill Clinton.

The Queen, of course, already knew Bush. She had been introduced by his mother, with whom Elizabeth II struck up an affinity as matriarchs of powerful dynasties trying to manage the privileges and pitfalls of bringing up children—and grandchildren—in the public gaze. Their previous run-in years before over black sheep and Texan footwear made a big impression on Bush, as he recalled before renewing his acquaintance with the monarch: "Mum and Dad invited Laura and me to a private lunch [with Queen Elizabeth]. . . . I found her charming. She was great, a wonderful sense of humor. My mother and I, we like to tease, and she fit right in. She was neat."

Bush felt so relaxed in the Queen's company that, during her state visit in 2007, he slipped easily into family dynamics. During his welcoming speech outside the White House, he stumbled over the timing of an earlier state visit: "You helped our nation celebrate its bicentennial in 17 . . ." He caught himself and quickly said, "in 1976." As laughter came from the crowd on the South Lawn, he turned and winked at Elizabeth as they exchanged glances.

"She gave me a look that only a mother could give a child," he said, to more laughter. It was a reminder that a generational difference between leaders need not be any barrier to a warm relationship, and nor was the informal manner Bush brought to the White House.

On Tuesday, September 11, 2001, Queen Elizabeth II was on vacation at Balmoral when the shocking news came through of passenger airliners flying into the Twin Towers of the World Trade Center in New York City, the Pentagon near Washington, DC, and a field near Shanksville, Pennsylvania. Her son Andrew was on a US-bound British Airways flight that was turned around back to London.

Andrew's ex-wife, Sarah Ferguson, was much closer to the tragedy. She had an 8:45 a.m. meeting at her Chances for Children charity office on the 101st floor of the World Trade Center's North Tower but arrived slightly late, moments after the first plane struck at 8:46 a.m., and quickly left the scene with her colleagues who were waiting in the lobby to meet her. Everyone on their floor was killed in the attack.

President Bush vowed that the United States and its allies would "win the war against terrorism" and "defend freedom and all that is good and just in our world." Elizabeth II immediately conveyed her profound sympathy and support to the president and the American people: "It is with growing disbelief and total shock that I am learning of the terrorist outrages in New York and Washington today. On behalf of the British people, Mr. President, may I express my heartfelt sympathy to the very many bereaved and injured [and] our admiration for those who are trying to cope with these unfolding tragedies. Our thoughts and prayers are with you all."

Elizabeth traveled back from Scotland to London to attend a special service for Americans in London at St. Paul's Cathedral. She also ordered a gesture at Buckingham Palace that resonated powerfully on the other side of the Atlantic. For the first time in the 160-year history of the Changing of the Guard ceremony, the Band of the Coldstream Guards, dressed in their scarlet tunics and tall black bearskin hats, played "The Star-Spangled Banner" as well as the British national anthem as the thousands who were gathered outside the palace gates looked on, many bowing their heads and clutching miniature US flags. Americans in the crowd sang along and shed tears at the emotionally charged occasion attended by William Farish, whom Bush had made the US ambassador to Britain, and Prince Andrew. After the anthem finished, the crowd applauded before falling quiet to observe two minutes of silence.

"The United States is not the only nation that mourns," said

Ari Fleischer, the White House press secretary, noting that Britain also lost citizens in the al-Qaeda attacks. "It's a further expression of the wonderful solidarity that the world is showing with the United States." Blair pledged that Britain would stand "shoulder to shoulder" with America.

Just as at JFK's memorial at St. Paul's thirty-eight years earlier and at Churchill's funeral service, "Battle Hymn of the Republic" resonated around the iconic cathedral during London's 9/11 commemoration. According to one observer, the Queen "struggled to hold her own emotions in check—tears came to her eyes and she bit her lip." She was among a congregation of 2,600 Britons and Americans, along with Prince Philip, Prince Charles, Blair, and three former prime ministers. Outside, more than five thousand people listened to the service as it was relayed on speakers. It was the first time "The Star-Spangled Banner" was heard in the cathedral and the first time the seventy-five-year-old Queen was seen singing the anthem of a foreign nation (or, indeed, any anthem, as she never sang her own). Prince Philip read the lesson, and Farish read from Isaiah 61: "And they shall build the old wastes, they shall raise up the former desolations, they shall repair the waste cities, the desolations of many generations."

Sir Christopher Meyer, the British ambassador to the US, read out a message from the Queen at a service in New York on September 20 to commemorate British victims. "These are dark and harrowing times for families and friends of those who are missing or who suffered in the attack—many of you here today," she wrote. "Nothing that can be said can begin to take away the anguish and the pain of these moments."

Then came one of the most memorable phrases of Elizabeth II's entire reign: "Grief is the price we pay for love." It really captured the moment, as Bill Clinton, who was sitting in the front pew alongside Blair as Meyer read it aloud, later remarked. "It was a stunning sentence, so wise and so true. It somehow made people feel better, making us understand that we were grieving because we had had that love," Clinton said.

The 9/11 tragedy touched Britain and its leaders deeply; Blair, on his flight to New York, told reporters, "This was not just an atrocity in which Americans died. This was the worst terrorist atrocity perpetrated against British citizens in our country's history." Sixty-seven British citizens were among the 2,977 victims. Buckingham Palace said that the Queen donated an undisclosed sum to the main 9/11 fund.

Before terror struck, the Queen had the chance to renew her relationship with George W. Bush in happier times, over lunch at Buckingham Palace in July 2001, on his first trip to the UK as president ahead of a G8 summit in Italy. Just as his father had done twelve years earlier, Bush set off around the quadrangle in the palace yard with Prince Philip to inspect the Guard of Honor of the First Battalion of the Devonshire and Dorset Regiment, but on this occasion the British summer delivered a sudden rain shower that gave them a soaking. Philip appeared to find it hilarious and jokingly blotted the president's suit. The Queen, who stayed dry, apologized for the weather. Bush tried to ignore it. "Perfect day!" he said. "We really appreciate your hospitality."

Barbara Bush, the nineteen-year-old twin daughter of the US president, wearing a casual denim jacket and trousers, came along to the palace "not exactly dressed for lunch with the Queen," according to *The Times*. "She had all the appearance of a girl traveling light, and on a last-minute whim," it added.

While her father and mother met the monarch in the grand 1844 Room, Barbara joined other members of the presidential party for lunch in the only slightly less grand Billiard Room, hosted by Vice Admiral Tom Blackburn, master of the household.

A post-lunch stroll in the garden was canceled due to the inclement weather. On his way to the palace, Bush had passed several hundred protesters against his environmental policies, including a banner declaring, "Wanted for crimes against the planet—the outlaw known as the Toxic Texan." As his motorcade pulled up at the palace gates, a male streaker ran from the crowd and was apprehended by police. Bush failed to secure Blair's backing for his idea of a global missile defense system. Nevertheless the prime minister was polite, prophetically so. "President Bush is right to raise the issue" of the growing risk of missile attacks from rogue states and terrorist organizations, Blair said. "It's a huge threat facing the whole of the world."

Bush also toured the Churchill War Rooms, the former prime minister's operational headquarters in an underground complex in Whitehall, little realizing that he was about to become a wartime leader himself. "I really admire Winston Churchill," Bush said, sitting in his hero's wooden chair. "He was a great leader and a great man who stood on principle throughout his career. And also he brought humor to the process." Knowing his interest, Blair had already arranged for the loan of a bronze bust of Churchill for display in the Oval Office.

Polls in October 2001 showed that around two-thirds of Britons backed the military action in Afghanistan launched by the US in the wake of 9/11 with support from British troops to remove the Taliban from power and root out al-Qaeda. However, by the time that Bush returned to the UK in November 2003, attitudes toward military intervention overseas were changing after the invasion of Iraq in March of that year, with the British population split down the middle. More than a million people joined an antiwar march in February 2003 in London, the biggest street protest the country had ever seen. The president put a positive spin on it: "I am so pleased to be going to a country which says that people are allowed to express their mind. That's fantastic. Freedom is a beautiful thing."

Bush was the first US president to receive a full state visit during the Queen's reign, an invitation suggested by Blair before the attack on Iraq because of the relationship he was building with his counterpart. It was only the second state visit to Britain by a US president after Woodrow Wilson in 1918.

The format for such visits under Elizabeth II was well-established: three or four days of activities, including a welcome on Horse Guards Parade and a carriage ride to Buckingham Palace; a white-tie dinner there, and a return hosted by the visitor; a big speech, usually to the joint Houses of Parliament; a day on tour outside London—all while staying at Buckingham Palace or Windsor Castle. Britain organized the most elaborate security of any state visit for Bush, at a cost to the taxpayers of £10 million.

Changes to the usual format had to be made because of protests planned by opponents of the War on Terror. Due to deep divisions in Blair's own Labour Party as well as opposition from some other parties, there would be no joint address to Parliament—as given by Reagan and Clinton on trips that did not have the status of a full state visit—nor would there be the usual public welcome on Horse Guards Parade by the Queen followed by a carriage ride down the Mall to Buckingham Palace, as enjoyed by President Vladimir Putin of Russia in an open landau that June. This was ruled out because of security fears, although the official explanation given at the time was that, as the American visitors would arrive in the evening and spend the night in the Belgian Suite at Buckingham Palace, it would look strange to send them down the road to Horse Guards only to come straight back. Instead, there was another odd spectacle: the Bushes rolled up to the front entrance of the palace in the Beast, the presidential limousine, having jumped into the vehicle moments earlier just around the corner of the building.

The start of the visit was formally heralded by a forty-one-gun salute from nearby Green Park fired by the King's Troop, Royal Horse Artillery, beginning as soon as the Bushes stepped out of the palace side entrance for their vehicle. The thirteen-pounder field guns dating back to the First World War boomed across the capital. VIPs including Secretary of State Colin Powell and National Security Advisor Condoleezza Rice watched as the president exited the car and waited for the First Lady to join him before climbing four steps up to a platform to greet Elizabeth II, who offered him her black-gloved hand. After the Bushes were greeted by Prince Philip, Blair, and other members of the cabinet, the US national anthem was played, and Bush, accompanied by Philip, inspected the Guard of Honor from the Household Division. They returned to the dais for a ride-past by the Household Cavalry.

The Queen led the First Couple inside the palace to peruse an exhibition of American memorabilia with royal connections. She pointed out a copy of *Uncle Tom's Cabin* by Harriet Beecher Stowe, together with an extract from Queen Victoria's diary about the antislavery novel: "To what can human nature descend. . . . It quite pains me." The exhibit that Bush appeared to scrutinize most closely was an 1892 sepia photograph of William Frederick Cody. The showman also known as Buffalo Bill brought his Wild West show to Britain in 1887, the golden jubilee year of Queen Victoria, who attended a performance.

The main speech of Bush's visit was delivered at the Banqueting House, Whitehall, completed in 1622. He began, characteristically, with a quip, referencing a recent stunt by the Brooklyn-born illusionist David Blaine, who spent forty-four days in a transparent box suspended in midair. "It was pointed out to me that the last noted American to visit London stayed in a glass box dangling over the Thames. A few might have been happy to provide similar arrangements for me," Bush said, to laughter. "I thank Her Majesty the Queen for interceding. We're honored to be staying at her house."

His main message was a robust defense of the Iraq war: "In some cases, the measured use of force is all that protects us from a chaotic world ruled by force. . . . We will use force, when necessary, in the defense of freedom. And we will raise up an ideal of democracy in every part of the world." He also urged European leaders to do more to fight anti-Semitism and to take steps to advance peace in the Middle East by pushing Palestinian leader Yasser Arafat from power. "Leaders in Europe should withdraw all favor and support from any Palestinian ruler who fails his people and betrays their cause," he said. Bush later met privately at the US embassy with families of some of the British citizens killed on 9/11 after the White House canceled plans for him to lay a wreath at the Memorial Garden, again due to security concerns.

The white-tie dinner that night took place after Buckingham Palace had been shaken by revelations in that day's *Daily Mirror*, edited by Piers Morgan, that one of its reporters spent two months as a royal footman after giving a false reference. The reporter, Ryan Parry, wrote how he laid out the Queen's breakfast table following strict guidelines on the positioning of every utensil, condiment, and Tupperware box of different cereals. He revealed that her toast was spread lightly with marmalade and much of it fed under the table to her corgis. Parry was there to welcome Bush at 8:00 p.m. the previous evening and would have served the president a 7:00 a.m. breakfast if he had not broken cover to publish his story along with photos of various palace rooms.

"Had I been a terrorist intent on assassinating the Queen or American President George Bush, I could have done so with absolute ease," he wrote. The White House was informed of the security breach after Bush's arrival, but the First Couple decided to remain at the palace.

The famously no-fuss president did not possess his own white tie and tails (in an echo of his father's famous campaign promise, he had once quipped "Read my lips—no new tuxes"), and so he rented an outfit for the state dinner for 170 guests, including thirteen members of the royal family. The menu was written in French, including *potage germiny* (cream of sorrel soup) and *délice de flétan rôti aux herbes* (herb-roasted halibut). A drumroll announced it was time for the Queen's toast.

Resplendent in a glittering diamond tiara and other jewels, she stood while others remained seated, and, after exchanging a quick sidelong glance with Bush, drew laughter by quipping that she had welcomed no fewer than seven of his predecessors to dinner because "the British head of state is not limited to two terms of four years." She acknowledged a certain continuity in the presidency by mentioning "your father," the forty-first president, for his role in overseeing the end of the Cold War and for his inaugural address statement that "we know what is right. Freedom is right."

Having seen plenty of ups and downs in the Special Relationship, the Queen said, "Despite occasional criticism of the term, I believe it admirably describes our friendship. Like all special friends, we can talk frankly and we can disagree from time to time—even sometimes fall out over a particular issue. But the depth and breadth of our partnership means that there is always so much we are doing together, at all levels, that disputes can be quickly overcome and forgiven."

The Queen's longevity was highlighted by Bush in his brief toast, which also dwelled on the wars that the two countries were once again fighting together. "We are grateful for your personal commitment across five decades to the health and vitality of the alliance between our nations," he said. His own laughter line came next: "Of course, things didn't start out too well." Reconciliation was possible because the two nations "shared a basic belief in human liberty," he said. "And now our two countries are carrying out a mission of freedom and democracy in Afghanistan and Iraq. Once again, America and

Britain are joined in the defense of our common values. Once again, American and British service members are sacrificing in a necessary and noble cause. Once again, we are acting to secure the peace of the world."

The two countries may have been in sync, but their heads of state were not quite. Having finished his remarks, Bush, who was standing, picked up his glass to complete his toast. Not so fast—the Queen rose from her seat but stared ahead, waiting for the British national anthem. Bush put his glass back on the table. After a musical rendition of "God Save the Queen" by military musicians dressed in red tunics on a balcony up behind them, only then did Elizabeth reach for her glass, signaling the consummation of the toast.

The second day of the visit was marked by a demonstration of at least one hundred thousand antiwar protesters in central London, culminating in the toppling of a seventeen-foot papier-mâché effigy of Bush in Trafalgar Square (a direct reference to the fall of Saddam Hussein, when a giant statue of the Iraqi dictator was pulled down in Baghdad). *The Times* insisted in an editorial that "the protesters did not speak for Britain" and a poll in the *Guardian* showed that 43 percent of Britons welcomed Bush's visit, compared to 36 percent who preferred him not to come and 21 percent who did not know. In any case, it was a relaxed Bush who hosted a return dinner for the seventy-six-year-old Queen at Winfield House, residence of Ambassador Farish, her old friend. She appeared to relish the Tex-Mex offerings of tortilla chips and jalapeño peppers followed by herb-crusted cannon of lamb and chocolate fudge brownies. Among the guests were actor Michael Caine and his wife, Shakira.

It was only on day three of the visit, an away day from the capital in Blair's parliamentary constituency in the northeast, that Bush finally came into contact with ordinary British people. This first occurred at the Blairs' home in Trimdon, County Durham, when Cherie Blair, the prime minister's wife, invited their neighbor, twenty-six-year-old Jemma Grieves, to meet the president. She had a Stars and Stripes embroidered on her jumper but was visibly so nervous that Bush gave her a "nice tight hug."

After they had moved on to the Dun Cow Inn for lunch, washed down for Bush with a pint of alcohol-free lager, six schoolchildren were ushered over for a word. Stuart Perceval, twelve, asked the president about Iraq.

"He said, 'That's a long story. I will have to tell you about that at another time,'" Stuart said afterward. "Whatever the protesters have to say about Mr. Bush, they are wrong. He isn't the number one terrorist in the world. He is the number one good man."

The day was shaken by news of bombings on two British targets in Istanbul, Turkey—the consulate and an HSBC bank building—which killed thirty-one people, including the consul general. A grim-faced Bush said that the US and UK were determined to "hunt these killers down," while Blair added that it "should make us all the more determined to do what we need to do to restore order and justice, to bring peace and freedom and democracy to people all over the world."

Bush left for Washington directly from the northeast. His parting words were: "I am fortunate to have a friend like Tony Blair. America is fortunate to have friends like the people of Great Britain because the people of Great Britain have got grit and strength and determination, and are willing to take on a challenge."

The Queen was eighty-one and included on *Time's* 100 Most Influential list as she arrived for her final state visit to the United States in May 2007. The institution of the monarchy was "solid, thanks largely to Elizabeth's steady hand," the magazine wrote, ten years after some called it into question over its uncertain handling of Diana's death. The Queen understood the need for reforms like cutting costs, "but she has never compromised her identity," it concluded. By this stage in her life, Elizabeth was simply The Queen, her constancy and dignity providing reassurance to Brits and Americans alike.

Her longevity contributed to the timeless sense of the Anglo-American relationship: it endured, just like her. This was emphasized when Jamestown, Virginia, celebrating its four-hundredth anniversary, was chosen for one of the early stops on her 2007 visit; she had been there as Queen a whole half century earlier, in 1957, on her first US state visit for its 350th commemoration. Just two and a half weeks beforehand the state was plunged into mourning over a shooting massacre at Virginia Tech. Flags were still flying at half-staff when Elizabeth II arrived.

After the first official engagement of her six-day tour, a speech to the Virginia general assembly in Richmond, Buckingham Palace arranged for Elizabeth to meet three students wounded in the atrocity. Katelyn Carney, who was shot in the hand, presented the Queen with a bracelet with thirty-two jewels, one for each person killed, in the school's maroon and orange colors. "My heart goes out to the students, friends, and families of those killed and to the many others who have been affected," Elizabeth said.

The gesture meant a great deal to some of the grieving community. Cathy Holland, a retired schoolteacher wearing a hat displaying Virginia Tech's Hokie mascot and a ribbon memorializing a victim, summed up her feelings: "It's been sad, but everybody has responded, including the Queen. It's connecting England to America to Virginia to Virginia Tech."

The Queen's first speech of the visit was also notable for the way she captured the continuity of Anglo-American relations while at the same time highlighting just how much the world had changed. "Over the course of my reign and certainly since I first visited Jamestown in 1957, my country has become a much more diverse society just as the Commonwealth of Virginia and the whole United States of America have also undergone a major social change," she said. In 1957, Virginia was defying a 1954 Supreme Court order to desegregate public schools. Tim Kaine, the governor of Virginia during this most recent visit, said that her message was timely. "This is a moment that brings Virginia together . . . in the aftermath of a hard time," he said. "The positive welcome for the Queen could be a good therapeutic thing for Virginians right now."

Elizabeth II was escorted by Kaine and Dick Cheney, the vice president, through a replica of a fortress from America's first permanent English settlement. "Half a century has done nothing to diminish the respect and affection this country holds for you. We receive you again today in that same spirit," Cheney told the Queen. They went on to Historic Jamestowne, where archaeologists had found remains of the original fort since her previous visit. At a museum of artifacts, she stopped to look at a display of medical instruments, including a long iron spatula for the treatment of constipation. "David!" she called to Commander David Swain, a Royal Navy doctor traveling with her. "You ought to have some things like that."

The Queen was a week early visiting Jamestown before the exact date of its anniversary, and the reason became clear with her next stop. She was off to the races, fulfilling a long-held desire to see the Kentucky Derby. Dressed in a lime green coat with a matching silk dress and a lime green hat with a fuchsia trim, she arrived two hours ahead of the 133rd running of the famous race with its $2 million purse. She was greeted by Farish, now retired as ambassador to the UK, and with a kiss on both cheeks from his wife, Sarah, in a rare sign of familiarity never seen in Britain. Elizabeth watched from a balcony in a private suite as Street Sense, the 9–2 favorite, came from back in nineteenth place to win a memorable victory. Farish was spotted having a flutter, but not so the Queen. She took an extremely close interest in the horses but did not place any bets, Buckingham Palace said. After the race she spent the rest of the weekend privately at Lane's End Farm with the Farishes.

The Queen's arrival at the White House lawn on Monday morning for her fifth and final visit to the presidential mansion was announced with a twenty-one-gun salute before Bush "demonstrated his well-documented talent for flubbing lines," as the *Los Angeles Times* put it, when he almost aged the Queen by two hundred years. It was taken in the best of humor, and the Queen had her revenge the next day at a dinner for Bush at the British ambassador's residence. Rising to give her toast, she began, "I wondered whether I should start this toast saying, 'When I was here in 1776 . . .'"

First, though, after the formal arrival ceremony, it was time for a private White House lunch of wild asparagus velouté, seared baby sea bass, and raspberry meringue, attended by the First Couple, Bush's siblings Dorothy and Marvin, and Sir David Manning, the British ambassador. "It was just a family, relaxing luncheon," Laura Bush said.

Afterward the Bushes accompanied the royal couple across Pennsylvania Avenue to Blair House, the traditional guest quarters for visiting dignitaries, stopping to accept flowers from a group of excited schoolchildren. Manning and his wife, Lady Catherine, hosted a garden party in the afternoon at the British embassy, where the choice was Pol Roger champagne or Earl Grey tea with cucumber sandwiches and scones with blackcurrant jam, while the Band of the Coldstream Guards—which had so movingly played the American national anthem at Buckingham Palace the day after 9/11—played the James Bond theme tune as well as "Rule, Britannia!"

The "no new tuxes" president was resistant to white tie and tails for that evening's five-course state dinner, but Laura Bush was determined. She enlisted the help of Condoleezza Rice, now secretary of state. "Dr. Rice and I took it upon ourselves to talk him into it, because we thought if we were ever going to have a white-tie event, this would be the one," Mrs. Bush said.

Just as at the Johnson White House, a royal visit was the spur for a rare lavish party. The First Lady added that her guests were "probably having to go out and rent" their white-tie outfits. This was a lot easier for the male guests, even at around

$125 for the night: "Cheap when you consider the women have to buy their dresses, formal, floor-length ball gowns," said Charlie Gibson of *ABC News*. "Things get very formal when the Queen comes to town."

This was the first such White House occasion of his presidency, nearly six and a half years in. With just 134 guests, the scarce seats were once again seen as the hottest tickets for a generation in Washington, DC. Unusually, there were no Hollywood stars on the list, but there was a last-minute invitee: Calvin Borel, the jockey who won the Kentucky Derby. Others who made the cut included Nancy Pelosi, Speaker of the House from the Democratic Party; Nancy Reagan; golfer Arnold Palmer; and Indianapolis Colts quarterback Peyton Manning. The thirteen tables were adorned with "historically significant pieces" from the White House collection, including gold-rimmed china, the president's "house crystal," and English vermeil gilded silver.

Precautions were also taken to avoid a repeat of the "talking hat" episode: Amy Zantzinger, the White House social secretary, provided a custom-made step for the Queen's remarks. Laura Bush also took no sartorial chances after three women came to a Kennedy Center reception in December wearing the same red Oscar de la Renta gown as her. She commissioned de la Renta to create a one-off dress of embroidered turquoise silk faille with a matching embroidered bolero, having the designer coordinate with the Queen's dresser to ensure they wore complementary colors. Elizabeth wore a jeweled tiara given to her as a wedding gift by her grandmother Queen Mary, a three-strand diamond necklace, and the blue sash of the Order of the Garter. Bush beamed as he escorted the monarch into the

White House grand foyer while the US Marine Corps band played music that included the Beatles' "Here Comes the Sun."

The president observed that this was "the fourth state dinner held in Your Majesty's honor here at the White House. On previous such occasions, you've been welcomed by President Eisenhower, President Ford, and another president named Bush. Over your long reign, America and Britain have deepened our friendship and strengthened our alliance."

This was another presidential toast dwelling on the post-9/11 wars, on this occasion emphasizing the positive progress Bush hoped his presidency had made following the sacrifices of many American and British troops. "Together we are supporting young democracies in Iraq and Afghanistan. Together we're confronting global challenges such as poverty and disease and terrorism. And together we're working to build a world in which more people can enjoy prosperity and security and peace," he said. "We're confident that Anglo-American friendship will endure for centuries to come." The Special Relationship had shown it could stand the test of time and the vicissitudes of war; however, the nation-building in Afghanistan would not endure.

In reply, Elizabeth II, perhaps cognizant this would be her last such formal occasion in the White House, cast an eye over her fifty-five-year reign as well as those wartime experiences, which did so much to establish her deep respect for the United States. "I would like to recognize that steadfast commitment your country has shown, not just in the last sixteen years [since the fall of the Berlin Wall], but throughout my life, in support of a Europe whole and free," she said. "I grew up in the knowledge that the very survival of Britain was bound up in that vital wartime alliance forged by Winston Churchill and President

Roosevelt. On my first visit to Washington in 1951, your predecessor, President Truman, welcomed me to the White House,
and it was his administration which reached out to Europe
through the Marshall Plan to help our tired and battered continent lift itself from the ruins of a second world war. In the
years that followed, successive administrations here in Washington committed themselves to the defense of Europe, as we
learned to live with the awesome responsibilities of the nuclear age."

Her conclusion reflected a lifetime's appreciation of the
strength of sticking together through thick and thin. "For
those of us who have witnessed the peace and stability and
prosperity enjoyed in the United Kingdom and the rest of Europe over these postwar years, we have every reason to remember that this has been founded on the bedrock of the Atlantic
Alliance. All the many and varied elements of our present relationship, be they in the fields of education, business, culture,
sports, politics, or the law, have continued to flourish, safe in
the knowledge of this simple truth," she said. "Divided, all
alone, we can be vulnerable. But if the Atlantic unites, not di-
vides us, ours is a partnership always to be reckoned with in the
defense of freedom and the spread of prosperity. That is the
lesson of my lifetime."

It was a stunning valediction but also a warning to maintain
the bond. Nor could it be lost on anyone in the room that it was
delivered by the living embodiment of endurance in transatlantic relations who was now nearing the end of her remarkable
diplomatic career.

CHAPTER 12

She is truly one of my favorite people.

—Barack Obama, April 22, 2016

Barack Obama had many fans in Great Britain when he came to the presidency, but it was less clear how popular the country was with him. In the run-up to his victory in 2008 it was revealed that his paternal grandfather was imprisoned and tortured by the British during the violent struggle for Kenyan independence, leading the grandfather to detest the colonial regime.

One of Obama's first acts was to remove from the Oval Office the bronze bust of Churchill that had been loaned to George W. Bush by Tony Blair in 2001. Churchill had been prime minister when the British declared an emergency in Kenya in 1952—the year Elizabeth II came to the throne—ordering troops to crush the rebellion against colonial rule, killing thousands of Kenyans. It was also Churchill who popularized the phrase "Special Relationship"—and when the first visit of Gordon Brown, the prime minister, was announced to see the new president, British ears detected a shift in the dynamic. Robert Gibbs, Obama's press secretary, referred to the "special partnership" between the two nations, a subtle shift in wording that suggested something more transactional and somehow less close.

A change in foreign policy focus to the Pacific region was signaled by Obama when he invited Japanese prime minister Taro Aso to Washington the week *before* Brown. When the two did sit down together, Brown brought Obama a thoughtful gift of a pen holder crafted from the timbers of the nineteenth-century British antislavery patrol warship HMS *Gannet* (whose sister ship, HMS *Resolute*, provided the wood for the Oval Office desk gifted by Queen Victoria). In return, Obama gave Brown twenty-five DVDs of classic American movies, a present viewed by the British media as unimaginative.

The DVDs were reportedly not even formatted for British players.

Queen Elizabeth II was once again required to be part of the rescue mission for the Special Relationship. She sent Obama a personal message upon his inauguration, and two months later a royal audience was arranged during his first trip to the UK for a G20 summit.

The president showed what this invitation meant to him—and to First Lady Michelle Obama, who accompanied him—during a news conference with Brown in London ahead of his Buckingham Palace rendezvous. Asked what he liked most about Great Britain, he mentioned the affinity between the people of the US and UK, then said: "There's one last thing that I should mention that I love about Great Britain, and that is the Queen. I'm very much looking forward to meeting her for the first time later this evening. And as you might imagine, Michelle has been really thinking that through, because I think in the imagination of people throughout America, I think what the Queen stands for and her decency and her civility, what she represents, that's very important."

From that moment on, it was clear that here was another US president with sincere respect for Britain's head of state, who took a real delight in meeting her, despite the ancestral pain caused by the former British Empire in her family's name. Senior UK diplomats believe the relationship that developed— one of the warmest between the Queen and any US president— played an important role in enhancing Obama's view of Britain.

Obama's fascination with the British monarchy went back to his early travels to Britain as a young man, according to his stepmother, Kezia Obama, his father's first wife and the mother of his older half sister, Auma. She settled in the town of Bracknell, in Berkshire, a short drive west of London, to be near her daughter.

"I remember him coming to London, standing outside the gates of Buckingham Palace, sightseeing along with the other tourists," sixty-seven-year-old Kezia recalled in March 2009, in an echo of President Carter's first view through the railings. "Now he is invited inside as the guest of the Queen," she added proudly. "I think they will have a very good conversation."

She was right. Not even a much-discussed breach of protocol got in the way of the Obamas' instant rapport with the much older royal couple—in fact, it was a sign of growing affinity. The Duke of Edinburgh was eighty-seven and the Queen a few weeks shy of her eighty-third birthday, while the president was forty-seven, eighteen months younger than their second son, Prince Andrew, and his wife forty-five, when the couples met for the first time for a twenty-minute private chat. "It is a great honor to be here," Obama said as he was greeted by Sir Christopher Geidt, the Queen's private secretary, upon arrival at the palace. It was an honor not extended to any of the other nineteen leaders in town for the G20 talks.

After taking an elevator up to her private rooms, the president nodded his head after shaking the outstretched hand of the monarch, then he and the First Lady flanked her for a photograph. Jet lag was discussed.

"We're still trying to stay awake," Michelle said.

Obama was overheard saying, "I had breakfast with the prime minister, I had meetings with the Chinese, the Russians, and David Cameron [leader of the opposition Conservative Party], and I'm proud to say I did not nod off in any of the meetings."

The Duke of Edinburgh, chuckling, quipped: "Can you tell the difference between them?"

The president waved a hand and joked back: "It's all a blur."

It was a slightly awkward first meeting, as staged diplomatic encounters can be. "Sitting with the Queen, I had to will myself out of my own head—to stop processing the splendor of the setting and the paralysis I felt coming face-to-face with an honest-to-goodness icon," Michelle Obama noted in her autobiography, *Becoming*. "I'd seen Her Majesty's face dozens of times before, in history books, on television, and on currency, but here she was in the flesh, looking at me intently and asking questions. She was warm and personable, and I tried to be the same."

Her husband also warmed to Elizabeth despite the ornate surroundings. "It was a wonderful visit. Her Majesty is delightful," he said afterward. Later he added, "My first impression was she looked just like my grandmother, and same attitude," referring to his maternal grandmother, Madelyn Dunham. The woman he affectionately called Toot was on his mind, having passed away at eighty-six in Hawaii just two days before his election victory.

After the president's DVDs for the prime minister, there was huge interest in his offering to the Queen. This time Obama thought he hit the bull's-eye. "I wanted her actually to be able to use the gift," Obama recalled. "I thought, let's get an iPod and fill it with British show tunes. The British tabloids thought it was entirely inappropriate, but I think she used it quite a bit."

It was when the Queen was hosting a reception for leaders of the twenty nations at Buckingham Palace later that day, and while the president was deep in conversation across the room with Chancellor Angela Merkel of Germany, that cameras caught the moment that really excited the British press. Michelle Obama put her left arm around the monarch's shoulder. Crikey! What would the Queen do? Call the palace guards? In most of the previous rare moments of uninvited physical contact, all the way back to that first public embrace she received from another friendly American lady, Alice Frazier, eighteen years earlier, the Queen appeared uncomfortable and unresponsive.

Not this time. Almost immediately, Elizabeth II extended a

gloved hand across the small of the First Lady's back. British media, so often quick to condemn those who dared to touch their Sovereign, were more puzzled than horrified. "No-one—including the ladies-in-waiting standing nearby—could believe their eyes," wrote the *Daily Mail*. "In 57 years, the Queen has never been seen to make that kind of gesture and it is certainly against all protocol to touch her." What was going on?

The pair had been observed shortly beforehand chatting and gesturing at their shoes. Mrs. Obama later revealed all. Finding themselves standing next to each other toward the end of the reception, after endless rounds of polite conversation with world leaders and a game of not forgetting which spouse was with whom, the Queen opened the conversation: "You're so tall," she said, looking up.

The First Lady replied that her shoes gave her a couple of inches. "But yes, I'm tall." The subject of footwear thus raised, the Queen looked down at Michelle's black Jimmy Choos and shook her head.

"Those shoes are unpleasant, are they not?" The Queen then motioned at her own black pumps, and they shared that their feet were hurting. Michelle wrote that they exchanged glances, suggesting, *When is all this standing around . . . going to finally wrap up?* at which point Elizabeth II "busted out with a fully charming laugh."

The First Lady added that, in that instant, they were simply "two tired ladies oppressed by our shoes" and so "I then did what's instinctive to me any time I feel connected to a new person" and "laid a hand affectionally across her shoulder." The incident "revived some of the campaign-era speculation that I was generally uncouth and lacking the standard elegance of a

First Lady," Michelle wrote, adding, "If I hadn't done the proper thing at Buckingham Palace, I had at least done the human thing." She said she was not aware of any particular royal protocol at the time.

The royal website noted that "there are also no obligatory codes of behaviour when meeting the Queen or a member of the Royal Family," although it added that some people choose to observe a more traditional greeting of "a neck bow (from the head only)" for men while women "do a small curtsy." Others "prefer simply to shake hands in the usual way." Elizabeth II was not only unfazed by the First Lady's embrace but she reciprocated.

Times had certainly changed since the name-calling that greeted Paul Keating, the Australian prime minister, in 1992, when the London tabloids labeled him "The Lizard of Oz" for daring to put his arm around the Queen.

Michelle Obama worried that she had "distracted from Barack's efforts abroad." She need not have done. The palace was relaxed. "This was a mutual and spontaneous display of affection and appreciation between the Queen and Michelle Obama," said a palace spokeswoman. Instead of going for the jugular, the British press hailed her as the new Jackie Kennedy, and her solo appearance giving a pep talk at an inner-city girls' school was a big hit with all involved—including the First Lady, who described speaking to the "hopeful faces" of "girls whose skin made up every shade of brown" as the moment she discovered her purpose in a role that involved "giving up one's privacy to become a walking, talking symbol of a nation." Two of her White House initiatives involved educational goals, one specifically for girls.

This was President Obama's debut on the world stage, amid anti-American protests in London blaming the US for a weak regulatory environment that led to the global financial crisis after the collapse of New York–based Lehman Brothers investment bank in September 2008. Obama succeeded at least in keeping the G20 nations united in tackling the crisis amid threats of a walkout from French president Nicolas Sarkozy that did not materialize, pledging an extra $100 billion from the US to the International Monetary Fund.

The Brits were happy too that he referred to the Special Relationship in his press conference with Brown to signify that no downgrading was intended in the alliance with Britain. As they said goodbye at the end of the palace visit, the Queen was overheard asking Michelle Obama: "Now we have met, would you please keep in touch?"

They did. Just a couple of months later the First Lady was back in London on a private visit without her husband but with their two girls, Malia and Sasha, and her mother, Marian Shields Robinson. The Queen invited them over. As a treat for Sasha's eighth birthday, they were given a private three-hour tour that included a meeting with Elizabeth and a carriage ride around the forty-acre Buckingham Palace grounds. "There clearly is a personal warmth between the two of them," a royal source told Reuters. "It's a positive thing for relations between the two countries that the royal family and the president's family get along so well."

The chemistry between the new First Family and the old royal family—and the British government's desire to capitalize on it—was such that the wheels were set in motion for a full state visit by President Obama, only the second by a US president under Elizabeth II after George W. Bush in 2003. Obama arrived shortly after one of the memorable successes of his first term, the special forces mission in Pakistan to kill or capture Osama bin Laden, which resulted in the death of the al-Qaeda leader behind the 9/11 attacks.

Just before heading to the UK, which stood so squarely with the US in the aftermath of that fateful day, Obama reflected that "if you have met with families who lost loved ones on 9/11—if you think about what an extraordinary trauma it was for the country as a whole, the sacrifices that had been made by troops—not only from the United States but also from Great Britain and other members—in Afghanistan and you think that all traces back to this maniacal action by al-Qaeda. For us, to be able to say unequivocally that the mastermind behind that event had been removed was a powerful moment."

In the same previsit interview he also praised the Queen and Duke of Edinburgh as "extraordinarily gracious people," recalling their welcome for his wife and daughters. "Michelle and the girls actually visited London again and went to Buckingham Palace. She could not have been more charming and gracious to the girls. They actually had a chance to ride in the carriage on the grounds. I think what the Queen symbolizes not just to Great Britain, but to the entire Commonwealth, and obviously the entire world is the best of England. And we're very proud of her."

Obama's first stop was Ireland, where he was the sixth US president to visit after JFK, Nixon, Reagan, Clinton, and George W. Bush. In time-honored fashion, he met a distant relative and visited an ancestral village—Moneygall in County Offaly—birthplace of his great-great-great-grandfather Falmouth Kearney, a shoemaker who left in 1850 for a new life in New York. After meeting with Taoiseach Enda Kenny, Obama had warm words for the first-ever state visit to Ireland by Queen Elizabeth II the previous week, made possible by progress in the Northern Ireland peace process.

"To see Her Majesty, the Queen of England, come here and to see the mutual warmth and healing that, I think, took place as a consequence of that visit, to know that the former Taoiseach, Dr. FitzGerald, was able to witness the Queen coming here, that sends a signal not just in England, not just here in Ireland, but around the world," he said.

The Obamas arrived in the UK half a day earlier than expected when their flight was brought forward to the evening of May 23, 2011, rather than the following morning, because of the potential hazard posed by volcanic ash from an eruption in Iceland. They were met at Stansted Airport, north of London, on the Queen's behalf by lord-in-waiting Viscount Brookeborough and by Louis Susman, the US ambassador, spending their extra night in England at his residence in Regent's Park. Obama took time before his arrival at Buckingham Palace to mark the "heartbreaking" mile-wide tornado that struck Joplin, Missouri, killing 158 people. No president could afford to neglect domestic matters while overseas, and he pledged to visit as soon as he returned.

Prince Charles, who had seen the president on a short visit to the US just a few weeks earlier, traveled to Winfield House to greet the Obamas in the morning before joining their motorcade to the palace, where their first meeting was with Prince

William and his new bride, Kate Middleton, just back from honeymooning in the Seychelles. Their wedding ceremony at Westminster Abbey had been watched by almost twenty-three million viewers in the United States—more than the seventeen million who watched Charles's marriage to Diana in 1981 and a testament to Americans' enduring fascination with the British monarchy.

A forty-one-gun salute—twenty-one rounds fired at ten-second intervals for a head of state, with an additional twenty rounds because the salute came from a royal park—announced to the capital that it was time for the formal meeting between the US president and the Queen. It was a windy day, and the gusts played havoc with the First Lady's hair and the skirt of her Barbara Tfank–designed floral-print dress, both of which she battled to keep under control in front of the unforgiving cameras. Even the normally serene monarch was holding on to her hat. The royal clothes, however, remained firmly in place. The secret? Small weights sewn unobtrusively into her hems to keep them looking perfect.

After Obama and the Duke of Edinburgh inspected the troops, the Queen showed the First Couple around the six-room Belgian Suite at Buckingham Palace, the traditional guest rooms that had also hosted the Bushes. In the wake of the bin Laden operation, the White House demanded extremely high security, bringing two hundred Secret Service agents and insisting on the installation of bombproof double-glazing to the Belgian Suite windows. Its most recent previous occupants were William and Kate on their wedding night. A palace aide told reporters: "It may not be the same bed. It is the same suite."

After all the fuss about gifts on his first UK visit, President Obama gave the Queen a handmade leather-bound album with rare memorabilia and photographs of the 1939 US visit by her parents. Prince Philip, a competitive carriage driver, received a custom-made set of Fell pony bits and shanks, and original horseshoes worn by the recently retired champion carriage horse Jamaica. Charles and Camilla were given a selection of plants and seeds from the gardens of Mount Vernon, Monticello, and the South Lawn of the White House, as well as jars of honey from the White House beehive.

There was yet another gift: a petite green flower brooch for the Queen crafted in 1950 from fourteen-carat yellow gold, diamonds, and moss agate, selected by the Obamas from the Tiny Jewel Box store in Washington, DC. The Obamas were given facsimiles of letters from the Royal Archives from a number of presidents to Queen Victoria, including a letter from John Quincy Adams when she was a princess in 1834, and one from William McKinley in 1897 marking Victoria's Diamond Jubilee year. Mrs. Obama was given an antique brooch in the form of roses made of gold and red coral, presented in a red leather jewel box. This was placed inside a larger box that also included fine chocolates and tea—although the Secret Service did not allow First Families to sample any gifted food.

Following a private lunch, the Obamas were off in the Beast to Westminster Abbey to lay a wreath at the Grave of the Unknown Warrior, honoring the fallen of the First World War. The president went to Downing Street for initial talks with Prime Minister David Cameron and then went with him to the Globe Academy school, where they teamed up for a table tennis match against two sixteen-year-old students. The two left-handed leaders appeared to have trouble coordinating their game.

"Are we keeping score?" Obama asked at one point.

When Cameron missed a shot, Obama joked: "Tennis is his sport." Eventually they won a couple of points, sharing high fives.

The 170 guests for that evening's white-tie state banquet, sitting at a huge U-shaped dining table in the grand Buckingham Palace Ballroom, included Secretary of State Hillary Clinton and American actors Tom Hanks and Kevin Spacey, as well as Helena Bonham-Carter (who would go on to play Princess Margaret in *The Crown*), along with her partner, director Tim Burton. There were three former prime ministers—Sir John Major, Gordon Brown, and Tony Blair—and one future PM, Boris Johnson, then mayor of London.

The Queen's toast emphasized the close cultural, military, and economic ties between the US and the UK. Obama's visit "inevitably reminds us of our shared history, our common language, and our strong intellectual and cultural links. It also reminds us that your country twice came to the rescue of the free and democratic world when it was facing military disaster. On each occasion, after the end of those destructive wars, the generosity of the United States made a massive contribution to our economic recovery," she said.

"Over the years, we have enjoyed some of America's most spectacular musical productions and any number of what we call films, which you might prefer to call movies. In return, British films and theatrical productions have achieved considerable success in your country. This exchange of people and projects has enlarged and invigorated our common language,

although I think you will agree, we don't always use it in quite
the same way."

With that, she returned to the well-worn phrase usually
heard more from British lips than American: "We are here to
celebrate the tried, tested, and, yes, special relationship between our two countries."

Obama's response was notable for its warm personal touches
but also a palace faux pas. Rising to speak with the Queen
seated on his left and Camilla on his right, he started out by
thanking his hostess "for the warm friendship that you've
shown both Michelle and myself on both of our visits to Buckingham Palace. I bring warm greetings from tens of millions of
Americans who claim British ancestry, including me, through
my mother's family. I bring warm greetings from Malia and
Sasha, who adored you even before you let them ride on a carriage on the palace grounds." He noted that Elizabeth II had
seen about a dozen presidents and prime ministers, which
"makes you both a living witness to the power of our alliance
and a chief source of its resilience."

Obama sought to allay British sensitivities about any downgrading of the alliance by name-checking "this great country . . .
and this special relationship" and also the wartime prime
minister whose bust he removed at the start of his administration. "Our alliance is a commitment that speaks to who we are.
As Winston Churchill said on a visit to the United States,
'Above all, among the English-speaking peoples, there must be
the union of hearts based upon convictions and common ideals.'" His attempt to name-check another great Briton was,
however, drowned out by the premature start of the British
national anthem by the string orchestra of the First Battalion

Scots Guard, which began playing when he announced: "To Her Majesty the Queen."

However, he had not finished his speech. As the room stood to attention, Obama persevered over the first bars of the anthem, saying: "For the vitality of the special relationship between our peoples, and in the words of Shakespeare, 'To this blessed plot, this Earth, this realm, this England,' to the Queen." Elizabeth II did not return the gesture of his raised glass but turned slightly toward him and said: "That's very kind." She resumed staring resolutely ahead. Obama placed his glass on the table and stared ahead too. As the music ended, the Queen picked up her water and turned toward him, signifying that now was the time to raise glasses.

Obama joked afterward, "I thought it was, like, out of the movies where the soundtrack kind of comes in."

President Obama's reelection year in 2012 coincided with another of Elizabeth II's personal landmarks, the Diamond Jubilee of her accession. Obama recorded a video message in which he described the Queen as "a steadfast ally, loyal friend, and tireless leader . . . an example of resolve that will be long celebrated."

American TV networks gave extensive coverage to commemorative events in Britain, although not always in such reverent tones as their president. Jon Stewart of *The Daily Show* ridiculed the rainy Diamond Jubilee concert held outside Buckingham Palace on June 4, 2012, making the famously soggy British summer the butt of the joke. "It was a magnificent spectacle that you could almost see through the inside of a car wash that is England in June," Stewart said, showing members of the royal family tapping their feet in time with the music. "They're not dancing—they're shivering. People can't tell the difference between fun and hypothermia."

There was sadly no time for the Queen to see Obama on her final visit to the United States, a five-hour stop in New York in July 2010 on a quick detour from a Canada tour, when she addressed the United Nations, visited Ground Zero, and formally opened the British garden memorial to 9/11 victims. However, there was an opportunity to renew their acquaintance on June 6, 2014, the seventieth anniversary of D-Day, which both attended in Normandy. They were seated next to each other at a lunch hosted by President François Hollande of France. The Obamas also saw other members of the royal family, with Prince Harry striking up a friendship with the First Lady in 2013 over her support for his Invictus Games for wounded veterans; Prince William making his first Oval Office appearance in December 2014 for a fifteen-minute discussion with Obama on wildlife conservation and "world issues"; and his father, Prince Charles, posing for photos with the president in Washington in March 2015.

Obama was dismayed when he heard that the Queen had decided to cease foreign trips, stepping back after a lifetime of travel that saw her visit 116 countries. Her final state visit was to Germany in June 2015. According to Sir Peter Westmacott, Britain's ambassador in Washington from 2012 to 2016:

"President Obama so enjoyed his state visit to London in 2011 in that he did his best to get the Queen to pay a return visit to Washington before he left office. When he learned that she had stopped making long-distance trips he simply went to London to bid her farewell, and a happy ninetieth birthday."

Obama's pilgrimage to see Queen Elizabeth II in April 2016, sandwiched between attendance at a Gulf Cooperation Council summit in Saudi Arabia and a meeting with European leaders in Germany, was manna for Cameron as he fought to make the argument for Britain to remain in the European Union in the high-stakes referendum on membership he called for June that year. Obama, who had established a good relationship with Cameron cooperating on the global economic recovery and removing Muammar Gaddafi in Libya, was happy to oblige, but first he and Michelle had a lunch date at Windsor Castle. They helicoptered in from the ambassador's residence on Marine One, which itself had arrived on a military transport plane from the US, along with the Beast.

Greeting them from the Marine Corps Sikorsky on the grass with handshakes, the Queen and the Duke of Edinburgh were dressed quite informally, she in a floral silk headscarf and powder blue jacket and skirt, black patent leather handbag over her left arm as usual, he in a beige mackintosh. The president was in a dark suit, white shirt, and tie, and his wife wore an Oscar de la Renta print dress and dark blue Narciso Rodriguez coat.

After a short walk, the ninety-four-year-old Duke motioned the First Couple to hop into a black Range Rover as he climbed into the driver's seat. Obama walked around the vehicle toward the back to sit alongside the Queen as he had been briefed by the White House protocol team. Meticulous transatlantic planning had gone into the short drive, not least because it was the first time in eight years the Obamas had not been chauffeured by the Secret Service or entered a vehicle without their protection agents, who could be seen dotted around the grounds. The best-laid plans, however, went awry. The president realized that the monarch was preparing to clamber in next to Michelle and so took the front seat next to Philip. Staff closed the car doors. Off they drove to the castle, Philip at the wheel.

Michelle Obama later confessed that she was worried about committing another faux pas by sitting next to the Queen, as the heads of state were usually paired off together. "The Queen abruptly threw a wrench into everything by gesturing for me to join her in the backseat," she wrote. "I froze, trying to remember if anyone had prepped me for this scenario."

Picking up on her hesitation, the Queen waved her hand, saying: "Did they give you some rule about this? That's rubbish. Sit wherever you want."

The private lunch lasted about an hour before it was time to say goodbye. Speaking after talks with Cameron later that afternoon, Obama delivered exactly what the prime minister hoped for—support for his side of the argument in the referendum. Using a very English phrase, he warned that if Britain left the EU, it would find itself "in the back of the queue" for a trade deal with the US, especially as one was already being considered with the much larger European group. Also at the press conference, Obama showed once again his fondness for the royals, saying that he "conveyed the good wishes of the American people" to Elizabeth II on her landmark birthday.

"I have to say I have never been driven by a Duke of Edinburgh before," Obama added, to laughter. "And I can report that it was very smooth riding. As for Her Majesty, the Queen has been a source of inspiration for me, like so many people around the world. She is truly one of my favorite people. And should we be fortunate enough to reach ninety, may we be as vibrant as she is. She's an astonishing person, and a real jewel to the world and not just to the United Kingdom."

Much was written during his eight years in office, analyzing whether the US was turning away from its transatlantic friends for a new focus on the Pacific. On this valedictory UK visit, Obama again sought to underline the importance of traditional relationships.

"The alliance between the United States and the United Kingdom is one of the oldest and one of the strongest that the world has ever known," he said. "When the US and the UK stand together, we make our countries more secure, we make our people more prosperous, and we make the world safer and better. That's one of the reasons why my first overseas visit as president more than seven years ago was here to London, at a time of global crisis. And the one thing I knew, as green as I was as a new president, was that it was absolutely vital that the United States and the United Kingdom, working together in an international forum, tackle the challenges that lie ahead. Our success depended on our ability to coordinate and to be able to leverage our relationship to have an impact on other countries."

Before he left Britain for the last time as president, there was one final royal encounter—one that appeared to symbolize American commitment to the future of the Special Relationship. In the evening rain the Obamas paid a home visit to Prince William and Kate, the Duke and Duchess of Cambridge, meeting for the first time with their son George, the boy in line to be king one day.

Prince Harry was there too, enjoying an evening with his sibling's family in happier times before they would start to drift apart. It was the two-year-old prince who stole the show, wearing a white dressing gown over checked pajamas. George was allowed to stay up late to meet his special American visitors, showing them the rocking horse they gave him at his birth. Obama later used their interaction to poke fun at his ebbing presidential power during his final appearance at the White House Correspondents' Association annual dinner.

"It's not just Congress. Even some foreign leaders, they've been looking ahead, anticipating my departure," he joked. "Last week, Prince George showed up to our meeting in his bathrobe. That was a slap in the face. A clear breach of protocol."

Photos of the meeting at Kensington Palace were widely broadcast and published in the US, showing how the younger royal family members were becoming as important as the Queen to the soft diplomacy that enhanced the image of Britain abroad, driving priceless publicity that helped to fuel tourism, investment, and a sense of confidence in their nation. The Obamas also lent a hand to a promotional video for Prince Harry's second Invictus Games, to be held in Orlando in 2016, which involved a message being sent from Michelle Obama in which she asked: "Hey, Prince Harry, remember when you told us to 'bring it at the Invictus Games'?" Her husband added: "Careful what you wish for" as a military officer mimicked a "mic drop" saying, "Boom."

In the sketch, Harry showed this to the ninety-year-old Queen, who smiled and said: "Boom. Really? Please." The prince then delivered his own mic drop, saying: "Boom" back at the Obamas.

At ninety, Elizabeth II was indeed the undisputed "jewel" of UK diplomacy, as Obama put it, embodying a comforting continuity like no other global head of state. She had begun reluctantly to step back from the front line of her country's outreach to the world as her immediate heirs grew into the roles they were expected to assume. Political events at home and in the United States later in the tumultuous year of 2016 meant, however, that her reassuring presence and star power would remain as vital as at any point in her long reign.

CHAPTER 13

There are those that say they have never seen the Queen have a better time.

—Donald Trump, June 7, 2019

Britain voted to leave the European Union on June 23, 2016, creating political upheaval that included the resignation of David Cameron following his unsuccessful campaign to remain. Another electoral surprise was in store across the pond in November, when Donald Trump defied most predictions and won the presidency. It was a reminder that every four or eight years, the United States had the chance to make a complete change not only in its head of government but also in its head of state, as the two roles were combined in the same person.

Not so in Britain, where its head of state was in her sixty-fifth year in the job, despite the political upheaval. Theresa May became her thirteenth prime minister shortly before Trump became the thirteenth US president of her reign. There was a mood of almost revolutionary change in the electorates of both countries, but the British still had their Queen.

Brits looking for clues to the new president's view of their

country could find one in the autobiographical book that helped
to make him famous, *The Art of the Deal*, published in 1987. In it,
Trump described a childhood memory of watching his Scottish-
born mother, Mary Anne MacLeod, "sitting up in front of the
television set to watch Queen Elizabeth II's coronation and not
budging for the whole day. She was just enthralled by the pomp
and circumstance, the whole idea of royalty and glamour."

While his father was not at all interested in the spectacle of
monarchy, Trump suggested that he inherited traits from both
parents, including his mother's love of "splendor and magnifi-
cence" that underpinned her fascination with the royal family.
"My mother was very ceremonial, I think that's where I got this
aspect because my father was very brick-and-mortar," Trump
told *The Times* shortly before his inauguration. "She loved the
Queen—she was so proud of the Queen. She loved the ceremonial and the beauty, because nobody does that like the English.
And she had great respect for the Queen, liked her. Anytime
the Queen was on television, an event, my mother would be
watching. Crazy, right?"

Unchanging in a time of disruption on both sides of the
Atlantic, Elizabeth would prove to be the biggest attraction of
post-Brexit Britain for a president who generally had little regard for establishment traditions but the greatest respect for
"the personal embodiment of nearly a century of British history," as he later described her.

When Trump came to office, the recent Brexit decision was the
main topic on British minds. As he had voiced support for the

policy, there were high hopes that the Special Relationship would mean a preferential trade deal between the two nations that would capitalize on Britain's departure from the European Union trading arrangement. However, a conflicting force was also at play—Trump's "America First" credo, which prioritized domestic production and was hostile to advantages being granted to overseas nations.

Other clues were sought to Trump's personal feelings about the land of his mother's childhood. He owned two golf courses in Scotland but had battled for years against plans for an eleven-turbine wind farm in the North Sea in sight of his Trump International Golf Links at Balmedie, Aberdeenshire, ultimately appealing all the way to the UK Supreme Court—where he lost in 2015. On the other hand, a positive signal was detected, at least by the British media, on his very first day, when he brought back the bronze bust of Churchill to the Oval Office. British officials worked hard to ensure that Theresa May was the first foreign leader to visit the new president, and she was on the plane to Washington at the end of his first week. She brought the most prestigious gift a British prime minister could offer—an invitation to meet the Queen.

Elizabeth II was in a regular pattern of hosting two foreign heads of state annually for three or four full days of the most elaborate ceremony her country could offer. When May stood alongside Trump in the White House on January 27, 2017, she announced that he had accepted Her Majesty's invitation, which originated from her government, for a prestigious state visit. But while May was on her way back to the UK, Trump signed a controversial executive order banning travel to the US for citizens from seven predominantly Muslim countries. It triggered an outcry across the British political spectrum and calls to rescind the invitation.

Lord Ricketts, who served as Cameron's national security advisor, said: "It would have been far wiser to wait to see what sort of president he would turn out to be before advising the Queen to invite him. Now the Queen is put in a very difficult position." A petition to block the visit "because it would cause embarrassment to Her Majesty the Queen" was signed by more than 1.8 million people and triggered a debate in the House of Commons.

The British government did not back down but, as the weeks and months went by, no date was announced. Trump attended a NATO summit in Belgium in May, adding on a trip to Italy but not Britain. Ahead of July's G20 meeting in Germany, he visited Poland. The following week he went to France for its Bastille Day celebrations. While First Lady Melania Trump met Prince Harry at his third Invictus Games in Toronto in September, the year passed with just one state visit to the UK, by King Felipe VI of Spain in July.

That year, 2017, was a difficult one in Britain, scarred by three terrorist atrocities carried out by Islamist extremists: a vehicle and knife attack in Westminster in March that left six dead and fifty injured; a suicide bombing at an Ariana Grande concert in Manchester in May that killed twenty-two people; and a vehicle-ramming and stabbing by three men in June in the London Bridge area who killed eight people. Trump used the violence to justify his travel ban policy and exchanged criticism over Twitter with Sadiq Khan, the London mayor, as their relations soured. It was reported that Trump told May in a phone call that he did not want to come to Britain if there were going to be large protests, and there was annoyance in the White House that the October date being considered was when Parliament was not sitting so there would be no joint address like the one made by Obama in 2011. The state visit was on hold.

Instead, plans were discussed for Trump to make a "working visit" in February 2018 to open the new US embassy building in London and meet the Queen in less formal circumstances, without staying with her at Buckingham Palace. The US ambassador to the UK, Woody Johnson, told the BBC: "Absolutely, I think he will come. It hasn't been officially announced but I hope he does." A month later Trump pulled out, tweeting that the new embassy was a "bad deal." Once again he was criticized by Khan: "It appears that President Trump got the message from the many Londoners who love and admire America and Americans but find his policies and actions the polar opposite of our city's values of inclusion, diversity, and tolerance."

The Special Relationship was beginning to look anything but. Trump had gone against core UK foreign policies by pulling out of the Iran nuclear deal and the Paris (climate) Agreement, and there was no sign of a trade deal. Almost exactly a year after she first invited him to Britain on behalf of the Queen, Theresa May emerged from "a great discussion" with Trump at Davos in Switzerland to announce that a new date was being explored for later in 2018. This visit would not be a full state visit, but it would nevertheless involve the Queen— and Trump would be kept away from protesters in the center of London by helicoptering into the US ambassador's residence in Regent's Park, then meeting May at her countryside retreat of

Chequers, and finally convening with Elizabeth II at Windsor Castle, twenty-two miles to the west of Buckingham Palace, outside the city.

What did the Queen make of the delayed on-off Trump visit after the unprecedented rush to invite him? Of course, she would never say anything publicly, but close observers detected a possible clue to her thoughts. On the day that the First Couple flew into Stansted Airport after another NATO summit in Brussels, Elizabeth II had an audience in the morning with the Archbishop of Canterbury and the Grand Imam of Al-Azhar, Egypt, at Windsor Castle. There, pinned on her dress, was a brooch that had not been seen for more than seven years. It was the vintage green flower made from fourteen-carat yellow gold, diamonds, and moss agate given to her by the Obamas and worn just once before, when she hosted the return dinner of their state visit—the kind of trip that was proving so difficult to arrange for Trump. Was she trolling the president? One royal courtier said: "These things do not happen by accident."

Her choice was highlighted by the blog *From Her Majesty's Jewel Vault*, which documented every item of jewelry she wore. "I thought this brooch would be a one-and-done thing, never to be seen after its original 'courtesy' appearance—only because it's not really Her Maj's style—so this was a big surprise!" the blog wrote about the reappearance of the brooch. "You'll note I'm pretty specifically NOT making a comment on why she may have chosen to wear this brooch today. That's because I like to keep politics away from here."

By the time Elizabeth II welcomed the Trumps for tea at the castle the following afternoon, she was wearing a delphinium blue coat with a blue-and-yellow floral silk dress and matching hat. The last time she wore this outfit, for the state opening of Parliament, the hat featured blue flowers with yellow centers, which the media pointed out were the colors of the European Union flag. This time the flowers had gone. A comment upon Brexit, which Trump so strongly supported? Her outfit was adorned with her mother's Cartier palm leaf brooch fashioned out of diamonds, most famously worn by the Queen Mother at the lying-in-state of her husband, George VI, at Westminster Hall.

The president had already been hosted the previous evening by Theresa May to a black-tie dinner at Blenheim Palace in Oxfordshire, the birthplace and ancestral home of Sir Winston Churchill, spending the night at Winfield House. But the day of his first royal audience began in controversy over an interview with *The Sun*. In it Trump criticized May's Brexit plans, which had already led to the resignation of her foreign secretary, Boris Johnson, four days earlier.

"If they do a deal like that, we would most likely be dealing with the European Union instead of dealing with the UK, so it will probably kill the [British and US trade] deal," he told the newspaper. "I would have done it much differently. I actually told Theresa May how to do it, but she didn't agree, she didn't listen to me."

He talked up Johnson, saying: "I'm not pitting one against the other, I'm just saying I think he [Johnson] would be a great prime minister."

He also continued his feud with London's Mayor Khan, saying: "You have a mayor who has done a terrible job in

London. I think he has done a very bad job on terrorism." Khan had authorized the flying of a large balloon in London in the form of a baby Trump wearing a diaper and carrying a phone.

If anyone could smooth things over and restore a sense of calm, it was the Queen, for whom Trump had fresh praise: "She is a tremendous woman, I really look forward to meeting her. I think she represents her country so well. If you think of it, for so many years she's represented her country, she's really never made a mistake. You don't see, like, anything embarrassing. She's just an incredible woman. My wife is a tremendous fan of hers."

The Trumps arrived in a dark Range Rover at 5:00 p.m. to an immaculate Windsor Castle scene of neatly arranged scarlet-tunicked Coldstream Guards on pristine green grass in the British summer sunshine. There appeared to be a very slight bowing gesture from Trump, dressed in a dark blue suit with a blue-and-red striped tie, as he stepped out of the vehicle and faced Elizabeth II for the first time. Then with First Lady Melania, wearing a chic Christian Dior cream skirt suit, they walked up to the royal dais under a white fabric awning and took turns shaking the Queen's extended hand as she smiled broadly.

After a few words she asked them to stand on either side of her for a stirring rendition of "The Star-Spangled Banner." As Prince Philip had retired from public duties the previous summer at the age of ninety-six, the ninety-two-year-old Queen took on his role of reviewing the Guard of Honor with the president. They paced across the lawn together to begin the line of inspection, but as they got to the starting point, Trump did not appear to see the Queen gesturing with her right hand for him to take up a position to her left and came to a stop standing right in front of her—in breach of protocol that no one should turn their back on the monarch. Without any more fuss, the Queen walked around him to begin the formal inspection side by side. Predictably there was an outcry on social media over another in a list of faux pas by presidents unfamiliar with royal custom. A royal source said it was not entirely Trump's mistake and that the Queen had not stopped in quite the right spot either. "It was as much her fault as his," the courtier said. Another source said: "There was some embarrassment in the palace that it turned into a bad story for Trump."

Arguably a bigger breach of protocol came later, when Trump divulged some of his conversation with Elizabeth II from their forty-five-minute tea (which was way over the allotted twenty-five minutes and had taken place inside the castle, away from the cameras and microphones). Royal confidants were never supposed to spill the beans on what was discussed privately. Trump confirmed in an interview with Piers Morgan that they spoke about Brexit, although his recounting of her answer illustrated just how diplomatic she was, giving a reply that could not easily be characterized as on one or the other side of the argument.

"She said it's a very—and she's right—it's a very complex problem, I think nobody had any idea how complex that was going to be. . . . Everyone thought it was going to be 'Oh it's simple, we join or don't join, or let's see what happens.'" However, when Morgan pushed him, asking, "Did she give you any clue as to which way she thinks about it?" Trump did the right thing, saying: "You just don't talk about that conversation with the Queen, right? You don't wanna do that."

Trump also sang the praises of the monarch: "The Queen is a fantastic woman; so much energy and smart and sharp. She was amazing! Such a wonderful lady and so beautiful! It was such an honor to finally meet her. To have a Queen like that is great." Asked what was going through his mind when they first met, Trump unhesitatingly said, "My mother."

Clearly the royal encounter meant a great deal to Trump. As he left for a weekend at Turnberry, one of his golf courses in Scotland, ahead of a meeting with President Putin in Helsinki that would quickly overshadow his UK visit, the big question for the Brits was whether the royal diplomacy would translate into policy dividends. Although Trump left after expressing renewed support for the Special Relationship in a press conference (during which he made up with May and called the US-UK bond "the highest level of special"), the deeper problem was that the British government and the European Union could not work out their own new relationship between themselves, making a trade deal with the US harder to arrange.

The EU rejected May's plans in September, and although a withdrawal agreement was reached in November, the House of Commons rejected it three times in early 2019, leading Theresa May to announce her intention to resign, to take effect shortly after President Trump's long-awaited state visit in June. Once again the Queen, now ninety-three, was viewed on the world stage as the fulcrum of stability in volatile times, especially with May in her lame duck period when the president and First Lady arrived at Stansted Airport.

⁓

Notwithstanding the domestic political turmoil in the UK, the cachet of the royal family made the state visit the most anticipated overseas trip of Trump's presidency, according to Sarah Huckabee Sanders, his press secretary, who accompanied him on the three-day tour timed to coincide with commemorations for the seventy-fifth anniversary of D-Day.

"For White House staff, this was the most coveted foreign trip on which to join the president, by far, and I couldn't wait," she said. Sanders and most of the White House party arrived at Buckingham Palace by motorcade and watched from the White Drawing Room on the second floor as President Trump, the First Lady, and US ambassador Woody Johnson landed in Marine One on the vast and immaculate lawn, part of the largest private garden in London. Prince Charles and his wife, Camilla, walked out of the palace to escort the Trumps over to meet the Queen. As they wandered back across the grass, a rare eighty-two-gun salute rang out, fired from nearby Green Park—forty-one shots to welcome the President from a royal park and forty-one more to mark the sixty-sixth anniversary the previous day of the Queen's coronation.

A smiling Elizabeth II, dressed in a pastel green outfit with pearls and an emerald brooch, shook hands with Trump, who wore a dark blue suit and light blue tie, before he introduced Melania, who was in a Dolce & Gabbana white dress with midnight blue collar and belt. Inside, the Americans, including all four of the president's adult children, lined up to meet three generations of royals: the Queen, followed by Prince Charles and Prince Harry, the Duke of Sussex, although he was unaccompanied by his Los Angeles–born wife, Meghan, who was caring for their month-old son, Archie. In a previsit interview with *The Sun*, Trump had hit back at the Duchess over her 2016 election criticism of him, saying "I didn't know that she was nasty." Any chance of them meeting was avoided by maternity leave and, according to Huckabee Sanders, Harry was "charming and gracious" to everyone.

Buckingham Palace staff had arranged a display of artifacts from the Queen's Collection for the visitors to view in the Grand Hall that illustrated the ties between Britain and the United States, including a British copy of the Declaration of Independence and a model pewter horse that the Trumps gifted the monarch on their 2018 visit. Asked if he recognized it, the president said he did not, but the First Lady came to his rescue. "I think we gave that to the Queen," she said. Tim Knox, director of the Royal Collection, later said: "We just asked him whether he recognized it and he said 'no,' but the First Lady did recognize it, which is rather nice. One horse is very much like another."

After lunch at the palace the Trumps laid a wreath at the Grave of the Unknown Warrior in Westminster Abbey before tea with Prince Charles and Camilla at Clarence House, where Trump was also greeted by Sir Kim Darroch, the British ambassador to Washington, who played a key role organizing the visit. Then it was time for the most ornate and eagerly awaited event: the state banquet. Huckabee Sanders set out just what it meant: "The day had already been spectacular, but that evening was something every girl dreams of. . . . It felt to us in the US delegation like we were royalty for the night."

The chief visitors were individually escorted by royals along the red-carpeted East Gallery and into the ballroom for steamed halibut, watercress mousse, and a saddle of new-season Windsor lamb with herb stuffing for 170 guests, including sixteen members of the royal family and eight Trumps. The president, accompanied by the Queen, wore a large white waistcoat as part of his white-tie outfit, which drew plenty of comment on social media, as they led the procession to the giant horseshoe table.

The excited Trump children shared photos of the occasion on social media: eldest daughter, Ivanka, tweeted a picture with her husband alongside brothers Donald Jr. and Eric; half sister, Tiffany; and First Lady Melania with the words, "Beyond wonderful to share this unforgettable evening with this crew. . . ."

Trump tweeted of his own delight: "London part of trip is going really well. The Queen and the entire Royal family have been fantastic. The relationship with the United Kingdom is very strong. Tremendous crowds of well-wishers and people that love our Country. Haven't seen any protests yet, but I'm sure the Fake News will be working hard to find them. Great love all around. Also, big Trade Deal is possible once U.K. gets rid of the shackles [of the European Union]. Already starting to talk!"

As with George W. Bush and Barack Obama on their state visits, there had been no royal welcome at Horse Guards Parade nor carriage ride down the Mall, due to the heightened security threat that uniquely denied the leaders of Britain's closest ally the same pageantry as other heads of state. Also like Bush, Trump was not invited to address Parliament, an honor afforded to Obama, Clinton, and Reagan. There was opposition from the Speaker of the House of Commons, John Bercow, who cited the "racism" of the ban on travelers from mainly Muslim countries. The "Trump baby" blimp was once again flown by protesters in central London, and several prominent politicians turned down banquet invitations, notably Jeremy Corbyn, leader of the opposition Labour Party. Trump's Twitter sparring partner Sadiq Khan was not invited, unlike in

2011, when his predecessor as London mayor, Boris Johnson, attended Obama's state banquet.

A brief drumroll announced the Queen's toast. "Visits by American presidents always remind us of the close and long-standing friendship between the United Kingdom and the United States, and I am so glad that we have another opportunity to demonstrate the immense importance that both our countries attach to our relationship," she began. Elizabeth II referenced the coming D-Day commemorations, the first major anniversary for which she was not traveling to Normandy, although she would join Trump at the British ceremony in Portsmouth.

Her toast also included a rejection of isolationism with a reference to the importance of multilateral institutions like the United Nations and NATO that Trump had criticized and, in the case of NATO, threatened to withdraw the US unless other allies contributed more to defense spending. "As we face the new challenges of the twenty-first century, the anniversary of D-Day reminds us of all that our countries have achieved together," she said. "After the shared sacrifices of the Second World War, Britain and the United States worked with other allies to build an assembly of international institutions, to ensure that the horrors of conflict would never be repeated. While the world has changed, we are forever mindful of the original purpose of these structures: nations working together to safeguard a hard-won peace."

Trump rose to give a toast underscoring his admiration of the Queen and full of warm words about the US-UK relationship. "In April of 1945, newspapers featured a picture of the Queen Mother visiting the women's branch of the army, watching a young woman repair a military truck engine," he said.

"That young mechanic was the future Queen—that great, great woman." He also paid tribute to the absent Prince Philip for his "distinguished and valiant service in the Royal Navy during the Second World War." Trump added: "From the Second World War to today, Her Majesty has . . . embodied the spirit of dignity, duty, and patriotism that beats proudly in every British heart." He closed with "a toast to the eternal friendship of our people, the vitality of our nations, and to the long, cherished, and truly remarkable reign of Her Majesty the Queen." As Elizabeth and the other dinner guests stood for the British national anthem, Trump briefly extended his left arm behind her back in a gesture of affection. While this was seen by some media as a potential breach of protocol, it was not even clear if he touched the Queen, who gave him a smile.

The evening was a great success, and the banquet ended with the ceremonial procession of twelve bagpipers around the room, a royal tradition begun by Queen Victoria. "The president loved it," Huckabee Sanders recalled. "He was a big fan of the bagpipes and had a piper play every night at his golf club in Scotland. After dinner we went through another receiving line and thanked the Queen for having us." Afterward Trump tweeted: "Could not have been treated more warmly in the United Kingdom by the Royal Family or the people. Our relationship has never been better, and I see a very big Trade Deal down the road." This was exactly what British diplomats and politicians were hoping for and a sign of the royal magic working again in the national interest.

The Queen did not join the return black-tie dinner the following evening, when Prince Charles and Camilla were the star royal guests at Winfield House. Trump sat in between the prince and Theresa May at a table for ten, including Foreign Secretary Jeremy Hunt. Huckabee Sanders, next to the Prince of Wales, asked fellow guests to sign the menu card, and Trump obliged with a gold Sharpie he produced from his jacket pocket. The prince initially demurred, but then, unlike his aunt Princess Margaret at the White House five decades earlier, he obliged with a simple "Charles." It was an unconventional move—palace staff had never seen him give an autograph before.

The state visit concluded with Trump flying to Portsmouth on Marine One for the D-Day anniversary. He read an excerpt from the prayer that FDR delivered by radio to the troops on June 6, 1944, before the largest invasion force in history—73,000 Americans and 83,115 British and Canadians, as well as smaller numbers from ten other countries—landed by sea and air in Normandy to take the fight to Hitler's Nazi war machine. The Queen, next to her son, told the three hundred veterans and dignitaries, including President Emmanuel Macron of France and German Chancellor Merkel, "When I attended the commemoration of the sixtieth anniversary of the D-Day landings, some thought it might be the last such event. But the wartime generation—my generation—is resilient, and I am delighted to be with you in Portsmouth today." It was to be her last major commemoration of the event that more than any other single joint operation showed the value of the transatlantic alliance.

"It is with humility and pleasure, on behalf of the entire country—indeed the whole free world—that I say to you all, thank you," she concluded.

Trump posed for a photo with the Queen, telling her: "It was a great honor to be with you." Elizabeth II replied: "I hope you come to this country again soon." As he and Melania headed to Marine One for Southampton Airport and their next stop in Ireland, Trump was heard saying: "Great woman. Great, great woman."

Trump told Fox News that there was "automatic chemistry" between himself and the monarch. "We had a really great time. There are those that say they have never seen the Queen have a better time, a more animated time. We had a period where we were talking solid straight, I didn't even know who the other people at the table were, never spoke to them. We just had a great time." One senior British official involved in the visit said: "It was a very big deal for Trump. He's not normally a man who cares massively about protocol but for the state visit he really made sure he got it all right, turning up on time, doing the right thing. It went off by the book."

How long would the royal effect last? Unfortunately a controversy blew up just one month later, during the final stretch of the Conservative leadership contest between Boris Johnson and Jeremy Hunt, that undid some of the goodwill. Secret diplomatic cables written by Kim Darroch were leaked to the *Mail on Sunday*, setting out the UK ambassador's candid and often unflattering views of the Trump administration.

"As seen from here, we really don't believe that this Administration is going to become substantially more normal; less dysfunctional, less unpredictable, less faction-riven, less diplomatically clumsy and inept," Sir Kim wrote. Britain's Foreign Office defended its man, saying: "Our team in Washington have strong relations with the White House and no doubt these will withstand such mischievous behavior." But Trump was riled. "Their ambassador has not served the UK well," he told reporters. "We're not big fans of that man."

Trump took to Twitter the next day to decry both Darroch and May: "What a mess she and her representatives have created. I told her how it should be done, but she decided to go another way. I do not know the Ambassador, but he is not liked or well thought of within the U.S. We will no longer deal with him. The good news for the wonderful United Kingdom is that they will soon have a new Prime Minister. While I thoroughly enjoyed the magnificent state visit last month, it was the Queen who I was most impressed with!" The following morning Trump tweeted that Darroch was "wacky," "a very stupid guy," and "a pompous fool." Never mind that he spent six months helping to arrange the state visit—his position was becoming untenable. May and Hunt stood by him, but Johnson, the front-runner to become prime minister, declined to support Darroch during a TV debate, and the ambassador announced his resignation the next day.

It was a wretched episode for UK-US relations, but it could not extinguish the royal effect nor break the numerous security, trade, economic, and cultural ties between the two nations. When Johnson emerged victorious to become PM, Trump hailed him as "Britain Trump" and the Special Relationship seemed restored. The president added: "They like me over there. . . . He'll get it done. Boris is good. He's gonna do a good job."

Trump had one further royal encounter when he attended a NATO summit in London in December 2019, reconnecting with Prince Charles and the Duchess of Cornwall at Clarence House, where Melania and Camilla exchanged an informal kiss on the cheek. At a Buckingham Palace reception that evening for the twenty-nine national leaders, host Elizabeth II greeted the Trumps warmly upon their arrival.

Background events were difficult for all concerned at the time, with the royal family reeling from Prince Andrew's recent BBC interview when he failed to quash allegations about his relationship with the late financier Jeffrey Epstein, causing the prince to step back from royal duties. In Washington, the House of Representatives' Judiciary Committee held its first impeachment hearing into Trump's treatment of Ukraine. Nevertheless, the Queen and the president looked perfectly relaxed in each other's company and chatted as they walked together to the "family photo" of the leaders for the alliance's seventieth anniversary.

A video clip would later go viral from the reception showing Justin Trudeau, the Canadian prime minister, apparently joking about Trump with Johnson, President Macron of France, Dutch prime minister Mark Rutte, and Princess Anne. Trump, who had already clashed with Macron, left abruptly the next day without holding his expected press conference, saying he had already spoken at length to the media. It was an unsatisfactory final UK trip for Trump, where once again the most enjoyable moments were spent with the British royals.

Despite the efforts of officials on both sides, there would be no comprehensive US-UK free trade deal, as had seemed so important to the British government in the immediate aftermath of Brexit. As Darroch observed in one of his leaked cables, Trump and his team were "dazzled" by the royal attention but, under Trump, "This is still the land of America First." Even when America decided it wanted a change of president, the transatlantic difficulties were not entirely over yet.

CHAPTER 14

I don't think she'd be insulted, but she reminded me of my mother.
—Joe Biden, June 13, 2021

President Joseph R. Biden Jr. first met the Queen as part of a congressional delegation visiting London when he was a senator in 1982. Thirty-nine years later, he was invited for tea at Windsor Castle, after a G7 summit, for the Queen's first meeting with a fellow head of state since the death of her husband, Philip, at ninety-nine.

Biden divulged that ninety-five-year-old Elizabeth II maintained her interest in international affairs, asking him about Presidents Putin of Russia and Xi of China. Just as with his two immediate predecessors, there was initial nervousness among British politicians and officials about the new president's true feelings toward the UK. Biden had an antagonistic history with Boris Johnson, having called him a "kind of a physical and emotional clone" of President Trump after Johnson won the 2019 UK general election. It was not meant as a compliment. Nor was he a fan of Brexit, a policy championed by Johnson, which Biden said the day after the UK voted in favor of it in 2016 was "not how we would have preferred."

Biden was extremely proud of his Irish heritage and made occasional references to Britain's historical suppression of Irish nationalism in his speeches. That said, Biden's personal attitude toward Britain was never as clear-cut as some of its media portrayed, and he also talked of the UK as a "true and faithful" ally of the United States and rejected the "senseless killings" carried out by the Provisional Irish Republican Army in the name of uniting the island of Ireland. If there had been concerns that the anti-Englishness of Biden's mother, Jean Finnegan, would translate into an aversion to that country's head of state, then these were misplaced. After becoming the thirteenth sitting US president to meet Elizabeth II, Biden invoked his late mother but in wholly positive terms, suggesting that Jean and the Queen shared essential characteristics including a "generosity" of spirit.

The main source of Biden's fierce pride in his roots was his mother's wholly Irish side of the family—the Blewitts of County Mayo and the Finnegans of County Louth. He recalled being told by his great-aunt Gertie, "Your father's not a bad man. It's not his fault he's English." (Joseph Sr.'s parents were of English, French, and Irish descent; his ancestor William Biden emigrated to the US from his native Sussex in southern England.)

Biden was a forty-year-old senator in the British-American Parliamentary Group when they met the Queen in November 1982. As he was leaving for London, Catherine Eugenia Finnegan

Biden, known as Jean, called him on the phone. "Don't you bow down to her," she told him, according to his autobiography, *Promises to Keep*. Biden recounted in a speech to Irish Americans in New York, while being inducted into the Irish American Hall of Fame in 2013, that his mother also said: "Joey, be polite, but do not kiss her ring. Nobody is better than you." This sentiment was not reserved just for the Queen, however. She also told him not to kiss the ring of Pope John Paul II.

Biden shared more details of his mother's views with Georgia Pritchett, a British scriptwriter, while she was researching the comedy *Veep* when he was vice president. "Noticing I was English, he changed the subject to how much his mother hated the English," she wrote in her memoir, *My Mess Is a Bit of a Life*. "She had written several poems about her hatred of the English. He went off to find them and returned with hundreds of poems describing how God must smite the English and rain blood on our heads." Biden also told her how Jean once visited the UK and spent a night in a hotel room where, she was told, the Queen had once stayed. "She was so appalled that she slept on the floor all night, rather than risk sleeping on a bed that the Queen had slept on," Biden told her.

Biden was politically aware enough to know that Jean's anti-Englishness, learned from her Pennsylvania-born Irish American parents and nurtured by a close-knit émigré community, proved in his own words that "Irish Americans think they're more Irish than the Irish, and that's kind of how I was raised, like so many Americans of Irish heritage."

His own approach to Britain was mixed, reflecting the political and moral questions of the day. In 1982, the year of his first royal audience, Biden grew impatient with the Reagan administration's lengthy period of public evenhandedness following Argentina's invasion of the Falkland Islands and sponsored a resolution in the Senate calling on the US to get fully behind the UK in the conflict.

A few years later, Biden led Senate opposition to a revised extradition treaty drawn up by the Thatcher government to limit the ability of suspected Irish republican terrorists to claim a political defense to avoid being sent from the US to Britain to face trial. In a 1987 interview with *Irish America* magazine, Biden paid tribute to Britain as "a true, faithful and legitimate real ally" of the US but also spoke about his opposition to the extradition treaty.

"It was a reflection on how we have never—I'm going to get myself in real trouble here—come to grips with our relationship with Great Britain," he said. "There is an overwhelming admiration and awe for the British jurisprudential system, a phenomenal respect for British majesty and power. In the sense that many Irish are ambivalent about the IRA, we have been ambivalent about Britain. We have fought them and we have loved them. As they are in the twilight of their position as a world power, we are reluctant to take issue with them."

Biden was clear while campaigning for the presidency in 2020 about his overriding priority before considering a US trade deal with Britain, saying: "We can't allow the Good Friday Agreement that brought peace to Northern Ireland to become a casualty of Brexit. Any trade deal between the US and UK must be contingent upon respect for the Agreement and preventing the return of a hard border. Period."

British concerns about Biden's approach were not alleviated

when, on the day he was named president-elect in November 2020, a BBC journalist tweeted a clip of Biden's response on the campaign trail in Iowa when he was asked for a quick word. In a busy corridor heading into a meeting room, Biden quipped: "The BBC? I'm Irish," before breaking into a smile and turning through the door.

When Biden came to office, the Johnson government was in a showdown with the EU over the border arrangements between Northern Ireland (part of the UK) and the Republic of Ireland (part of the EU). As she did for every new president, the Queen sent a private message for his inauguration. Soon the British tabloids were quick to identify a snub when Biden removed the bronze bust of Churchill, opting for one of civil rights icon Rosa Parks.

"Fury as Joe Biden REMOVES bust of Boris Johnson's hero Winston Churchill from the Oval Office," the conservative *Daily Mail* headlined. It felt like déjà vu after Obama also made the same change. The British government tried to calm the storm.

"It's of course up to the President to decorate the Oval Office as he wishes," a UK spokesperson told reporters. "We're in no doubt about the importance President Biden places on the UK-US relationship." Johnson publicly welcomed Biden's inauguration and his return of the US into the Paris Agreement. "When you look at the issues that unite the UK and the United States right now, there's a fantastic joint common agenda," Johnson said. "It's a fantastic thing for America, a step forward for the country that has been through a bumpy period."

There was another perceived dig at the British in the new president's first full press conference in March, however. Asked about the exodus of immigrants fleeing difficult conditions in Latin America and putting pressure on the US southern border, Biden recalled that his great-great-grandfather had been forced to leave Ireland "because of what the Brits had been doing," referring to the Great Famine of 1845–52 that resulted from British policies. He added: "They were in real, real trouble. They didn't want to leave. But they had no choice. So . . . I can't guarantee we're going to solve everything, but I can guarantee we can make everything better."

The Queen had a turbulent start to the year. On February 19, 2021, Buckingham Place announced that, after a twelve-month review of the future role of her grandson Harry and his American wife, Meghan, "the Duke and Duchess of Sussex have confirmed to Her Majesty The Queen that they will not be returning as working members of The Royal Family." Harry was stripped of his royal patronages and honorary military appointments, but the pair kept their Duke and Duchess titles.

A few weeks later they gave an interview to Oprah Winfrey that deepened the pain of the rift and was watched on CBS by 17.8 million viewers in the US and one of Britain's biggest TV audiences of the year of 13.3 million. Meghan told Winfrey that, while she was pregnant with their first child, Archie, there had been "concerns and conversations about how dark his skin might be when he's born . . . several conversations." Meghan would not say who said this, but Winfrey clarified the next day that Harry told her it was not the Queen or Prince Philip.

After all the British media suspicions about the forty-sixth president's attitude toward the UK, Biden showed his compassionate side toward its head of state when Elizabeth's husband of seventy-three years passed away on April 9, 2021, two months short of his hundredth birthday. "On behalf of all the people of the United States, we send our deepest condolences to Her Majesty Queen Elizabeth II, the entire royal family, and all the people of the United Kingdom on the death of His Royal Highness Prince Philip, the Duke of Edinburgh," Biden and First Lady Jill Biden said in a joint message.

"Over the course of his ninety-nine-year life, he saw our world change dramatically and repeatedly. From his service during World War II, to his seventy-three years alongside the Queen, and his entire life in the public eye, Prince Philip gladly dedicated himself to the people of the UK, the Commonwealth, and to his family. The impact of his decades of devoted public service is evident in the worthy causes he lifted up as patron, in the environmental efforts he championed, in the members of the Armed Forces that he supported, in the young people he inspired, and so much more."

In the atmosphere of social distancing and limited in-person contacts during the height of the Covid-19 pandemic, there had been no prime ministerial sprint to Washington to meet the new president as there had been with Blair, Brown, and May soon after the inaugurations of Bush, Obama, and Trump. Instead, there was a fortuitous chance to meet because Britain held the annual rotating presidency of the G7 and hosted a return to an in-person leaders' summit in Cornwall after the pandemic forced the cancellation of the 2020 gathering. The Queen insisted on going along for her first meeting with world leaders since being widowed two months earlier.

Biden once again showed his respect for his host by offering further thoughts on her loss when he arrived in Cornwall on June 10, 2021, recognizing that the day held special significance: "First, I want to express our condolences on behalf of Jill and I to Her Majesty, Queen Elizabeth II, the entire royal family, and the people of the United Kingdom. Today would have been Prince Philip's one hundredth birthday, and I know there are a lot of people feeling his absence today."

Biden was again at odds with Johnson's Conservative government in the run-up to the summit. Just a week earlier he had sent his top diplomat in London, Yael Lempert, the chargé d'affaires, to issue a strongly worded warning known as a démarche to Lord Frost, the Brexit minister, against "inflaming" tensions in Northern Ireland and the Republic of Ireland after the failure of talks on updating border transit arrangements. However, in his first speech in Cornwall, Biden added that he had "a good first full day here in the UK" and "a very productive meeting" with Johnson. "We affirmed the Special Relationship—and it's not said lightly—the Special Relationship between our people, and we renewed our commitment to defending the enduring democratic values that both our nations share that are the strong foundation of our partnership." This made him the latest in a long line of presidents to use Churchill's phrase. Britain and the US had agreed to a "revitalized" Atlantic Charter, the agreement that the UK and the US would "meet the challenges of their age and they would meet it together" first made between Churchill and FDR eighty years earlier. The latest version was aimed at "the key challenges of this century: cybersecurity, emerging technologies, global health, and climate change."

The following day First Lady Jill Biden, a lifelong educator, teamed up with Kate, the Duchess of Cambridge, a mother of three who has made early education one of her special projects, for a preschool visit in Cornwall. It was the first meeting between the pair, who later published a joint article pledging to work together to improve early-years education globally.

Kate joined a large contingent of royals for an afternoon reception for the world leaders at the Eden Project, an eco-charity that re-creates a rain forest environment under giant domes. The royal party was led by the Queen in a white-and-pink floral dress and included Charles and Camilla—appropriately, as they were the Duke and Duchess of Cornwall—as well as William and Kate, in a rare turnout of the three generations closest to the throne. It was Charles who gave the welcoming speech to the G7 leaders on behalf of the British royals and hosted that evening's dinner, further signs that Elizabeth II was stepping back from the front line of diplomatic duty for her country. She still managed to raise a laugh from her guests as they assembled with her for the socially distanced "family photo."

"Are you supposed to be looking as if you're enjoying yourself?" she asked.

"Yes," Prime Minister Johnson replied. "We have been enjoying ourselves in spite of appearances."

An American president attending an international summit of numerous leaders in the UK was once again singled out for special treatment by the British monarchy, just as Obama had received a private audience at Buckingham Palace ahead of the G20 meeting in 2009. As soon as the G7 in Cornwall wrapped up, the Bidens flew by Air Force One to Heathrow and from there in Marine One for a private meeting with Elizabeth II at Windsor Castle.

They landed in glorious sunshine on a hot day in the Home Park next to the royal residence west of London. The Queen, wearing a pink floral dress and hat, white gloves, and her distinctive black handbag over her left arm, was serenaded with "God Save the Queen" when she emerged with a military escort to take up her place under a white awning in front of the private apartments facing the red-tunicked troops. The Bidens were driven from the helicopter in a dark green Range Rover through the George IV gateway and around the quadrangle, where they disembarked in front of the Queen and removed black cloth coronavirus face masks, climbed three steps, and greeted her on the dais.

The Queen began to offer her gloved hand but kept it back upon noticing that Jill was holding her husband's hand, and there was no handshake. After a few private words, the president stood on her left and the First Lady, dressed in a powder blue skirt suit, on her right for the playing of "The Star-Spangled Banner." Biden, dressed in a dark blue suit and blue tie, kept on his aviator-style sunglasses.

The Queen had stood in for her husband when President Trump inspected the troops in 2019, but this time she remained in place alongside the First Lady while Biden set off to view the Guard of Honor accompanied by the commanding officer, Major James Taylor, and Chris Ghika, major general of the Household Division. Before walking onto the grass, he finally removed his sunglasses. The British tabloids, on constant gaffe watch, saw the aviators as a breach of protocol, but the Queen did not seem to mind at all.

Once the inspecting was done and the troops had marched past in formation, Elizabeth took her American guests through the Sovereign's Entrance for tea in the Oak Room in her private quarters, a setting adorned with mementos and family photos. Afterward the president said he had invited the Queen back to the White House, even though her traveling days were behind her.

"I don't think she'd be insulted, but she reminded me of my mother. In terms of the look of her and just the generosity," Biden said, adding that she asked what it was like inside the White House now. He divulged a little more of what they talked about, including his forthcoming meeting with Russian leader Vladimir Putin in Geneva. Speaking at Heathrow Airport before heading to Brussels for a NATO meeting, he added: "She's extremely gracious. That's not surprising, but we had a great talk. She wanted to know what the two leaders that I—the one I'm about to meet with, Mr. Putin, and she wanted to know about Xi Jinping, and we had a long talk."

President Biden brought along a thoughtful gift—a specially designed rectangular, lined sterling silver box from Tiffany & Co. personalized with an engraving of Windsor Castle on top, with flowers representing different Commonwealth countries on the sides. There was an inscription inside the box commemorating the meeting and expressing support for the continuation of the US-UK relationship. The Bidens were the fifth First Couple received at the castle after the Trumps in 2018, the Obamas in 2016, George and Laura Bush for a valedictory tea in 2008, and the Reagans in 1982. As with other presidential visits, the White House team was thrilled. Jen Psaki, the press secretary, was asked beforehand if Biden wanted a royal encounter and quipped, "Who wouldn't want to meet the Queen?"

The Times summed up the importance of having such a

long-serving and iconic figure to host visiting dignitaries and make allies feel even more special. "The US president and the first lady found themselves participating in a seemingly timeless ritual, and not just because the Queen offered them afternoon tea," it wrote. "Mr. Biden became the thirteenth sitting president to have met the monarch, continuing a rite of passage for US leaders that began when Harry Truman entertained Princess Elizabeth in Washington DC in 1951. . . . It is a remarkable record that has been invaluable in maintaining goodwill between Britain and the US through good and less good times."

The monarchy was "an effective weapon" in Britain's diplomatic armory, it added. "At a time when trust in Boris Johnson's government, and therefore Britain itself, is being openly questioned by its closest allies, including the US, the continuity that the Queen brings to the country's international relationships has never been more vital. That she continues to do her duty with such diligence and dignity is a blessing for which we should all be grateful."

Biden was back in the UK in November for COP26, the United Nations climate change conference in Glasgow, which the Queen was due to attend, but just a week before, she was forced to pull out after a hospital visit. She was advised to rest but recorded a powerful video message at Windsor Castle that was relayed to an evening reception for the leaders in Scotland. The four-minute address was notable not merely for Elizabeth II staking out a strong position in support of global climate action, in a departure from the studiously neutral approach she usually took on major topics of the day, but also for her reflection on mortality in the wake of her husband's passing and her own more delicate health.

"The impact of the environment on human progress was a subject close to the heart of my dear late husband, Prince Philip, the Duke of Edinburgh," she said, seated next to a photograph taken of Philip looking at a swarm of butterflies, and herself wearing a butterfly brooch on her lime green outfit, along with her favorite three-strand pearl necklace. Back in 1969, she said, Philip told a conference that failure to address pollution would make all other problems "pale into insignificance."

Seemingly in better health after her hospital visit, she went on: "It is a source of great pride to me that the leading role my husband played in encouraging people to protect our fragile planet lives on through the work of our eldest son Charles and his eldest son, William. I could not be more proud of them." She drew on her long career on the global stage to stiffen the leaders' resolve, saying: "For more than seventy years, I have been lucky to meet and to know many of the world's great leaders and I have perhaps come to know a little of what made them special. . . . What leaders do for their people today is government and politics, but what they do for the people of tomorrow— that is statesmanship."

It was "time for action," she said. In her poignant closing lines, she concluded: "We none of us will live forever. But we are doing this not for ourselves but for our children and our children's children, and those who will follow in their footsteps."

Just as Britain prepared to celebrate the Queen's Platinum

Jubilee in 2022, marking seventy years since coming to the throne, Elizabeth II was awarded the annual Ruth Bader Ginsburg Woman of Leadership Award from the Dwight D. Opperman Foundation. The award recognized "an extraordinary woman who has exercised a positive and notable influence on society and served as an exemplary role model in both principles and practice." In a letter addressed to Her Majesty, President Biden acknowledged her "strength and integrity through an era of unprecedented global challenges" that "set an example for the world that will continue to inspire leaders for generations to come."

On Accession Day—February 6, 2022—the royal family posted a video of the Queen at Sandringham working through one of her red boxes containing official papers, handed to her by Sir Edward Young, her private secretary. They included a report from the UK ambassador in Washington, Dame Karen Pierce, about the Woman of Leadership Award ceremony.

"You will see, ma'am, there's some extremely nice comments, including one from President Biden," said Sir Edward.

The Queen replied: "Oh that's very kind, isn't it."

That same day, the White House posted on Twitter: "Today we honor Her Majesty Queen Elizabeth II on the historic occasion of her Platinum Jubilee. Throughout the past 70 years, she has strengthened the ties of friendship, shared ideals, and faith in democracy that forever unite our countries."

In June, during the main celebrations in Britain and the Queen's realms of her extraordinary reign, the Bidens recorded a video message to thank her for her "solidarity" with America. "Your Majesty, congratulations on your Platinum Jubilee. For seventy years, you've inspired people with your selfless devotion and service to the people of the United Kingdom and the Commonwealth," the president said. "Throughout your reign, the relationship between the United Kingdom and United States has grown stronger and closer than ever."

Jill Biden finished up the message: "Congratulations, Your Majesty, and have a wonderful Platinum Jubilee celebration."

The last time that Elizabeth II was seen in public was for the formal appointment of her fifteenth prime minister, Liz Truss, at Balmoral—the first time she affirmed the new head of her government in Scotland. Although she had increasingly been relying on Prince Charles and other family members, this was one duty that she was determined to perform and appeared cheerful, if frail, with official photographs showing her dressed informally in a light blue blouse and gray cardigan with a Balmoral tartan skirt and holding a cane, with noticeable bruising on the backs of her hands.

Two days later members of her immediate family were suddenly summoned to Balmoral. Her son and heir, Charles, was at Dumfries House, an eighteenth-century country estate owned by his educational charity the Prince's Foundation, 150 miles to the southwest in Ayrshire. During the morning Jenna Bush Hager, daughter of George W. Bush, arrived at Dumfries House under a long-standing arrangement to interview the Duchess of Cornwall for NBC about her book club. Showing the extended links that the royals made with presidential families, Bush Hager's friendship with the royal couple dated back to her father's presidency—when her own relationship with her future husband, Henry Chase Hager, became public on their first appearance together at a White House dinner for Charles and Camilla in November 2005.

"At twelve thirty we heard sort of running up and down the halls and it was her team and his team," Bush Hager later recounted to *Today*. "They came in and said, 'Can you please be quiet there's a call'—we were right by then Prince Charles's, now King Charles III's, office . . . And then all of a sudden we heard a helicopter. . . . They said the Queen is ill and they have gone and rushed off to be with her."

Elizabeth II, Queen of the United Kingdom and fourteen other Commonwealth realms, passed away aged ninety-six at 3:10 p.m. British Summer Time on September 8, 2022, with Charles and Anne, her eldest children, by her side. Her reign of 70 years and 214 days was the second longest in world history after Louis XIV of France.

President Biden canceled an afternoon event on Covid-19 booster shots and issued a Proclamation on the Death of Queen Elizabeth II, ordering the US flag to be flown at half-staff over the White House, all public buildings and lands, and military and naval stations from that moment until sunset on September 19, the day of the Queen's funeral.

"Her Majesty Queen Elizabeth II was more than a monarch. She defined an era," the proclamation stated. "In a world of constant change, she was a steadying presence and a source of comfort and pride for generations of Britons, including many who have never known their country without her. Queen

Elizabeth II led always with grace, an unwavering commitment to duty, and the incomparable power of her example. She
was a stateswoman of unmatched dignity and constancy who
deepened the bedrock Alliance between the United Kingdom
and the United States. She helped make our relationship special. The seven decades of her history-making reign bore witness to an age of unprecedented human advancement and the
forward march of human dignity. Her legacy will loom large in
the pages of British history, and in the story of our world."

The Queen's death appeared to make a deep impression on
Biden. That evening, at a Democratic National Committee
event in Maryland, he told the audience: "Before I begin I want
to say a few words about Queen Elizabeth. I just stopped by the
British embassy to sign the condolence book in her honor. I had
the opportunity to meet her before she passed, and she was an
incredibly gracious and decent woman. And the thoughts and
prayers of the American people are with the people of the
United Kingdom and the Commonwealth in their grief."

In the UK, elaborate plans known as Operation London
Bridge were activated, with a ten-day period of national mourning leading up to a state funeral. Invitations went out to world
leaders, and Biden broke with precedent to accept—no sitting
American president had attended a British state funeral. In
1965, Eisenhower went in a personal capacity to the one for
Sir Winston Churchill, and in 1910, Theodore Roosevelt, who
left office the previous year, was at the state funeral for Edward VII.

During the evening before the service at Westminster Abbey, the president and First Lady attended the lying-in-state of
Elizabeth II's coffin in Westminster Hall, with Biden making

the sign of the cross as he arrived on a viewing platform to stand in between Jill and US ambassador Jane Hartley. More than 250,000 people queued for as long as fourteen hours to pay their respects over five days, in a line that stretched up to five miles. The next day in the abbey there was only room for a maximum delegation of two per country and the Bidens joined representatives from 168 countries, including 18 monarchs, 55 presidents, and 25 prime ministers. Almost all of them traveled in a fleet of buses, because it would have taken hours for them to arrive individually. The US president was among a very select band, including Israel's President Isaac Herzog, who received a special concession to travel in their own vehicle—in Biden's case, the Beast—because of security concerns.

Biden's thoughts again returned to his mother, Jean, who passed away in 2010, just as they had when he met Elizabeth II at Windsor Castle for tea. He also referred back to the values of his Irish American upbringing when considering the British Queen's core character. "I think the thing that is—maybe it's too much, excuse the expression, the Irish of it—but it's about treating people with dignity," he said, after signing the official book of condolence in London.

"I talk about how my mother and father thought that everyone, no matter who they were, no matter what their station, no matter where they were from, deserved to be treated with dignity. And that's exactly what she communicated. . . . It was an honor to meet her—an honor to meet her."

CONCLUSION

Two centuries after George III lost the colonies, Queen Eliza-
beth II is in danger of winning them back. . . . She is, after all, the
closest Americans will ever get to a genuine queen of their own.

—*The Washington Post*, May 13, 1991

I n March 2015, the then Prince Charles was making chit-
chat with President Obama in the Oval Office when their
conversation was picked up by a boom microphone despite
their lowered voices.

"Everybody's so friendly," said Charles, a nice line in diplomatic small talk.

Obama leaned toward him and replied: "Well, I think it's
fair to say that the American people are quite fond of the royal
family."

Charles chuckled. "Awfully nice to know," he said.

Obama added: "They like them much better than they like
their own politicians."

It was true. A CNN survey put the Queen on an approval
rating of 82 percent, Prince William on 77 percent, and Prince
Charles 57 percent, ten points more than his host's rating with
Gallup.

Americans' respect for Queen Elizabeth II was also evident in her frequent appearance on the top ten list of most admired women living anywhere in the world. None featured more often than the Queen, who held that distinction fifty-two of the seventy-one times Gallup asked the question between 1948 and 2020. And the esteem in which she was held by the American people seemed only to grow after her death.

All five living past presidents paid warm tributes following her passing. President Clinton said: "Throughout her remarkable seventy-year reign, she led Britain through great transformations with unfailing grace, dignity, and genuine care for the welfare of all its people. In sunshine or storm, she was a source of stability, serenity, and strength."

George W. Bush said that he and Laura "were honored to have known Her Majesty Queen Elizabeth II. She was a woman of great intellect, charm, and wit. Spending time at Buckingham Palace, and having tea with Her Majesty—and her corgis—is among our fondest memories of the presidency."

The longest tribute came from President Obama, praising her as "a beacon of hope and stability for the people of the United Kingdom and the world" and recalling that she not only made presidents feel at ease during potentially stuffy ceremonial events but had a sense of fun, as shown in the video she made with Daniel Craig as James Bond for the opening of the London Olympics in 2012. "From the day of her coronation seventy years ago—the first one ever televised—to this very moment, as countless tributes are being posted online in her honor, Her Majesty Queen Elizabeth II has captivated the world," Obama wrote. "Her Majesty was just twenty-five years old when she took on the enormous task of helming one of the world's great democracies. In the decades that followed, she would go on to make the role of Queen her own—with a reign defined by grace, elegance, and a tireless work ethic, defying the odds and expectations placed on women of her generation."

Obama reflected on the incredible span of Elizabeth's seventy-year reign. "During World War II, she became the first-ever female royal to serve on active military duty. And through periods of prosperity and stagnation—from the moon landing, to the fall of the Berlin Wall, to the dawn of the digital age—she served as a beacon of hope and stability for the people of the United Kingdom and the world. . . . She listened deeply, thought strategically, and was responsible for considerable diplomatic achievements." He confirmed what British diplomats also realized: that the Queen personally increased the appeal of her country for a president who thought the United States should reorient its focus more toward the Pacific than the Atlantic.

"Michelle and I were lucky enough to come to know Her Majesty, and she meant a great deal to us. Back when we were just beginning to navigate life as president and First Lady, she welcomed us to the world stage with open arms and extraordinary generosity. Time and again, we were struck by her warmth, the way she put people at ease, and how she brought her considerable humor and charm to moments of great pomp and circumstance. Like so many, Michelle and I are grateful to have witnessed Her Majesty's dedicated leadership, and we are awed by her legacy of tireless, dignified public service."

President Trump, in a tribute posted on his social media site Truth Social, said, "Queen Elizabeth's historic and remarkable reign left a tremendous legacy of peace and prosperity for Great

Britain. Her leadership and enduring diplomacy secured and advanced alliances with the United States and countries around the world. However, she will always be remembered for her faithfulness to her country and her unwavering devotion to her fellow countrymen and -women. Melania and I will always cherish our time together with the Queen, and never forget Her Majesty's generous friendship, great wisdom, and wonderful sense of humor."

The briefest statement came from the living president she knew least well: "Rosalynn and I extend our condolences to the family of Her Majesty Queen Elizabeth II and the citizens of the United Kingdom," President Carter said. "Her dignity, graciousness, and sense of duty have been an inspiration, and we join the millions around the world in mourning a remarkable leader."

Underlining just how extensive Queen Elizabeth's connections were with US presidents and their families, the Franklin D. Roosevelt Presidential Library and Museum also posted a tribute that included the thoughts of Eleanor Roosevelt from her daily diary on May 15, 1957, shortly after Elizabeth's thirty-first birthday: "I have the greatest respect for this young woman who must combine the responsibilities of a Queen with the requirements and emotional stresses of a young mother. I think, too, the British people are fortunate in having the royal family to hold them together. Everywhere you go, you see that the Queen, Prince Philip, the Queen Mother, and Princess Margaret are loved as well as deeply respected."

Perhaps the president who captured Elizabeth II's distinctive contribution as hereditary monarch and champion of democracy the best was Bill Clinton, who in 2002 put it like this: "I think she understands that even though many people may think the position is an anachronism, it serves quite a useful purpose, particularly at critical times in the nation's history. And she has, I think, done everything she possibly could to elevate her role in the best sense, but to still try to show a common touch, a sense of being in tune with the people. I don't think it's very complicated. I think she has done her duty. You know, life thrust her into certain circumstances, and she did an excellent job of dealing with the hand she was dealt in life. We should all do so well."

Did she have a favorite president? The Queen would never be heard expressing a view.

President Trump was curious enough to ask her directly. "'Can I ask you a question?' 'Yes, yes you may, anything you like,'" said Trump, recounting their dialogue. "'Who was your favorite president? Was it Ronald Reagan?' 'No, no, everybody, I liked them all.' 'Did you like Nixon?' 'Oh yes, I liked him very much.' 'But did you like Reagan the most?' 'No, I liked them all, I liked them very much.' . . . And I realized how smart she was. . . . She was like a steel trap," he said.

Trump was certainly right that the Queen was a smart diplomat—her seven decades representing her country had made her an expert at putting everyone she met at their ease and making them feel like the most special person she had encountered. He continued: "You know she has her favorites because that's the way life works. Many people have said that I was her favorite president, I will tell you, I have heard from everybody."

Four presidents stand out as particularly special to the British sovereign, spanning the three distinct generations of her reign: President Eisenhower knew her parents and was indelibly and heroically associated with her formative wartime years—he was the only one invited to stay at Balmoral and the only one who put her up in the White House private quarters; from her own Greatest Generation, Elizabeth formed especially close relationships with Presidents Reagan, who shared her love of horses, and George H. W. Bush; and from the baby boomer generation of her children, her favorite was probably President Obama. These US leaders were not only good company: their wives clicked with the royal couple and, perhaps most importantly, they also worked at the relationship with letters, phone calls, and visits that went beyond standard diplomatic obligations. In addition they all paid close attention to the other royal generations: in Eisenhower's case, he remained close to the Queen Mother and painted portraits of two of Elizabeth's children; Reagan and Bush both hosted Charles and Diana separately to the Queen; while the Obamas met several times with Elizabeth's grandsons William and Harry, and their own daughters were invited to Buckingham Palace when in London with their mother. As for a favorite First Lady, officials who saw the relationships up close single out Barbara Bush, a fellow matriarch and animal lover.

There was no downside for US presidents in appearing alongside such a beloved figure as the Queen. The British system of distinct heads of state and government gave her an enviable platform, as John Bolton, a former UN ambassador and national security advisor, identified: "Her separation from the often-unpleasant reality of day-to-day affairs of state . . . allowed national divisions of opinion, even deep and bitter ones, to be subsumed under a unifying figure that had only the British national interest at heart. While a president can certainly be a unifying figure, he is always at risk of accusations that he is putting party priorities above those of the nation as a whole, invoking its sacred symbols not for higher purposes, but for those very crass partisan interests that are always getting in the way."

But it is a myth that, as politically neutral as she strove to be in public, Elizabeth was indifferent. Far from it. In naming the US-UK bond the Special Relationship, Churchill not only recognized the crucial wartime alliance but dearly hoped to perpetuate deep transatlantic ties as the anchor of English-speaking nations and democracies everywhere. This became one of Queen Elizabeth II's most important missions. Her personal link to that era gave her a firm belief in the "assembly of international institutions" built out of "shared sacrifices" of wartime "to ensure that the horrors of conflict would never be repeated," as she said at her 116th and final state visit banquet, hosting President Trump in 2019. This made her the living embodiment of that Special Relationship, herself becoming the unique element that helped keep American presidents emotionally connected to her own country as the world changed beyond belief from the beginning of her reign in 1952 until her death more than seventy years later.

Many Americans liked and respected Queen Elizabeth II, and she was very fond of the United States, enjoying the freedom it gave her to relax on private visits—and in the company of the presidents she knew the best—to a degree that was almost unimaginable back in Britain. As *The Washington Post* wrote when she arrived for her third American state visit: "She's not our queen, but before we're through with her, she'll probably think she is. Two centuries after George III lost the colonies, Queen Elizabeth II is in danger of winning them back.... She is, after all, the closest Americans will ever get to a genuine queen of their own."

She did as much as she could to usher her children and grandchildren onto the stage to continue her work, but her passing inevitably raises difficult questions about whether the British monarchy can continue to provide the same combination of celebrity, diplomatic relevance and experience, and personal allure. After all, she was a woman who met so many in public life—from Marilyn Monroe (they were born six weeks apart) to Lady Gaga (two years younger than Prince Harry). She was the last head of state who had served during World War II, she visited fifteen US states as well as the District of Columbia, and she knew thirteen sitting US presidents (fourteen presidents in all, counting her meeting with Hoover in 1957), and fourteen First Ladies.

King Charles III, for his part, made sure to meet many of the presidents while growing into the role that was destined to be his by birth—from boyhood encounters with Eisenhower to his emergence as Prince of Wales with his first American visit hosted by Nixon, then meeting every commander in chief from Carter onward, nine in all by the time he succeeded his mother at seventy-three. At the time of writing, he has a popular heir in Prince William, who enjoys a higher favorability rating than his father in the US and the UK alike.

This all suggests that the modern representatives of an ancient hereditary system will continue its traditions for the foreseeable future, including the Churchillian mission to keep their nation closely bound to the United States. But neither they nor the people of the US and the UK are likely to take for granted that they walk in the footsteps of a royal role model who charmed and fascinated America and its presidents for so long.

ACKNOWLEDGMENTS

Growing up in Britain, watching Elizabeth II's televised address at 3:00 p.m. on Christmas Day was just as much a part of our family's annual holiday ritual as decorating the tree and exchanging gifts. The Queen was a constant presence who became even more treasured as the years went by and she shared in years both good and bad at the national and personal level. It was only when I moved to Washington, DC, in 2018 that I realized just how much she also meant to Americans—my British accent was often an invitation to discuss the latest royal news, and whatever the views expressed on her family members, I heard a near-universal respect for the Queen in the country that had rebelled against her forebears.

The concept for this book sprang from an article I wrote for *The Times* about her relations with successive US presidents as she prepared to meet her thirteenth, Joe Biden, in June 2021. Discussions with British and American officials past and present confirmed that there was a wealth of stories out there just waiting to be brought together in one place.

Special thanks are due to Amberley Lowis at the Viney Agency for her enthusiasm for the idea and to Michelle Howry and Ashley Di Dio for sharing a passion for the project and steering it through to reality along with their fantastic team at Putnam.

The book would not be half as much fun without the recollections of those close to the action. I am very grateful to the relatives of presidents who took the time to talk to me about memories of the Queen, including Clifton Truman Daniel, Susan Eisenhower, and Luci Baines Johnson, as well as those who served presidents and the Queen, including Lloyd Hand, Sir William Heseltine, and Dickie Arbiter, and other diplomats and officials who spoke off the record.

The presidential libraries were a great source of information, and I would like to thank the knowledgeable staff at them who took the time to answer queries and help with factual and photo research. I would also like to thank Dr. Tessa Dunlop, historian and royal author, for invaluable help and suggestions.

I owe my parents special thanks for encouraging me throughout my career as a journalist, even as it has taken me further away from where it all began.

Lastly there would be no book without the wonderful support and patience of Michelle, Leo, and Kim, who deserve the greatest thanks of all for putting up with the lost weekends, disrupted vacations, and other annoyances associated with pressing deadlines. As Elizabeth II reflected in her 1976 Christmas message on the theme of reconciliation, after her warm welcome during America's bicentenary celebrations that July, "It is not something that is easy to achieve. But things that are worthwhile seldom are."

NOTES

Introduction

2 **John Adams:** John Adams, *The Works of John Adams* (Boston: Little, Brown, 1853), 8:256–57.

3 **By 1830:** John Spencer Bassett, ed., *Correspondence of Andrew Jackson* (Washington, DC: The Carnegie Institution of Washington, 1929), 4:159.

3 **She wasted no time:** Mryan, "Your Good Friend, Victoria R," *Pieces of History* (blog), US National Archives, March 20, 2015, https://prologue.blogs.archives.gov/2015/03/20/your -good-friend-victoria-r.

4 **Eventually, though, the American media:** James Gordon Bennett, "Message to Both Houses of Congress," *New York Daily Herald*, December 24, 1839.

4 **In her speech:** "The Queen's Speech," *The New York Times*, February 20, 1861.

5 **Both sides:** "Letter of Condolence from President Lincoln to Queen Victoria, 1 February 1862," Royal Collection Trust, accessed July 8, 2023, https://www.rct.uk/sites/default/files /ra_vic_main_m_65_63.pdf.

5   **The Queen would turn:** Queen Victoria to Mrs. President
     Lincoln, Library of Congress, accessed July 8, 2023, https://
     www.loc.gov/resource/lprbscsm.scsm0727.

5   **Mrs. Lincoln replied:** "Mary Lincoln's Response to Queen
     Victoria," The White House Historical Association, accessed
     July 8, 2023, https://www.whitehousehistory.org/photos
     /mary-lincolns-response-to-queen-victoria.

6   **Victoria's son:** "Letter from King Edward VII to Theodore
     Roosevelt," Theodore Roosevelt Center at Dickinson State
     University, accessed July 8, 2023, https://www
     .theodorerooseveltcenter.org/Research/Digital-Library
     /Record?libID=o156190.

6   **Roosevelt wrote back:** "Letter from Theodore Roosevelt to
     Edward VII, King of Great Britain," Theodore Roosevelt
     Center at Dickinson State University, accessed July 5, 2023,
     https://www.theodorerooseveltcenter.org/Research/Digital
     -Library/Record?libID=o191290.

6   **Reporting Wilson's reception:** "London's Memorable
     Boxing Day," The Guardian, December 27, 1918.

7   **Calling in at the White House:** "President Enjoys Chat with
     Prince," The New York Times, November 14, 1919.

8   **The day after the abdication:** "Roosevelt Good Wishes
     Are Sent to New King," The New York Times, December 13,
     1936.

8   **Roosevelt won reelection:** "FDR Campaigns for Reelection
     1940," History Central, accessed July 5, 2023, https://www
     .historycentral.com/FDR/FDR_1940Election.html.

9   **"King Tries Hot Dog . . .":** Felix Belair Jr., "King Tries Hot
     Dog and Asks for More," The New York Times, June 12, 1939.

12 **Wartime searchlights:** "Nurse Who Helped Operate on
     King George VI to Celebrate 100th Birthday," West Sussex
     Today, January 13, 2017.

12 **This modern advance:** Maurice Jefferies, "Hint Crowd Of
     100,000 At Landing," The Windsor Star, October 6, 1951.

12 **The fifty-five-year-old:** "Princess 'Tired, Nervous' as Victoria
     Salutes Her," The Windsor Star, October 23, 1951.

12   **Her father had been:** United Press, "Princess Off on Air Trip to Canada, US," *The Philadelphia Inquirer*, October 8, 1951.

12   **In his briefcase:** Ben Pimlott, *The Queen: Elizabeth II and the Monarchy* (London: HarperCollins, 2002), 170.

13   **warning of the "Iron Curtain":** Sir Winston Churchill, "The Sinews of Peace," (speech, Westminster College, Fulton, Missouri, March 5, 1946), https://www.nationalchurchill museum.org/sinews-of-peace-iron-curtain-speech.html.

13   **"I have never seen":** Associated Press, "Thrills to Royal Show," *The Kansas City Times*, June 8, 1951.

13   **Clifton Truman Daniel:** Interview with author, April 12, 2021.

14   **As expectation built:** Hedda Hopper, "Hollywood," *New York Daily News*, October 15, 1951.

16   *The Des Moines Register:* Fletcher Knebel, "Capital Cheers Royal Couple," *The Des Moines Register*, November 1, 1951.

17   **As she pointed:** Pierre Berton, *The Royal Family* (New York: Knopf, 1954), 197.

19   **She left a lasting:** Dorothy Roe, "Marguerite Higgins Is Named Woman of the Year in AP Poll," *The Charlotte News*, July 14, 1951.

CHAPTER 2

22   **Back in June 1945:** "Order of Merit for Gen. Eisenhower," *The Daily Telegraph*, June 13, 1945.

23   **"We all dived under the table":** Chris Hastings, "Day That the Queen and George VI Hid from Eisenhower Under a Table: The Bizarre Royal Conversations That Didn't Make It into Landmark Film," *Daily Mail*, January 15, 2011, https:// www.dailymail.co.uk/news/article-1347513/Day-Queen -George-VI-hid-Eisenhower-table-bizarre-Royal -conversations-didnt-make-landmark-film.html.

27   **As *Life* magazine had pointed out:** "*Life* on the Newsfronts of the World," *Life*, October 2, 1942, 34.

27　**Eisenhower furiously threatened:** David J. Katz, "Waging Financial War," *The US Army War College Quarterly: Parameters* 43, no. 4, January 12, 2013.

27–28　**The day before she departed:** Pimlott, *The Queen*, 284.

28　**Capitol police chief Robert V. Murray:** "President Hails Free World Bond in Toast to Queen," *The Philadelphia Inquirer*, October 18, 1957.

28　**The Queen would stay:** Associated Press, "Queen Mother Is Guest at White House," *The Asheville Times*, November 5, 1954.

30　**"That was the gayest, prettiest dinner":** Jacqueline Cochran, "Gift of Personal Statement to the Dwight D. Eisenhower Library," 60–63, https://www.eisenhowerlibrary.gov/sites /default/files/research/oral-histories/oral-history-transcripts /cochran-jacqueline.pdf.

31　**Macmillan announced that very day:** "Macmillan-Ike Parley Set," *The Indianapolis Star*, October 18, 1957.

32　**The physicality of the sport:** "No Injury! Elizabeth Is Amazed," *The Charlotte Observer*, October 20, 1957.

32　**The store manager had been called:** "The Queen Walks to Give US Crowd Good View," *The Daily Telegraph*, October 21, 1957.

33　**"Why did she have to cross the Atlantic to become REAL?":** "Why Did She Have to Cross the Atlantic to Become REAL?," *Daily Herald*, October 23, 1957.

34　**the Queen remark to her husband:** Wiley T. Buchanan Jr., *Red Carpet at the White House* (New York: Dutton, 1964), 149–50.

36　**Elizabeth joined sailors at the rail:** Gwen Morgan, "Queen Gives Hand, but Ship Scrapes Again," *Chicago Tribune*, June 27, 1959.

36　**Prince Philip, who held the highest Royal Navy rank:** United Press International–Canadian Press, "Philip Guilty, He Bashed Yacht," *The Calgary Albertan*, June 25, 1959.

37　**This visit was all about relaxation:** Robert Young, "Queen Welcomes Ike to Chat at Fireside," *Chicago Tribune*, August 29, 1959.

39 **Susan Eisenhower:** Susan Eisenhower, interview with author, April 10, 2023.

40 **"At this moment":** John S. D. Eisenhower, *General Ike: A Personal Reminiscence* (New York: Free Press, 2003), 216.

40 **Describing his 1959 visit:** Dwight David Eisenhower, *Waging Peace* (New York City: Doubleday, 1965), 360.

41 **Jack Woodward:** Jack M. Woodward, interview with Dwight D. Eisenhower Library, May 28, 1992, https://www .eisenhowerlibrary.gov/sites/default/files/research/oral -histories/oral-history-transcripts/woodward-jack-512.pdf.

Chapter 3

44 **Asked by the New York stylist Simon Doonan:** Beth Teitell, "GOP Candidates Dress Down for the Campaign Trail," *The Boston Globe*, January 7, 2012.

45 **"Met the king this morning":** Will Swift, *The Kennedys Amidst the Gathering Storm: A Thousand Days in London, 1938–1940* (New York: Smithsonian Books, 2008), 138.

46 **Joe recorded that the princess:** Swift, *The Kennedys Amidst the Gathering Storm*, 153–54.

48 **He formally offered his resignation:** Louis M. Lyons, "Kennedy Says Democracy All Done," *Boston Globe Sunday*, November 10, 1940.

49 **Where Joe had scorned Churchill:** John F. Kennedy, "Remarks upon Signing Proclamation Conferring Honorary Citizenship on Sir Winston Churchill," The American Presidency Project, April 9, 1963, https://www.presidency .ucsb.edu/documents/remarks-upon-signing-proclamation -conferring-honorary-citizenship-sir-winston-churchill.

49 **"I worked at the American embassy":** HelmerReenberg, "June 5, 1961—President John F. Kennedy's Remarks to the Staff of the US Embassy in London, England," uploaded October 28, 2015, YouTube video, 5:51, https://www.youtube .com/watch?v=vlfmvt1EzFc.

50 **The prime minister had briefed the Queen:** Sally Bedell Smith, *Elizabeth the Queen* (New York: Random House Trade Paperback, 2012), 156.

50 **Ormsby-Gore recorded later:** Gary Ginsberg, *First Friends* (New York: Twelve, 2021), 259.

51 **told the Queen that Kennedy:** Bedell Smith, *Elizabeth the Queen*, 157.

52 **According to Gore Vidal's account:** Gore Vidal, *Palimpsest* (New York: Random House, 1995), 372.

53 **"The queen had her revenge":** Vidal, *Palimpsest*, 372.

53 **Jackie found Elizabeth "pretty heavy-going":** Craig Brown, *Hello Goodbye Hello: A Circle of 101 Remarkable Meetings* (New York: Simon & Schuster Paperbacks, 2013), 34.

53 **He later relayed to Margaret:** Craig Brown, *Ma'am Darling* (London: 4th Estate, 2017), 256.

54 **in his diaries published in 1976:** Cecil Beaton, *The Restless Years: Diaries 1955–63* (London: Weidenfeld and Nicholson, 1976).

54 **Nixon reportedly asked a Black guest:** Martin Meredith, *The Fate of Africa: A History of the Continent Since Independence* (New York: PublicAffairs, 2011), 26.

55 **She told Macmillan: "How silly I should look":** Lord Boateng, *Hansard* 824, column 458, September 10, 2022.

56 **Ghana's government-controlled press:** Bedell Smith, *Elizabeth the Queen*, 158.

56 **Macmillan enthused about:** Pimlott, *The Queen*, 307.

56 **Upon her return, he wasted:** Bedell Smith, *Elizabeth the Queen*, 159.

57 **One evening Jackie walked in:** Ginsberg, *First Friends*, 263.

CHAPTER 4

62 **The hubbub surrounding the visit of Margaret:** Lady Bird Johnson, Oral History Transcript, interview by Michael L. Gillette, LBJ Library Oral Histories, March 8, 1991, 2.

65   **Ormsby-Gore, now Lord Harlech:** Jonathan Colman, *A "Special Relationship"?: Harold Wilson, Lyndon B. Johnson and Anglo-American Relations "at the Summit," 1964–8* (Manchester, UK: Manchester University Press, 2018).

67   **As the ninety-year-old:** "President's Daily Diary Entry, 1/17/1965," LBJ Presidential Library, accessed August 12, 2022, https://discoverlbj.org/item/pdd-19650117.

67   **Johnson invited a small group of journalists:** Associated Press, Frank Cormier, "President Available in an Emergency," *The Arizona Republic*, January 24, 1965.

67   **However, what his doctor:** "President's Daily Diary Entry, 1/24/1965," LBJ Presidential Library, accessed August 12, 2022, https://discoverlbj.org/item/pdd-19650124.

68   **Hand recalled:** Lloyd Hand, interview with author, August 16, 2022.

71   **"When the visit was over":** Hand, interview with author.

72   **Garland left the messenger:** Hadley Meares, "Why Princess Margaret Was the Worst Party Guest," Biography.com, December 10, 2021.

73   **His official diary:** "President's Daily Diary Entry, 10/8/1965," LBJ Presidential Library, accessed August 12, 2022, https://discoverlbj.org/item/pdd-19651008.

74   **"In spite of the fact":** Luci Baines Johnson, interview with author, March 15, 2023.

76   **"Mark Twain once said":** "Toasts of the President and Princess Margaret," The American Presidency Project, November 17, 1965, https://www.presidency.ucsb.edu/documents/toasts-the-president-and-princess-margaret.

76   **One senior advisor:** "Folder, 'McGeorge Bundy, Vol. 12, July, 1965 [1 of 2],' Memos to the President, NSF, Box 4," LBJ Presidential Library, accessed August 12, 2022, https://www.discoverlbj.org/item/nsf-memos-b04-f01.

77   **Guests told Princess Margaret:** Christopher Warwick, *Princess Margaret: A Life of Contrasts* (London: Andre Deutsch, 2000).

77   **despite the late night:** "President's Daily Diary Entry, 11/18 /1965," LBJ Presidential Library, accessed August 12, 2022, https://discoverlbj.org/item/pdd-19651118.

79   **Arriving by Concorde:** John-Carlos Estrada, "#TBT: Queen Elizabeth & Prince Philip Historic Trip to Austin Three Decades Ago," CBSAustin.com, May 20, 2021, https://cbsaustin.com/news/local/tbt-queen-elizabeth-ii-historic -trip-to-austin-three-decades-ago.

79   **"Queen Elizabeth's ability":** Johnson, interview with author.

CHAPTER 5

81   **Charles recalled the visit:** Max Foster, "Spotlight: Charles and Camilla," CNN, March 14, 2015, https://transcripts.cnn .com/show/cspo/date/2015-03-14/segment/01.

84   **"In the three days":** William H. Stoneman, "Favorable Impression Made by Nixon on England Visit," *Fort Worth Star-Telegram*, November 28, 1958.

85   **"Winston Churchill called":** United Press Limited, "Nixon, Wilson Meet, Review World Problems," *The Greenville (SC) News*, February 25, 1969.

89   **"the science of opening:** "The Times View on Prince Philip: The Monarchy's Rock," *The Times*, April 10, 2021.

90   **"We go into the red next year":** "Royal Family 'May Move to Smaller Premises,'" *The Times*, November 10, 1969.

92   **Nixon had sent Tricia:** Associated Press, "Tricia Nixon Wants to Meet Prince of Wales," *Lancaster (PA) New Era*, July 1, 1969.

93   **"He conversed with the birds:** Christopher Lydon, "Prince Charles Talks with Nixon for over an Hour," *The New York Times*, July 19, 1970.

94   **Replying to a dinner toast:** George W. Bush, "Remarks at a State Dinner Honoring Prince Charles and Duchess Camilla of the United Kngdom," The American Presidency Project, November 2, 2005.

95 **When Nixon landed:** Associated Press, "Nixon Confers with Heath in Britain," *The Racine (WI) Journal-Times*, October 3, 1970.

CHAPTER 6

98 **In the delicate dance:** National Security Advisor Presidential Correspondence, "United Kingdom—Queen Elizabeth II," Gerald R. Ford Presidential Library, https://www.fordlibrarymuseum.gov/library/document/0351/1555868.pdf.

100 **On September 25:** "Queen Elizabeth's Visit (July 1976)," John Marsh Files, Gerald R. Ford Presidential Library, https://www.fordlibrarymuseum.gov/library/document/0067/1563326.pdf.

101 **"It has been our policy":** "7/7–10/76—State Visit of Queen Elizabeth II and Prince Philip (Great Britain) (3)," Betty Ford White House Papers, Gerald R. Ford Presidential Library, https://www.fordlibrarymuseum.gov/library/document/0018/81555793.pdf.

105 **"The Royal Yacht's function":** Susan Crosland, *Tony Crosland* (London: Coronet, 1983), 344.

106 **"One plants one's feet apart":** Crosland, *Tony Crosland*, 346.

108 **Ahead of lunch:** Stephan Salisbury, "My Day with the Queen," *The Philadelphia Daily News*, September 12, 2022.

109 **According to Gerald Bodmer:** Alice Cary, "The Story Behind the Queen's Lifelong Devotion to Launer Handbags," *Vogue*, September 17, 2022, https://www.vogue.com/article/the-story-behind-the-queens-lifelong-devotion-to-launer-handbags.

110 **Maintaining the polite inscrutability:** Sarah Bradford, *Elizabeth* (New York: Farrar, Straus and Giroux, 1996), 364–65.

110 **At one point during the evening:** Crosland, *Tony Crosland*, 347.

111 **Brown and his wife:** Crosland, *Tony Crosland*, 348.

113 **Betty Ford had put:** "Maria Downs," Gerald R. Ford Presidential Foundation, accessed August 2, 2022, https://

geraldrfordfoundation.org/centennial/oralhistory/maria
-downs.

116 **As Betty Ford admitted:** Donnie Radcliffe, "Being Dealt a Queen, a Jack and a Headache," *The Washington Post*, March 6, 1983.

117 **"We had two great hits":** Michelle Tauber, "Mr. President, 'It Was Muskrats': Toni Tennille on the Time She Sang 'Muskrat Love' for Queen Elizabeth—in the White House!," *People*, March 19, 2016.

CHAPTER 7

124 **On that occasion:** Graham Hovey, "Carter, in Warm Welcome to Callaghan, Affirms Special Ties to Britain," *The New York Times*, March 11, 1977.

126 **Armstrong explained:** "US President Jimmy Carter Visits Newcastle in 1977 and Becomes an Adopted Geordie," *Co-Curate*, accessed August 9, 2022, https://co-curate.ncl .ac.uk/resources/view/67378.

128 **Carter later recalled:** Jimmy Carter, "International Economic Summit Meeting Exchange with Reporters Following a State Dinner at Buckingham Palace," online by Gerhard Peters and John T. Woolley, The American Presidency Project https:// www.presidency.ucsb.edu/node/244115.

128 **For Carter, dressed in a black tuxedo:** London United Press International, "Carter Star at Royal Banquet," *The Shreveport Times*, May 8, 1977.

128 **In his own discussions:** International Economic Summit Meeting Exchange.

129 **It was only revealed to the general public:** Pendennis [pseud.], "Lèse-majesté," *The Observer*, February 13, 1983.

129 **In a conversation recounted by William Shawcross:** William Shawcross, *The Queen Mother: The Official Biography* (New York: Vintage Books, 2010), 900.

130 **He clearly felt:** Jimmy Carter, *A Full Life: Reflections at Ninety* (New York: Simon & Schuster, 2015), 147.

130–31 **the international talks in London:** "Mr. Carter's Summit," *The Times*, May 9, 1977.

131 **Five years later:** "Dylan Thomas Is Honored by Britain," *The New York Times*, March 2, 1982.

131 **Jimmy Carter's handwritten note:** Courtesy of the Jimmy Carter Presidential Library and Museum.

132 **They were invited:** Sally Quinn, "The Royal Jubilee; Elizabeth's Kingdom Celebrates Her Silver Jubilee," *The Washington Post*, June 8, 1977.

132 **Robert Fellowes, her assistant private secretary:** "Collection: Office of Staff Secretary; Series: Presidential Files; Folder: 6/25/77; Container 28," Jimmy Carter Presidential Library and Museum, June 25, 1977, https:// www.jimmycarterlibrary.gov/digital_library/sso/148878/28 /SSO_148878_028_01.pdf.

133 **When Walter Washington, the mayor of the District of Columbia:** Donnie Radcliffe, "Glimpses of a Gracious Princess Royal," *The Washington Post*, June 17, 1977.

134 **"I was delighted":** Courtesy of the Jimmy Carter Presidential Library and Museum.

CHAPTER 8

136 **"Rarely have I enjoyed myself":** Janice Kleinschmidt, "From Here to Eternity," *Palm Springs Life*, November 30, 2018, https://www.palmspringslife.com/sunnylands-history.

137 **Sheila Tate, Mrs. Reagan's press secretary:** Associated Press, "Nancy's Nod to Queen Confounds British Press," *The Shreveport Journal*, July 29, 1981.

137 **Linda Faulkner, the First Lady's social secretary:** Carolyn Lesh, "The Particulars of Princely Etiquette," *The Dallas Morning News*, February 16, 1986.

137 **The elder Elizabeth:** Bedell Smith, *Elizabeth the Queen*, 302.

138 **Sir Nicholas "Nico" Henderson:** Gregory Katz, "Keep Queen Elizabeth II Waiting? Ronald Reagan Got Away with

It, Newly Released Papers Show," Associated Press, December 28, 2012.

138 **"I need hardly say that":** Katz, "Keep Queen Elizabeth II Waiting?"

139 **Reagan would also be the first:** George Skelton, "Parliament to Hear Reagan," *Los Angeles Times*, March 7, 1982.

139 **"It would look petty":** David Blair, "Ronald Reagan Ignored Queen's Windsor Castle Invitation," *The Telegraph*, December 28, 2012, https://www.telegraph.co.uk/news/uknews/9769558 /Ronald-Reagan-ignored-Queens-Windsor-Castle-invitation .html.

139 **Deaver underlined its importance:** Bedell Smith, *Elizabeth the Queen*, 311.

140 **Reagan asked Alexander Haig:** Times Wire Services, "US Cuts Off Aid to Argentina," *Los Angeles Times*, April 30, 1982.

141 **Its full extent was not revealed until:** Carlos Osorio, Sarah Christiano, and Erin Maskell, ed., "Reagan on the Falklands/ Malvinas: 'Give Maggie Enough to Carry On . . . ,'" The National Security Archive, April 1, 2012, https://nsarchive2 .gwu.edu/NSAEBB/NSAEBB374.

142 **Larry Speakes, the acting White House press secretary:** David Hewson, "Reagans Join the Queen at Windsor," *The Times*, June 8, 1982.

142 **In his personal diary:** White House Diaries, "Monday, June 7, 1982," Ronald Reagan Presidential Foundation & Institute, accessed December 19, 2022, https://www.reaganfoundation .org/ronald-reagan/white-house-diaries/diary-entry-06 071982.

142 **Reagan rode Centennial:** "RCMP and the Monarchy," Royal Canadian Mounted Police Veterans' Association, Vancouver Division, September 6, 2012, http://www .rcmpveteransvancouver.com/rcmp-and-the-monarchy.

143 **Two styles of horsemanship:** David Hewson, "Two Styles of Horsemanship," *The Times*, June 9, 1982.

147 **"Lee and I wanted":** "Sunnylands Spotlight: Queen Elizabeth and Prince Philip Visit the Annenbergs," Sunnylands,

February 27, 2014, https://sunnylands.org/article/sunnylands
-spotlight-queen-elizabeth-comes-to-lunch.

147 **Following a Caribbean tour:** Linnea Lannon, "Queen
Matron: Fashion Is Clearly Not Her Cup of Tea," *Detroit Free
Press*, March 2, 1983.

147 **while another thought the hat:** Fred Bruning, "Cloudy Calif.
Cheers the Queen," *Newsday*, February 27, 1983.

148 **The Queen noted that:** "Sunnylands Spotlight: Queen
Elizabeth and Prince Philip Visit the Annenbergs."

148 **"Acting is easy," Burns said:** Bob Thomas, "Hollywood Stars
Dish Out Royalty," Associated Press, February 27, 1983.

149 **"The queen was a wonderful sport":** Nancy Reagan with
William Novak, *My Turn: The Memoirs of Nancy Reagan* (New
York: Random House, 1989), 262.

149–50 **"The royal visit chewed":** Lou Cannon and Donnie Radcliffe,
"Taking the Coast by Storm," *The Washington Post*, March 2,
1983.

150 **The Queen appeared to enjoy:** Bedell Smith, *Elizabeth the
Queen*, 320.

150 **After accompanying the royals:** Donnie Radcliffe and
Katharine MacDonald, "Reigning on Her Parade; The
Reagan's Glittering Dinner After the Queen's Day on the
Town," *The Washington Post*, March 4, 1983.

150 **"It was not the Queen":** Bedell Smith, *Elizabeth the
Queen*, 320.

151 **"I was so excited":** Radcliffe and MacDonald, "Reigning on
Her Parade."

151 **Packard said the royals:** Radcliffe and MacDonald,
"Reigning on Her Parade."

151 **Visitors to Buckingham Palace:** Hayley Maitland, "The
Queen's Most Memorable Encounters with American
Presidents Through the Decades," *Vogue*, September 14, 2022.

152 **That night Elizabeth:** Radcliffe and MacDonald, "Reigning
on Her Parade."

152–53 **Diana Walker, a *Time* photographer:** "Walker Webcast:
History in Focus!: Diana Walker, *Time* Magazine White

House Photographer," interview by Willy Walker, *Walker Webcast*, November 1, 2022, https://www.walkerdunlop.com /insights/2022/11/01/history-focus-diana-walker-time -magazine-white-house-photographer.

154 **Ahead of the political and ceremonial meetings:** "London Red Carpet for Reagans," United Press International, June 5, 1984.

154 **Reagan wrote delightedly:** White House Diaries, "Sunday, June 3, 1984," Ronald Reagan Presidential Foundation & Institute, accessed August 7, 2022, https://www .reaganfoundation.org/ronald-reagan/white-house-diaries /diary-entry-06031984.

154 **Harold Brooks-Baker:** "Experts Link Reagan to Ancient Irish King," *The New York Times*, April 8, 1984.

157 **The Associated Press noted:** Edith M. Lederer, "Queen Bestows Knighthood on Former President," Associated Press, June 15, 1989.

157 **Sir William Heseltine:** William Heseltine, interview with author, January 15, 2023.

CHAPTER 9

158 **On a sweltering May morning:** Henry Allen, "Hail, and Thunder, to the Queen," *The Washington Post*, May 15, 1991.

159 **"All I got is a talking hat!":** Robert Hardman, "He Nicknamed the Queen the Talking Hat After She Was Hidden Behind Her Microphone," *Daily Mail*, December 2, 2018.

161 **The Queen, who originally:** Bedell Smith, *Elizabeth the Queen*, 324.

161 **"Open it!":** Knight Ridder News Service, "Bush Winds Up Trip with Thatcher's Praise," *Lexington Herald Leader*, June 2, 1989.

161 **"It's very quiet":** Terence Hunt, "Bush, Thatcher Disagree on Refugee Issue," *Honolulu Star-Bulletin*, June 1, 1989.

162 **She chatted with Elizabeth:** Barbara Bush, *A Memoir* (New York: Lisa Drew Books, 1994), 298.

164 **"The next morning":** Laurie Firestone, "An Affair to Remember," C-SPAN, April 21, 2007, https://www.c-span.org/video/?197550-1/an-affair-remember.

164 **Under questioning from the White House press corps:** "Public Papers: Question-and-Answer-Session with Reporters," George H. W. Bush Presidential Library & Museum, May 15, 1991, https://bush41library.tamu.edu/archives/public-papers/2990.

165 **he started treatment:** Timothy J. McNulty, "Bush Tones Down Activities on First Road Trip Since Heart Scare," *Chicago Tribune*, May 11, 1991.

166 **"I jokingly told Her Majesty":** Bush, *A Memoir*, 414.

166 **Barbara Bush quickly:** Mike Allen, "Dubya's Visit with QEII," *The Washington Post*, July 20, 2001.

166 **"I teased her that":** Bedell Smith, *Elizabeth the Queen*, 358.

167 **"She was very happy to watch":** "Queen Sighs, Enraptured Crowd Cheers Monarch's Arrival in U.S.," *South Florida Sun Sentinel*, May 15, 1991.

168 **Much to the relief:** Bush, *A Memoir*, 415.

169 **The historically impoverished:** Bush, *A Memoir*, 416.

170 **She greeted the Queen:** "Queen Tours Widely Differing Realms on 2nd Day of Visit," *The Baltimore Sun*, May 16, 1991.

170 **It had been Frazier's plan:** Linda Wheeler, "An Open-Arms Welcome for the Queen," *The Washington Post*, May 15, 1991.

170 **While "exhibiting faint alarm":** "Queen Tours Widely Differing Realms on 2nd Day of Visit."

170 **It was described:** Phil McCombs, "Warm Hugs and Cold Beer for the Royals," *The Washington Post*, May 16, 1991.

170 **"Alice was so innocent":** Martin Austermuhle, "Thousands of Miles from Buckingham Palace, Queen Elizabeth II Will Always Be Remembered on One D.C. Street," *DCist*, September 8, 2022, https://dcist.com/story/22/09/08/queen-elizabeth-ii-commemorated-dc-street-name.

171 **Prince Philip caused:** McCombs, "Warm Hugs and Cold Beer for the Royals."

171 **When Fellowes raised the possibility:** *Elizabeth R: A Year in the Life of the Queen*, directed by Edward Mirzoeff, aired February 6, 1992, on BBC One.

171 **"All that independence-from-England":** Jean Marbella, "Wild Applause Greets Monarch at Memorial Stadium," *The Baltimore Sun*, May 16, 1991.

172 **She spoke "the old-fashioned way":** Myron S. Waldman, "Pomp and Protest for Queen," *Newsday*, May 17, 1991.

174 **Motherwell composed:** Associated Press, "War Tribute March Keys Queen's Dinner for Bush," *Tulsa World*, May 17, 1991.

174 **"After I'd finished":** Robert Bieselin, "Queen's Piper Gives Concert 'Cross the Pond," NorthJersey.com, October 15, 2008.

175 **Ford, then aged seventy-seven:** *Elizabeth R: A Year in the Life of the Queen.*

176 **Out of office for almost a year:** Bush, *A Memoir*, 531.

CHAPTER 10

178 **Nevertheless there was:** Dickie Arbiter, interview with author, June 5, 2023.

178 **According to genealogists:** Eugene Robinson, "Born to Rule?," *The Washington Post*, October 22, 1992.

179 **Clinton joked:** Bill Clinton, *My Life* (New York: Alfred A. Knopf, 2004), 440.

179 **The tabloids had:** Joanne Merriweather, "London Papers Publish 'Camillagate' Love Tape," United Press International, January 26, 1993.

179 **Charles's popularity plummeted:** Amy Mackelden, "Yes, *The Crown*'s Tampongate Really Happened," *Harper's Bazaar*, November 12, 2022.

179 **This difficult time:** "UK Tories—Major Unaware of Aid to Bush Campaign," Reuters News, February 22, 1993.

180 **"After the election":** Clinton, *My Life*, 433.

180 *The Sunday Times* **berated:** "Adams and the Alliance—Clinton's Foreign Policy," editorial, *The Sunday Times*, February 6, 1994.

180 **The two leaders began:** Rick Sebak, "Bill Clinton's Most Unusual Visit to Pittsburgh," *Pittsburgh* magazine, December 21, 2015.

181 **"It would have been":** Walter R. Mears, "In Rain and Wind, Clinton Honors D-Day," Associated Press, June 4, 1994.

182 **Dressed in a blue gown:** The Court Jeweller, "The Belgian Sapphire Tiara," *The Court Jeweller*, September 1, 2016, www.thecourtjeweller.com/2016/09/the-belgian-sapphire-tiara.html.

182 **This was Clinton's first:** Clinton, *My Life*, 599.

183 **He described the royal yacht:** William Shawcross, "The Last Icon," *Vanity Fair*, June 2002.

183 **The First Lady recalled:** Anders Hagstrom, "Hillary Clinton Compares Nancy Pelosi to Queen Elizabeth II, Calls Her 'Gutsiest Woman in Politics,'" Fox News, September 12, 2022, https://www.foxnews.com/politics/hillary-clinton-compares-nancy-pelosi-queen-elizabeth-calls-her-gutsiest-woman-politics.

183 **As it happens:** "A Hairdo with Hold," *New York Daily News*, June 5, 1994.

184 **Captain Chuck Connor:** Terence Hunt, "Saluting the Queen, Elevating the Admiral," Associated Press, June 5, 1994.

184 **Clinton observed:** Clinton, *My Life*, 600.

185 **In her first international appearance:** WWD Staff, "Princess Di Draws the Spotlight at White House Super Sale Event," *Women's Wear Daily*, September 25, 1996.

186 **British officials scrambled:** Valentine Low, "Bill Clinton Turned Down Tea with the Queen and Jam with Blair," *The Times*, July 20, 2021.

187 **they ordered seared tuna:** Anton Antonowicz, "All the President's Menu," *Daily Mirror*, May 30, 1997.

188 **The day cemented relations:** James Landale, "A Controversial Guest," *Diplomat*, May 16, 2018, https://diplomatmagazine .com/a-controversial-guest.

188 **The Clintons heard the news:** Kathy Lewis, "Clinton Saddened by Death," *The Dallas Morning News*, September 1, 1997.

188 **Nancy Reagan also:** Nancy Reagan, "An American Favorite," *Newsweek*, September 15, 1997.

188 **"she was America's Princess":** John Whitesides, "Americans Mourn 'Fairy-Tale' Princess," Reuters, September 1, 1997.

188 **Elaine Showalter:** John Carlin, "Diana 1961–1997—Star of the States—Nothing Short of an American Dream," *Independent on Sunday*, September 7, 1997.

189 **"I am writing to say":** Queen Elizabeth letter to Hillary Clinton, William J. Clinton Presidential Library & Museum (OA/ID 1645), September 10, 1997.

190 **He arrived in Britain:** "Bill Clinton Has Made a Big Difference to Northern Ireland," *The Economist*, December 16, 2000.

191 **The president told fellow drinkers:** Helen Rumbelow, "What the President Bought His Women in Notting Hill . . . ," *The Times*, December 15, 2000.

191 **On Air Force One:** Deb Reichmann, "Clinton Talks with Queen Elizabeth II for Final Time as President," Associated Press, December 14, 2000.

192 **After Elizabeth's death:** Bill Clinton, interview by Rita Braver, CBS News, September 11, 2022, https://www.cbsnews .com/news/former-president-bill-clinton-on-queen-elizabeth -ii-she-was-an-amazing-woman.

Chapter 11

194 **Their previous run-in:** Ben Macintyre, "Bush Vows to Bury 'Obsolete' Missile Treaty," *The Times*, July 18, 2001.

195 **Andrew's ex-wife:** Jim Kresse, "Duchess Narrowly Escapes Disaster," *The Spokesman-Review* (Spokane, WA), September 21, 2001.

196 **President Bush vowed:** George W. Bush, "Statement by the President in His Address to the Nation," George W. Bush White House, September 11, 2001, https://georgewbush -whitehouse.archives.gov/news/releases/2001/09/20010911-16 .html.

196 **Elizabeth II immediately conveyed:** Jason Hopps, "Britain on High Alert After US Attacks," Reuters, September 11, 2001.

196 **"The United States is not":** Citizen News Services, "A World in Mourning: Thousands Turn Out to Express Sympathy," *Ottawa Citizen*, September 14, 2001.

197 **According to one observer:** Richard Kay, "Tears of the Queen," *Sunday Mail*, September 16, 2001.

197 **Prince Philip read:** Tim Reid, "Bells of St. Paul's Toll for the Dead," *The Times*, September 15, 2001.

197–98 **It really captured:** William Shawcross, "The Last Icon," *Vanity Fair*, June 2002.

198 **The 9/11 tragedy touched:** Ben Macintyre, "Outrage Led to 'Surge of Human Spirit'—Terror in America," *The Times*, September 21, 2001.

198 **Buckingham Palace said:** Jonathan Petre, "Queen Gives Cash to Aid New York Victims," *The Sunday Telegraph*, September 23, 2001.

198 **Philip appeared:** Mike Allen, "Dubya's Visit with QEII," *The Washington Post*, July 20, 2001.

198 **Barbara Bush, the nineteen-year-old:** Alan Hamilton, "Dry Bush Gets Soaked While Laughter Has a Sniff of the Port," *The Times*, July 20, 2001.

199 **Bush failed to secure:** Bob Deans, "US Goes into Summit Alone on Missile Defense, Blair Politely Declines to Endorse Proposal, Despite Another Pitch from Bush," *Austin American-Statesman*, July 20, 2001.

199 **"I really admire":** Jill Lawless, "WHITE HOUSE NOTEBOOK: Bushes Lunch with the Queen," Associated Press, July 19, 2001.

200 **More than a million:** Flora Holmes, "Public Attitudes to Military Interventionism," The British Foreign Policy Group, January 2020, https://bfpg.co.uk/wp-content/uploads/2020 /01/Public-Attitudes-to-Military-Intervention-1.pdf.

200 **The president put:** Jonathan Mann, Robin Oakley, and John King, "President George Bush Visits Britain," CNN International: Insight, November 18, 2003.

201 **This was ruled out:** Alan Hamilton, "Tradition Moves onto Safer Ground for President," *The Times*, November 19, 2003.

202 **She pointed out:** Paul Waugh, "A Day of Pomp, Pageantry and Protests as the President Proclaims His Mission to the World," *The Independent*, November 20, 2003.

203 **Bush later met privately:** Richard W. Stevenson, "Bush, in Britain, Urges Europeans to Fight Terror," *The New York Times*, November 20, 2003.

203 **"Had I been a terrorist":** Jill Lawless, "British Government Launches Investigation After Tabloid Journalist Hired as Royal Footman," Associated Press, November 19, 2003.

203 **The famously no-fuss:** David Frost, "Interview with Sir David Frost of BBC Television," *Weekly Compilation of Presidential Documents* 39, no. 47, November 24, 2003, 1625.

206 **She had a Stars and Stripes:** David Charter and Sam Lister, "Make Mine a Pint . . . of Alcohol-Free Lager," *The Times*, November 22, 2003.

206 **A grim-faced Bush:** Edwin Chen: "Bush Offers Help in 'New Front'; President Says Turkey Is Now a Battleground for Terrorists in Light of Bombings. He Promises US Aid in Hunting 'Al Qaeda–Type Killers,'" *Los Angeles Times*, November 22, 2003.

207 **The institution of monarchy:** Catherine Mayer, "Queen Elizabeth II," *Time*, May 3, 2007.

208 **Cathy Holland:** Adam Hochberg, "Reporter's Notebook: Queen Elizabeth Pays Tribute to Slain Students," NPR, *Weekend Edition*, May 5, 2007.

208 **The Queen's first speech:** Bob Lewis, "Britain's Queen Discusses Diversity in Virginia," Associated Press, May 4, 2007.

208 **Elizabeth II was escorted:** Sonja Barisic, "Virginia: Cheney Escorts Queen on Jamestown tour," Associated Press, May 5, 2007.

209 **She was greeted:** Camilla Tominey, "Queen of Inspiration," *The Express on Sunday*, May 6, 2007.

209 **Farish was spotted:** "Queen Fulfils Derby Dream with a Day at the Track; Monarch Joins Star-Studded Louisville Crowd," *Calgary Herald*, May 6, 2007.

210 **First, though:** Tamara Jones and Roxanne Roberts, "Capital Goes Gaga Over the Queen for a Day," *The Washington Post*, May 8, 2007.

210 **"Dr. Rice and I":** Mrs. Bush's Remarks in a Media Preview for the State Dinner in Honor of Her Majesty Queen Elizabeth II and His Royal Highness The Prince Philip Duke of Edinburgh, George W. Bush White House, accessed July 16, 2023, https://georgewbush-whitehouse.archives.gov/news /releases/2007/05/20070507-5.html.

210 **This was a lot easier:** Charles Gibson, "A Royal Visit: The White House Honors the Queen," *ABC World News with Charles Gibson*, May 7, 2007.

211 **With just 134 guests:** "Fit for a Queen: White House Prepares for State Dinner," *ABC World News Sunday*, May 6, 2007.

211 **The thirteen tables were adorned:** "White House Prepares Lavish Welcome for British Queen," Agence France-Presse, May 6, 2007.

212 **The president observed:** "President Bush Exchanges Toasts with Her Majesty Queen Elizabeth II," George W. Bush White House, May 7, 2007, https://georgewbush-whitehouse .archives.gov/news/releases/2007/05/20070507-13.html.

CHAPTER 12

214 **In the run-up:** Ben Macintyre and Paul Orengoh, "Beatings and Abuse Made Barack Obama's Grandfather Loathe the British," *The Times*, December 3, 2008.

216 **Obama's fascination:** Jane Ridley, "Family Is Proud of Bam's Royal Schedule," *New York Daily News*, March 31, 2009.

217 **Obama was overheard:** "President Obama at Buckingham Palace," C-SPAN, April 1, 2009, https://www.c-span.org /video/?285025-1/president-obama-buckingham-palace.

217 **The Duke of Edinburgh, chuckling:** Laura Dixon and *Times Online*, "Protocol Is Abandoned as Michelle Obama Cosies Up to Queen," *The Times*, April 2, 2009.

217 **"Sitting with the Queen":** Michelle Obama, *Becoming* (New York: Crown, 2018), 317.

218 **Later he added:** "Spotlight: A Conversation with President Barack Obama," Inbound Conference, Digitopia, accessed February 9, 2023, https://www.digitopia.agency/blog/inbound -2022-day-three.

219 **Finding themselves standing:** Obama, *Becoming*, 317.

219 **Michelle wrote that:** Obama, *Becoming*, 318.

220 **"This was a mutual":** Valentine Low, "Queen and Michelle Obama, the Story Behind a Touching Moment," *The Times*, April 2, 2009.

221 **Obama succeeded at least:** Donna Smith, "Obama's IMF Pledge Could Be Tough Sell in Washington," Reuters, April 3, 2009.

221 **As they said goodbye:** Valentine Low, "Obamas to Make State Visit (a Month After the Big Day," *The Times*, February 18, 2011.

221 **"There clearly is":** Reuters Staff, "Michelle Obama Finds a New Friend in Britain's Queen," Reuters, June 14, 2009.

222 **Just before heading:** Andrew Marr, "Transcript: Andrew Marr Interview with President Obama," BBC News, May 22, 2011, https://www.bbc.com/news/uk-13473065.

223 **"To see Her Majesty":** Giles Whittell, Philippe Naughton, and David Byers, "Ash Cloud Forces Obama to Leave Ireland Early," *The Times*, May 23, 2011.

223 **They were met:** Mark Hennessy, "US Ambassador in London Hosts Couple After Early Arrival," *The Irish Times*, May 24, 2011.

224 **Their wedding ceremony:** Nellie Andreeva, "23 Million Americans Watch Royal Wedding, Beating U.S. Audience for Charles and Di's; UK Viewership Can't Match 1981 Nuptials," *Deadline*, April 30, 2011, https://deadline.com /2011/04/so-how-were-the-royal-wedding-ratings-126926.

224 **The secret?:** Rebecca English, "Just £1.50, the Secret Weapon That Preserves Her Modesty," *Daily Mail*, April 14, 2012.

224 **In the wake of:** Chris Greenwood and Rebecca English, "The Car That Thinks It's a Tank: Inside Obama's 'Beast' Cadillac That Is Being Flown from the U.S. to Drive down the Mall," *Daily Mail*, May 23, 2011.

225 **Mrs. Obama was given:** Maureen Groppe, "Royal Bling to Handmade: 70 Years of Iconic Gifts US Presidents Exchanged with the Queen," *USA Today*, September 18, 2022.

225–26 **The two left-handed leaders:** David Byers, Jenny Booth, and Philippe Naughton, "Live: Obama at State Banquet," *The Times*, May 24, 2011.

228 **Obama joked afterward:** "Obama Makes Light of Toast Hiccup at Queen Banquet," BBC News, May 25, 2011, https://www.bbc.com/news/av/uk-13537972.

228 **Obama recorded a video:** Matt Compton, "President Obama's Message for Queen Elizabeth II," Barack Obama White House, June 5, 2012, https://obamawhitehouse .archives.gov/blog/2012/06/05/president-obama-s-message -queen-elizabeth-ii.

228 **Jon Stewart:** Ben Hoyle and Nico Hines, "Obama Pays Tribute to a Personal and Very Special Relationship," *The Times*, June 6, 2012.

229 **Obama was dismayed:** Victoria Murphy, "IT'S HAUL OVER; Queen Misses First Summit for 40 Years: She Sends

Charles to Avoid Long Flight," *The Daily Mirror,* May 8, 2013.

229 **According to Sir Peter:** Sir Peter Westmacott, interview with author, June 8, 2021.

231 **"The Queen abruptly":** Obama, *Becoming,* 404.

233 **In the evening:** Press Association Reporters, "A Late Night for George, the Pyjama Prince, as He Meets the Obamas," HuffPost, April 22, 2016.

233 **Obama later used:** Ben Hoyle, "George Gives Obama the Last Laugh," *The Times,* May 2, 2016.

233 **The Obamas also lent a hand:** Prince Harry (@KensingtonRoyal), "Unfortunately for you @FLOTUS and @POTUS I wasn't alone when you sent me that video 😊—H.," Twitter, April 29, 2016, https://twitter.com /KensingtonRoyal/status/726062251354914817?s=20.

CHAPTER 13

236 **In it, Trump described:** Donald J. Trump with Tony Schwartz, *Trump: The Art of the Deal* (London: Random House Publishing Group, 1987), 55.

236 **"My mother was":** Michael Gove and Kai Diekmann, "Full Transcript of Interview with Donald Trump," *The Times,* January 16, 2017.

236 **Unchanging in a time:** Donald J. Trump, "EXCLUSIVE: 'The Most Extraordinary Honor of My Life,'" DailyMail .com, September 10, 2022.

237 **When May stood:** "PM Press Conference with US President Trump: 27 January 2017," Prime Minister's Office, 10 Downing Street, January 27, 2017, https://www.gov.uk /government/speeches/pm-press-conference-with-us -president-donald-trump-27-january-2017.

238 **Lord Ricketts:** Francis Elliott, "State Visit Will Hurt the Queen, May Is Told," *The Times,* January 31, 2017.

238 **A petition to block:** "Petition: Prevent Donald Trump from Making a State Visit to the United Kingdom," accessed

February 10, 2023, https://petition.parliament.uk/archived
/petitions/171928.

238 **It was reported that:** Toby Harnden, "White House Gets
Cold Feet over Trump State Visit," *The Sunday Times*, June 11,
2017.

239 **The US ambassador:** Nicholas Cecil, "Trump Will Visit
London Early Next Year, Says American Ambassador,"
London Evening Standard, December 12, 2017.

239 **Once again he was criticized:** Stephen Castle and Austin
Ramzy, "Trump Won't Visit London to Open Embassy. His
U.K. Critics Say He Got the Message," *The New York Times*,
January 12, 2018.

240 **One royal courtier:** Interview with author, June 23, 2023.

240 **Her choice of attire was highlighted by:** "Audience at
Windsor Castle," *From Her Majesty's Jewel Vault* (blog), July
12, 2018, https://queensjewelvault.blogspot.com/2018/07
/audience-at-windsor-castle.html.

241 **But the day of his first:** Tom Newton Dunn, "TRUMP'S
BREXIT BLAST: Donald Trump Told Theresa May How to
Do Brexit 'But She Wrecked It'—and Says the US Trade
Deal Is Off," *The Sun*, July 13, 2018.

243 **Trump confirmed in an interview:** Piers Morgan, "Up Close
and VERY Personal with The Donald on Air Force One:
DailyMail.com's PIERS MORGAN Finds Out What Trump
Really Thinks of the Putin, Brexit, Kim Jong-Un and the
Queen," *Mail Online*, July 15, 2018.

245 **"For White House staff":** Sarah Huckabee Sanders, *Speaking
for Myself* (New York: St. Martin's Press, 2020), 220.

245 **Any chance of:** Huckabee Sanders, *Speaking for Myself*, 221.

246 **Tim Knox:** Adam Carlson, "Donald Trump Didn't
Recognize the Gift He Brought Queen Elizabeth on Last
Year's U.K. Visit," *People*, June 3, 2019, https://people.com
/politics/donald-trump-didnt-recognize-gift-queen
-elizabeth.

246 **After lunch at the palace:** Bob Fredericks, "DON'TON
ABBEY," *New York Post*, June 4, 2019.

246 **Huckabee Sanders set out:** Huckabee Sanders, *Speaking for Myself*, 222.

247 **Also like Bush:** Jessica Elgot, "Trump Not Expected to Address Parliament During UK State Visit," *The Guardian*, April 30, 2019.

248 **A brief drumroll:** "Remarks by President Trump and Her Majesty Queen Elizabeth II at State Banquet, London, United Kingdom," White House Archives, June 3, 2019, https://trumpwhitehouse.archives.gov/briefings-statements/remarks-president-trump-majesty-queen-elizabeth-ii-state-banquet-london-united-kingdom.

249 **"The president loved it":** Huckabee Sanders, *Speaking for Myself*, 224.

250 **The prince initially demurred:** Huckabee Sanders, *Speaking for Myself*, 228.

250 **As he and Melania:** Daniel Binns, "Come Again Soon . . . Queen Bids Farewell to President," *Metro*, June 6, 2019.

251 **Trump told Fox News:** Laura Ingraham, Mollie Hemingway, Ari Fleischer, and Raymond Arroyo, "A Day of Remembrance; President Trump's One-on-One Interview with Laura Ingraham," *The Ingraham Angle*, June 6, 2019.

251 **One senior British official:** Senior British official, interview with author, December 22, 2022.

251 **Secret diplomatic cables:** Isabel Oakeshott, "Britain's Man in the US Says Trump Is 'Inept': Leaked Secret Cables from Ambassador Say the President Is 'Uniquely Dysfunctional and His Career Could End in Disgrace,'" *The Mail on Sunday*, July 6, 2019.

251 **Britain's Foreign Office:** "Trump Administration 'Uniquely Dysfunctional,' Says UK Ambassador to U.S.: Newspaper," Reuters, July 8, 2019.

252 **But Trump was riled:** Gregg Re, "Trump Fires Back at UK Ambassador Who Attacked Him: 'We Are Not Big Fans of That Man,'" Fox News, July 7, 2019, https://www.foxnews.com/politics/trump-uk-ambassador-leaked-cables-not-big-fans-of-that-man.

252 **The president added:** David Smith, "Trump Hails 'Good Man' Boris Johnson and Says of UK: 'They Like Me Over There,'" *The Guardian*, July 23, 2019, https://www .theguardian.com/us-news/2019/jul/23/trump-boris-johnson -britain-trump-uk-prime-minister.

252 **Trump had one further:** Mikhaila Friel, "Donald and Melania Trump Broke Royal Protocol Again While Greeting the Queen, Prince Charles, and Camilla at Buckingham Palace," *Insider*, December 4, 2019.

253 **As Darroch observed:** Oakeshott, "Britain's Man."

CHAPTER 14

254 **Nor was he a fan:** Joe Biden, "Remarks by the Vice President to the Irish People," White House Press Release and Documents, June 24, 2016.

255 **That said, Biden's personal:** Niall O'Dowd, "Fiery Joe Biden," *Irish America*, April 1987.

255 **He recalled being told:** Irish America, "Vice President Joe Biden Is Inducted into the Irish America Hall of Fame," March 21, 2013, YouTube video, 30:05, https://www.youtube .com/watch?v=PTM68gtBnYA&ab_channel=IrishAmerica.

256 **"Don't you bow":** Joseph R. Biden, *Promises to Keep: On Life and Politics* (New York: Random House, 2007), 11.

256 **Biden recounted in a speech:** "Vice President Joe Biden Is Inducted into the Irish America Hall of Fame."

256 **Biden shared more details:** Georgia Pritchett, *My Mess Is a Bit of a Life: Adventures in Anxiety* (New York: HarperCollins, 2021), 268.

256 **Biden was politically aware:** Joe Biden, "Remarks by President Biden at the Annual Friends of Ireland Luncheon," The White House, March 17, 2022, https://www.whitehouse .gov/briefing-room/speeches-remarks/2022/03/17/remarks -by-president-biden-at-the-annual-friends-of-ireland -luncheon.

256 **In 1982:** 97 Cong. Rec. S8016 (1982).

257 **In a 1987 interview:** O'Dowd, "Fiery Joe Biden."

258 **In a busy corridor:** Nick Bryant (@NickBryantNY), "'A quick word for the BBC?' 'The BBC? I'm Irish,'" Twitter, November 7, 2020, https://twitter.com/NickBryantNY/status /1325159843171201024.

258 **"Fury as Joe Biden":** Jennifer Hassan and Adam Taylor, "British Tabloids See Snub in Biden's Rejection of Churchill Bust amid Oval Office Makeover," *The Washington Post*, January 21, 2021.

258 **"When you look":** Sam Blewett, "Johnson Welcomes Biden's Inauguration as a 'Step Forward' After 'Bumpy Period,'" Press Association, January 20, 2021.

258–59 **Asked about the exodus:** "Remarks by President Biden in Press Conference," The White House, March 25, 2021.

259 **On February 19, 2021:** "Buckingham Palace Statement on The Duke and Duchess of Sussex," The Royal Household, February 19, 2021, https://www.royal.uk/buckingham-palace -statement-duke-and-duchess-sussex.

259 **A few weeks later:** David Bauder, "World Viewership of Royals' Interview Nearly 50 Million," AP News, March 9, 2021.

259 **Meghan would not say:** Sophie Lewis, "Prince Harry Clarifies That It Was Not Queen Elizabeth or Prince Philip Who Commented on Archie's Skin Color," CBS News, March 8, 2021, https://www.cbsnews.com/news/prince-harry -queen-elizabeth-prince-philip-archie-skin-color-oprah -interview-cbs.

260 **"On behalf of all":** "Statement on the Death of Prince Philip, Duke of Edinburgh, of the United Kingdom," GovInfo, April 9, 2021, https://www.govinfo.gov/content/pkg/DCPD -202100300/html/DCPD-202100300.htm.

261 **Biden once again:** "Remarks by President Biden on the COVID-19 Vaccination Program and the Effort to Defeat COVID-19 Globally," The White House, June 10, 2021, https://www.whitehouse.gov/briefing-room/speeches -remarks/2021/06/10/remarks-by-president-biden-on-the

-covid-19-vaccination-program-and-the-effort-to-defeat-covid
-19-globally.

261   **Just a week earlier:** Patrick Maguire and Oliver Wright, "G7
Summit 2021: Joe Biden Accuses Boris Johnson of Inflaming
Irish Tensions," *The Times*, June 10, 2021.

264   **Speaking at Heathrow:** "Biden Says Queen Elizabeth Asked
About Putin and Xi," Reuters, June 13, 2021.

264   **President Biden brought:** Diane Clehane, "The Exclusive
Story Behind President Biden's Gift for Queen Elizabeth,"
Yahoo!, June 14, 2021.

264   *The Times* **summed up:** "*The Times* View on the Queen's
Meeting with Joe Biden: Royal Diplomat," *The Times*, June 14,
2021.

265   **The four-minute address:** The Royal Family, "The Queen's
Speech at the COP26 Evening Reception," November 1,
2021, YouTube video, 4:12, https://www.youtube.com/watch
?v=eXvfqUe4EFQ.

267   **In a letter addressed:** Judy Kurtz, "Ruth Bader Ginsburg
Women of Leadership Award Given to Queen Elizabeth,"
The Hill, December 3, 2021.

267   **They included a report:** The Royal Family Channel, "Queen
Works from Red Boxes to Mark Accession Day," February 6,
2022, YouTube video, 3:20, https://www.youtube.com/watch
?v=IDW8xJ9iNXM.

267   **That same day:** Sky News, "Platinum Jubilee: Joe and Jill
Biden Congratulate the Queen," June 2, 2022, YouTube video,
0:58, https://www.youtube.com/watch?v=-GIRyuFztdo.

268   **Bush Hager's friendship:** *Today*, "Jenna Talks Dinner with
Charles Just Hours Before the Queen's Death," September 12,
2022, YouTube video, 4:10, https://www.youtube.com/watch
?v=0j9jQBQW7d8&ab_channel=TODAY.

269   **President Biden canceled:** "A Proclamation on the Death of
Queen Elizabeth II," The White House, September 8, 2022,
https://www.whitehouse.gov/briefing-room/presidential
-actions/2022/09/08/a-proclamation-on-the-death-of-queen
-elizabeth-ii.

270 **That evening:** "Remarks by President Biden at a Reception
for the Democratic National Committee," The White House,
September 8, 2022, https://www.whitehouse.gov/briefing
-room/speeches-remarks/2022/09/09/remarks-by-president
-biden-at-a-reception-for-the-democratic-national
-committee-4.

271 **He also referred back:** "Remarks by President Biden After
Signing the Official Condolence Book for Her Majesty
Queen Elizabeth II," The White House, September 18, 2022,
https://www.whitehouse.gov/briefing-room/speeches
-remarks/2022/09/18/remarks-by-president-biden-after-
signing-the-official-condolence-book-for-her-majesty-queen
-elizabeth-ii.

CONCLUSION

272 **"Everybody's so friendly":** "Obama Hosts Prince Charles,"
The New York Times, video, March 19, 2015.

272 **A CNN survey:** "Queen's Popularity Sky-high in America on
Eve of Diamond Jubilee," CNN, June 4, 2012.

273 **President Clinton said:** "Statement from President Clinton
on the Passing of Her Majesty Queen Elizabeth II,"
Clinton Foundation, September 8, 2022, https://www
.clintonfoundation.org/press-and-news/general/statement
-from-president-clinton-on-the-passing-of-her-majesty
-queen-elizabeth-ii.

273 **George W. Bush said:** "Statement by President George W.
Bush on Her Majesty Queen Elizabeth II," George W. Bush
Presidential Center, September 8, 2022, https://www
.bushcenter.org/newsroom/statement-by-president-george
-w-bush-on-her-majesty-queen-elizabeth-ii.

273 **The longest tribute:** Barack Obama, "Our Statement on the
Passing of Her Majesty Queen Elizabeth II," Medium,
September 8, 2022, https://barackobama.medium.com
/our-statement-on-the-passing-of-her-majesty-queen
-elizabeth-ii-e0b3ab49de86.

275   **The briefest statement:** "Statement from President Carter on the Death of Her Majesty Queen Elizabeth II," The Carter Center, September 8, 2022, https://www.cartercenter.org /news/pr/2022/statement-on-queen-elizabeth.html.

275   **Underlining just how:** "Queen Elizabeth II," Franklin D. Roosevelt Presidential Library and Museum, September 8, 2022, https://fdr.blogs.archives.gov/2022/09/08/queen -elizabeth-ii.

275   **Perhaps the president:** William Shawcross, "The Last Icon," *Vanity Fair*, June 2002.

276   **"Can I ask you":** "Trump: Queen Elizabeth Was an Incredible Woman," *Mark Levin Show*, April 28, 2023, https://rumble.com/v2l0ky4-trump-queen-elizabeth-was-an -incredible-woman.html.

277   **The British system:** John Bolton, "American Presidents Can Only Dream of What the Queen Accomplished," *The Telegraph Online*, September 9, 2022.

278   **As *The Washington Post*:** Donnie Radcliffe, "Festivities Fit for a Queen," *The Washington Post*, May 13, 1991.

PHOTO CREDITS

Page 1: (*top*) Abbie Rowe, National Park Service. Harry S. Truman Library; (*bottom*) Harry S. Truman Library

Page 2: (*top*) Dwight D. Eisenhower Presidential Library & Museum; (*bottom*) GBM Historical Images/Shutterstock

Page 3: (*top*) The John F. Kennedy Presidential Library and Museum; (*middle*) LBJ Library photo by Yoichi Okamoto; (*bottom*) Official White House photo by Ollie Atkins

Page 4: (*top*) Richard Nixon Presidential Library, photo by Robert Knudsen; (*middle*) Official White House photo by Ricardo Thomas; (*bottom*) Official White House photo

Page 5: (*top and bottom*) Courtesy Ronald Reagan Presidential Library

Page 6: (*top*) George H.W. Bush Presidential Library and Museum; (*bottom*) Official White House photo by William Vasta

Page 7: (*top left*) Official White House photo by Joyce Naltchayan Boghosian; (*top right*) Shutterstock; (*bottom*) Official White House Photo by Lawrence Jackson

Page 8: (*top*) Official White House Photo by Andrea Hanks; (*middle*) Andrew Parsons, 10 Downing Street; (*bottom*) Official White House photo

INDEX

Acland, Antony, 166
Acland, Jenny, 166
Adams, Gerry, 180
Adams, John, 2, 112
Adeane, Michael, 87–88
Afghanistan, 199–200, 204, 222
Agnew, Spiro, 91
Ahern, Bertie, 190
Albert (prince of Saxe-Coburg), 4, 5
Albert, Duke of York, 1. *See also*
    George VI
Albert Edward, Prince of Wales, 4
An American Life
    (Ronald Reagan), 146
Amies, Sir Hardy, 44
Andrew, Prince, 139, 179, 253
Andrews, Julie, 72
Anne, Princess, 86, 253
  divorce, 179
  media coverage of, 94
  visits to US, 80, 91–92, 94, 132–134
Annenberg, Lee, 136, 147–148
Annenberg, Walter, 136, 147–148
Armstrong, Anne, 104

Armstrong, Ernie, 126
Armstrong, Robert, 97
Armstrong-Jones, Antony, 66, 71–76
The Art of the Deal (Trump), 236
Associated Press, 17, 19–20, 33, 66
Astaire, Fred, 72
Attlee, Clement, 13
Australia, 65–66

Balmoral Castle, 21, 24, 37, 40
The Baltimore Sun, 170, 171
Baring, Rowland, 97
Barton, Philip, 186, 187
Bassett, Jim, 84
Beaton, Cecil, 54
Beatty, Warren, 72
Becoming (Michelle Obama),
    217–218, 219–220
Bellville, Belinda, 75
Bennett, James Gordon, 4
Bercow, John, 247
Berton, Pierre, 19
Betjeman, Sir John, 131

Biden, Jill, 261–262, 268, 269–270
Biden, Joseph R., Jr.
    bust of Churchill and, 258
    on death of Philip, 259–260, 261
    Elizabeth and, 254, 262–265,
        267–268, 269–271
    Falkland Islands conflict, 257
    Ireland and, 255, 257–258, 259
    Boris Johnson and, 254–255,
        258, 261
bin Laden, Osama, 222
Black, Shirley Temple, 152
Blackburn, Tom, 199
Blackwell, Richard, 113
Blaine, David, 202
Blair, Tony, 226
    George W. Bush and, 194, 206, 214
    Bill Clinton and, 177, 178, 194
    September 11, 2001 and, 197
Blumenthal, W. Michael, 125
Bolton, John, 277–278
Bonham-Carter, Helena, 226
Borel, Calvin, 211
Brexit, 230, 235, 236, 241, 243,
    254–255
Britannia, 13, 36, 104–106, 108, 147,
    149, 150, 153, 174, 182–183, 184
British-American relations
    John Adams and George III, 2
    Afghanistan and, 199–200
    Biden, 261, 264, 269–270
    British invasion of Egypt (1956), 27
    George H. W. Bush, 158, 168–169,
        173, 212
    George W. Bush, 212
    Carter, 124–132
    Churchill, 13, 212, 278
    Clinton, 180
    Eisenhower, 22
    Elizabeth's longevity and, 207, 208
    expressed during bicentennial
        celebrations, 107–108, 109,
        111–113, 116–117
    Falkland Islands conflict and,
        140–141, 257
    Good Friday Agreement, 189–190

Heath and, 81, 94
Jackson and William IV, 3
Lyndon Johnson, 65, 70–71, 75,
    76–77
John Kennedy, 43, 50
Nixon, 85–87, 91–93, 94
Obama, 214–215, 221, 222,
    226–228, 232–233
Reagan, 143–144, 145, 146, 148–149,
    153–157
Franklin Roosevelt, 212–213
Theodore Roosevelt and Edward
    VII, 6
Truman, 213
Trump, 237–242, 244, 248–250,
    251–252, 253
under Victoria, 3–6
Vietnam War and, 76–77, 78
Wilson and George V, 6–7
British Empire, 27
Brookeborough, Viscount, 223
Brooks-Baker, Harold, 154–155
Brown, George S., 110–111
Brown, Gordon, 214–215, 226
Bruce, David, 68, 69
Bryan, John, 103
Buchanan, James, 4
Bundy, McGeorge, 76–77
Burns, George, 148
Burton, Richard, 72
Burton, Tim, 226
Bush, Barbara (daughter of George
    W.), 198–199
Bush, Barbara (wife of George H.
    W.) and Elizabeth, 161–162,
    165–166, 169–171, 277
Bush, Dorothy, 210
Bush, George Herbert Walker
    on American-British
        relationship, 158
    Britain and re-election campaign
        of, 180
    Charles and, 163
    Diana and, 163
    Elizabeth and, 160, 161, 162,
        166–167, 173–174, 175, 277

Bush, George Herbert Walker (*cont.*)
  health, 165
  Philip and, 163
  protocol and, 164–165, 168
  Thatcher and, 162–163
Bush, George W.
  Blair and, 206, 214
  Charles and, 94
  Elizabeth and, 166, 168,
    194–195, 198, 199,
    204–205, 209–213, 273
  state visit to Britain, 200–206
Bush, Laura, 166, 210, 211
Bush, Marvin, 210
Bush Hager, Jenna, 268–269

Caine, Michael, 205
Caine, Shakira, 205
Callaghan, James "Sunny Jim," 119,
  124, 127
Cameron, David, 225–226, 230,
  231, 235
Camilla, Duchess of Cornwall, 225,
  245, 249, 252
  Eden Project, 262
  prior to marriage to Charles, 103
  Trump and, 246
Captain & Tennille, 117–118
Carney, Katelyn, 207
Carter, Caron, 132
Carter, James Earl "Chip" III, 132
Carter, Jimmy
  Elizabeth and, 122, 123,
    134, 275
  first visit to Britain, 124–132
  Queen Mother and, 122, 128–129,
    130
  Resolute Desk, 6
Carter, Rosalynn, 125
Castle, Barbara, 90
Catto, Henry, 102
Cawood, Hobie, 108, 109
Chalfont, Lord, 119–120
Chamberlain, Neville, 46, 47

Charles, Prince of Wales and Duke
  of Cornwall
  at America's bicentennial
    celebrations, 103
  autograph for Huckabee Sanders,
    250
  George H. W. Bush and, 163
  Camilla and, 103
  Diana and, 179
  Eden Project, 262
  first visit to US, 92–93, 94
  marriage, 103, 137
  Nixon and, 93
  Tricia Nixon and, 80–81,
    86–87, 92
  Barack Obama and, 223, 225,
    229, 272
  popularity of, in US, 272
  Reagans and, 136–137
  September 11, 2001 and, 197
  Trump and, 245, 246, 249–250
Charles III, 279
Charteris, Martin, 12–13
Charteris, Sir Martin, 97
Cheney, Dick, 208
Chicago Daily News, 84
Chicago Tribune, 128
Churchill, Sir Winston
  Eisenhower and, 40, 270
  Elizabeth and, 21, 22
  funeral of, 40, 65–66, 68–70
  John Kennedy and, 48, 49
  Obama and, 214
  postwar election of, 13
  "Special Relationship" between
    Britain and US, 13,
    214–215, 278
  Truman and, 19
  union of hearts among English-
    speaking peoples, 227
  World War II bond with
    Roosevelt, 212–213
Clinton, Bill
  Blair and, 177, 178, 186–188, 194
  British lineage of, 178–179

D-Day fiftieth anniversary visit,
    181–185
  Elizabeth and, 177, 178, 181–184,
    185–186, 190–193, 273, 275–276
  Major and, 180–181
  Northern Ireland and, 177, 180,
    185–186, 189–190
  September 11, 2001 and, 198
Clinton, Hillary, 181, 183, 186–187,
    189, 226
Cochran, Jacqueline, 30
Cold War, 50, 54, 56
Como, Perry, 148
Connor, Chuck, 184
Cooke, Alistair, 103
COP26, 265–266
Corbyn, Jeremy, 247
Cox, Edward, 93–94
Cromer, Esme, 97
Crosland, Anthony, 105
Crosland, Susan, 105, 106, 110
The Crown, 43

Daily Herald, 33
Daily Mail, 137, 219, 258
Daily Mirror, 203
Daily News (New York), 183
Daniel, Clifton Truman, 14
Darroch, Sir Kim, 246, 251–252, 253
D'Avanzo, Donald, 32
Deaver, Mike, 138, 139
The Des Moines Register, 16, 17
Deukmejian, George, 152
Deukmejian, Gloria, 152
Diana: Her True Story (Morton), 103
Diana, Princess of Wales, 103, 137,
    145–146, 150, 188–189
  George H. W. Bush and, 163
  Charles and, 179, 185
  D-Day anniversary celebrations,
    184
  Travolta and, 155
  visits to US, 185
Diefenbaker, John, 29, 35

DiMaggio, Joe, 152
dontopedalogy, 89–90
Doonan, Simon, 44
Douglas, Mic, 63
Douglas, Sharman, 71–72
Downs, Maria, 101, 113–114, 115
"drop scones" recipe, 38–39
Dunham, Madelyn Toot, 218

Eden Project, 262
Edward III, 6
Edward VIII
  abdication of, 8
  characteristics, 1–2
  Simpson and, 7–8
  visit to US by, 7
Eisenhower, David, 92
Eisenhower, Dwight D.
  on bonds between US and Britain,
    22, 29, 30
  British invasion of Egypt (1956)
    and, 27
  Churchill and, 270
  cooking and, 39
  deaths if George VI and Queen
    Mary, 24–25
  Elizabeth and, 21–22, 34–36,
    37–39, 40–41, 277
  Elizabeth's state visits to US and,
    26–27, 28–31, 34
  eulogy for Churchill by, 40
  George VI and, 22, 23–24
  Khrushchev and, 37
  Macmillan and, 37
  Order of Merit, 24, 29
  painting and, 39
  on personal relationship with
    Britain, 29
  popularity in Britain of, 22
  royal horse named after, 25
  as supreme commander of the
    North Atlantic Treaty
    Organization, 18
  during World War II, 22, 23–24

Eisenhower, John, 24
Eisenhower, Julie Nixon, 86–87
Eisenhower, Mamie, 24
Eisenhower, Susan, 39
Elizabeth (queen, wife of George
  VI), 8–9
  Carter and, 122, 128–129, 130
  Chamberlain and, 47
  Bill Clinton and, 182–183
  Eisenhower and, 39–40
  Joseph Kennedy's admiration for, 48
  Nixon and, 81–82
  Nancy Reagan and, 137
  at White House as Queen
    Mother, 28
Elizabeth, Duchess of Edinburgh.
  See also Elizabeth II
  birth of, 1
  characteristics, 14
  Eisenhower and, 22
  hobbies of, 18
  John Kennedy and, 44–46
  Joseph Kennedy and, 46–47
  likelihood of becoming Queen,
    1–2, 8
  Nixon and, 81
  preparation for role as Queen,
    12–13, 15, 21, 22, 46–47
  as storybook couple with Philip, 14
  Truman and, 15, 20
  visit to US, 15–18
Elizabeth II. *See also* Elizabeth,
  Duchess of Edinburgh
  abdication of, as possibility, 89
  American affinity for, 215–216
  American lunar landing and,
    87–88
  America's bicentennial celebrations
    and, 96–99, 100–103, 104,
    105–119, 120
  Anne Armstrong on, 104
  annus horribilis, 179
  behind-the-scenes documentary
    about, 86
  Joe Biden and, 254, 262–265,
    267–268

Barbara Bush and, 161–162,
  169–171, 277
George H. W. Bush and, 160,
  161, 162, 166–167, 173–174,
  175, 277
George W. Bush and, 166, 168,
  194–195, 198, 199, 204–205,
  209–213, 273
Carter and, 122, 123, 134, 275
Rosalynn Carter and, 125
Bill Clinton and, 177, 178,
  181–184, 185–186, 190–193,
  273, 275–276
clothes of, 224
Cold War and, 56
concern for Diana, 150
on constantly being on public
  view, 53
continuity in international
  relationships and, 265
COP26, 265–266
coronation of, 25
D-Day fiftieth anniversary visit of
  Clinton, 181–184
D-Day seventieth anniversary visit
  of Obama, 229
D-Day seventy-fifth anniversary
  visit of Trump, 248–249, 250
death of, 269–271
death of Churchill and, 69–70
Diamond Jubilee, 228–229
divorce of Charles and Diana, 185
Eden Project, 262
Eisenhower and, 21–22, 37–39,
  40–41, 277
football and, 31–32
Gerald Ford and, 110–113, 116–117,
  174–175
Ghanaian trip by, 55–56
gum chewing by, 33
horses and, 13, 32–33, 53, 56–57,
  135–136, 139–140, 142–143,
  146, 147, 151, 156, 160, 209
invitation to Trump by, 237–238
Jacqueline Kennedy and, 42–43,
  52, 53, 56–57, 59–60

as "jewel" of British diplomacy, 232, 234
John Kennedy and, 42, 57, 58–59, 60–61
Lyndon Johnson and, 64–66, 78–79
last visit to US, 229
as living embodiment of "Special Relationship," 278
Macmillan and, 55–56
Nixon and, 82–84, 95–96
non-state visits to US, 147–153, 156
Barack Obama and, 215–220, 222, 225, 230–232, 273–274, 277
Michelle Obama and, 216, 217–220, 221, 222, 231
Platinum Jubilee, 266–268
popularity of, in US, 16–18, 19–20, 25–26, 28, 34, 43–44, 272–273, 279
protocol for, 101–103
purse contents, 108–109
Nancy Reagan and, 137, 148, 149, 150
Ronald Reagan and, 135–136, 138–141, 142–143, 144–146, 149–151, 152–153, 154–157, 174–176, 277
recipe for "drop scones," 38–39
Ruth Bader Ginsburg Woman of Leadership Award, 267
Saint Lawrence Seaway opening, 34–36
September 11, 2001 and, 196–198
"soft diplomacy" and, 38
state visits to US, 25–27, 28–34, 158–159, 163–176, 195, 207–213
state visit to Ireland by, 223
supermarkets and, 32
Truman and, 15–17, 20, 213
Trump and, 236, 240–241, 242, 243–244, 245, 248–249, 250–251, 252, 253, 274–275, 276
Woodward and, 41
Epstein, Jeffrey, 253
Evening Standard (London), 54

Falkland Islands, 140–141, 143–144, 145, 146, 257
Farish, Sara, 161, 166, 209
Farish, William Stamps, III, 160–161, 166, 196, 209
"Favorable Impression Made by Nixon on England Visit" (Stoneman), 84
Feldman, Myer, 67
Fellowes, Robert, 132, 171, 172
Ferguson, Sarah, 179, 195–196
Fergusson, Ewen, 105
Finnegan, Catherine Eugenia, Jean, 255–256
Firestone, Laurie, 164
Fitzgerald, Ella, 115
Fleischer, Ari, 197
Fonda, Jane, 173
football and Elizabeth II, 31–32
Ford, Betty, 101–102, 113, 115, 116, 118–119, 147
Ford, Gerald
    assassination attempts on, 99–100
    Elizabeth and, 110–113, 116–117, 147, 174–175
    Philip and, 114
Ford, Jack, 115
Fortas, Abe, 73
Fortas, Carolyn, 73
Franks, Sir Oliver, 19
Frazier, Alice, 170–171, 218
Freeman, Morgan, 168
From Her Majesty's Jewel Vault (blog), 240
Fromme, Lynette, 99–100
Frost, David, 124

Garland, Judy, 72
Geidt, Sir Christopher, 217
George (son of William and Kate), 233
George III, 2, 3, 103
George V, 6–7
George VI
    assumption of throne by, 8
    death of, 20

George VI (*cont.*)
  Eisenhower and, 22, 23–24
  health of, 11–12, 13, 15
  Joseph Kennedy and, 48
  Kennedy family and, 45
  Franklin Roosevelt and, 8–9
  Truman and, 15, 18–19, 20
Germany, 229
Getty, Gordon, 152
Ghana, 54–55
Ghika, Chris, 263
Gibbs, Robert, 215
Gibney, Seamus, 151
Gibson, Charlie, 211
Good Housekeeping, 103
Graham, Billy, 152
Grant, Cary, 115
Grant, Ulysses, 5
Grenada, 153–154
Grieves, Jemma, 206
G20 summit in London, 215, 218, 221
The Guardian, 6, 205

Hager, Henry Chase, 269
Haig, Alexander, 140, 141
Haller, Henry, 117
Hamilton, George, 63, 74
Hand, Lloyd, 68, 71
Hanks, Tom, 226
Hardy-Roberts, Geoffrey, 85
Harry, Duke of Sussex, 229,
  233–234, 238, 259
Hartley, Jane, 271
Hayes, Rutherford B., 5–6
Heath, Edward, 81, 94
  Nixon and, 95
Henderson, Sir Nicholas "Nico,"
  138, 139
Herald-Sun (North Carolina), 125
Herzog, Isaac, 271
Heseltine, Sir William, 157
Higgins, Marguerite, 20
Holland, Cathy, 208
Hollande, François, 229
Holt, Harold, 78

Hoover, Herbert, 33
Hope, Bob, 76, 91, 115, 117, 148
Hopper, Hedda, 14
Huckabee Sanders, Sarah, 245,
  246, 250
Hughes, Ted, 131
Humphrey, Hubert, 68, 73, 84
Humphrey, Muriel, 73
Hunt, Jeremy, 250, 251

Invictus Games, 229, 233, 238
Iraq, 158, 200, 202, 204
Ireland
  Biden and, 255, 257–258, 259
  Elizabeth's state visit to, 223
  Kennedy and, 58
  Obama and, 222–223
  protests during Elizabeth's US
    visit, 107, 172–173
  Reagan and, 154
Irish America, 257
"Iron Curtain" speech, 13

Jackson, Andrew, 3
Jackson, Clayton, 113–114
Jobs, Steve, 152
John F. Kennedy Memorial
  (England), 59–60
Johnson, Boris
  Biden and, 254–255, 258, 261
  Eden Project, 262
  Obama and, 248
  Trump and, 241, 251, 252, 253
Johnson, Claudia Alta "Lady Bird,"
  62–63, 66, 75, 115
Johnson, Luci Baines, 74, 79
Johnson, Lynda, 74
Johnson, Lyndon B.
  characteristics, 62
  Churchill's funeral and, 68–69
  Elizabeth and, 64–66, 78–79
  health of, 67–68, 73
  Margaret and, 62–63, 66, 73–76
  Resolute Desk, 6

as Senator, 30
Wilson and, 63, 64, 65, 70–71, 78
Johnson, Woody, 239, 245

Kaine, Tim, 208
Kate, Duchess of Cambridge, 224, 262
Kaye, Danny, 72
Kearney, Falmouth, 223
Keating, Paul, 220
Kelly, Gene, 72
Kennedy, Caroline, 59, 60
Kennedy, Edward, 172
Kennedy, Jacqueline
    Elizabeth II and, 42–43, 52, 53, 56–57, 59–60
    Macmillan and, 53–54
    "private" visit to London, 50, 51–54
    protocol and, 52
Kennedy, John, Jr. "John John," 59
Kennedy, John F.
    assassination of, 58–59
    as assistant to ambassador in England, 45–46, 49–50
    characteristics, 51
    Churchill and, 48, 49
    Elizabeth and, 42, 44–46, 57, 58–59, 60–61
    Ireland and, 58
    Khrushchev and, 42, 50–51
    Macmillan and, 42, 50, 51, 57, 58
    Ormsby-Gore and, 42, 57
    "private" visit to London, 50, 51–54
    Resolute Desk, 6
    US-British relationships, 43, 50
    as wartime hero, 49
Kennedy, Joseph, Jr., 45, 49
Kennedy, Joseph, Sr., 44, 45–50
Kennedy, Joseph P., III, 172
Kennedy, Kathleen "Kick," 45, 58
Kennedy, Rose, 46
Kennedy family as "royal dynasty," 44, 54
Kenny, Enda, 223
Khan, Sadiq, 238, 239, 241–242, 247

Khrushchev, Nikita, 37, 42, 50–51
Kissinger, Henry, 94, 98, 110–111, 118
Klapthor, Margaret, 133
Kleppe, Glen, 108
Kleppe, Thomas, 108
Knapp-Fisher, Edward, 131
Knox, Tim, 246
Kuwait, 158

Lansbury, Angela, 168
Lascelles, Alan, 48
Lempert, Yael, 261
Lerner, Alan Jay, 60
Life magazine, 27
Lincoln, Abraham, 5
Lincoln, Mary Todd, 5
"The Lizard of Oz," 220
Longworth, Alice Roosevelt, 115
Los Angeles Times, 103, 138, 209
lunar landing, 87–88

MacLeod, Mary Anne, 236
Macmillan, Harold
    characteristics, 51
    Eisenhower and, 37
    Elizabeth II as monarch and, 55–56
    Elizabeth II's state visits to US and, 26–27, 31
    Jacqueline Kennedy and, 53–54
    John Kennedy and, 42, 50, 51, 57, 58
    reelection of, 38
Macron, Emmanuel, 250, 253
Mail on Sunday, 251
Major, Sir John, 180, 226
Manning, Lady Catherine, 210
Manning, Peyton, 211
Manning, Sir David, 210
Margaret, Princess
    George H. W. Bush and, 163
    Lyndon Johnson and, 62–63, 66
    Kennedy dinner and, 52, 53
    visit to US, 71–76, 77

Marina, Duchess of Kent (aunt of
     Elizabeth II), 52, 53, 54
Marsh, Jack, 100
Martin, Mary, 151
May, Theresa, 235
  resignation of, 244
  Trump and, 237, 239–240, 241,
     250, 252
McGrath, Raymond, 172–173
McGuire, Michael, 188
McIntire, Carl, 106–107
McKeldin, Theodore, 32
Meet the Press, 90
Meghan, Duchess of Sussex,
     245–246, 259
Mellon, Paul, 32–33, 115
Menuhin, Yehudi, 115
Merkel, Angela, 218, 250
Meyer, Sir Christopher, 197
Miami Herald, 159, 189
Middleton, Kate, 224. See also
     Kate, Duchess of
     Cambridge
Miklaszewski, Jim, 159
Mitchell, George, 189–190
Moore, Sara Jane, 100
Morgan, Piers, 243
Morton, Andrew, 103
Motherwell, Jim, 174
Murray, Robert V., 28
My Mess Is a Bit of a Life
     (Pritchett), 256

Newman, Paul, 72
The New York Times, 9, 25, 92, 108
New Zealand, 65–66
Nixon, Richard
  British press on, 84
  Charles and, 93
  Charles and Tricia, 80–81,
     86–87, 92
  election as president, 84–85
  Elizabeth and, 85–86, 95–96
  fascination with British
     royalty, 81
  Frost interview of, 124
  at Ghanaian independence
     celebration, 54
  Heath and, 95
  Philip and, 88–89, 91
  as vice president and royal family,
     81–84
  Wilson and, 85
Nixon, Thelma Catherine "Pat," 82,
     84, 93
Nixon, Tricia, 80–81, 86–87, 92,
     93–94
Nkrumah, Kwame, 54, 55
Norman, Jessye, 169
North Atlantic Treaty Organization
     (NATO), 18
Northern Ireland, 177, 180, 185–186,
     189–190

Obama, Auma, 216
Obama, Barack
  British press on, 218
  Cameron and, 225–226, 230, 231
  Charles and, 223, 229
  Churchill bust and, 214
  D-Day seventieth anniversary
     visit, 229
  Elizabeth and, 215–220, 222, 225,
     230–232, 273–274, 277
  fascination with British monarchy
     as young man, 216
  Ireland and, 222–223
  Lyndon Johnson and, 248
  Philip and, 216–217, 222, 224, 225,
     230–231
  reelection of, 228
  shift to Pacific focus by, 215
  state visit to Britain, 222–228
  Prince William and, 229
Obama, Kezia, 216
Obama, Malia, 221, 222
Obama, Michelle
  British press on, 218–219, 220
  Elizabeth and, 216, 217–220, 221,
     222, 231

Prince Harry and, 229
protocol and, 218–219, 220, 231
Obama, Sasha, 221, 222
Oberon, Merle, 115
Observer, 69
Operation Hope Not, 65–66
Ormsby-Gore, David, 42, 46, 50–51,
57, 65

Packard, David, 151
Palmer, Arnold, 168, 211
Parker-Bowles, Camilla, 103. *See also*
Camilla, Duchess of Cornwall
Parry, Ryan, 203
Peck, Gregory, 72
Pelosi, Nancy, 211
Perceval, Stuart, 206
The Philadelphia Inquirer, 26, 34
Philip, Duke of Edinburgh
America's bicentennial celebrations
and, 105, 114, 117, 118
assassination of John Kennedy, 58
Britannia mishap, 36
George H. W. Bush and, 163
death of, 259–260
Ford and, 114
hobbies of, 18
interview with Walters, 88–89, 91
Nixon and, 86–87, 88–89, 91
Barack Obama and, 216–217, 222,
224, 225, 230–231
popularity of, with American
public, 16–18
protocol for, 102, 103
on purpose of monarchy, 88
on royal finances, 90
September 11, 2001 and, 197
state visits to US, 26, 28–34
as storybook couple with
Elizabeth, 14
Trump and, 249
visit to US, for George VI,
15–18
Philips, Mark, 132–133, 179
Pierce, Dame Karen, 267

Powell, Colin, 168
Pratt, Sharon, 170–171
Pritchett, Georgia, 256
Promises to Keep (Biden), 256
Psaki, Jen, 264

Queen Mother. *See* Elizabeth (queen,
wife of George VI)

Radziwill, Anna Christina, 50
Radziwill, Lee, 50, 52, 53, 56
Radziwill, Stanisław Albrecht "Stas,"
50, 52, 53, 56
Reagan, Nancy
Charles and, 136–137
Diana's funeral, 188
Elizabeth and, 137, 148, 149, 150
protocol and, 137, 141–142
Queen Mother and, 137
Reagan, Ronald
Charles and, 136–137
Elizabeth and, 135–136, 138–141,
142–143, 144–146, 149–151,
152–153, 154–157, 174–176, 277
Falkland Islands conflict and,
140–141, 143–144, 145,
146, 257
Ireland and, 154
Thatcher and, 141, 144, 153–154
Reed, Joseph, 165, 168
Rice, Condoleezza, 210
Ripley, Sidney Dillon, 133
Rizzo, Frank, 110
Robinson, Marian Shields, 221
Rockefeller, Nelson, 73
Roosevelt, Eleanor, 275
Roosevelt, Franklin D., 8–9,
212–213
Roosevelt, Selwa, 147
Roosevelt, Theodore, 6
Rourke, Russell, 100
Rumsfeld, Donald, 100
Rusk, Dean, 69
Rutte, Mark, 253

Saint Lawrence Seaway, 34–36
Sarkozy, Nicolas, 221
Savalas, Telly, 115
Schwarzkopf, "Stormin' Norman," 168
Scripps-Howard news agency, 31–32
September 11, 2001, 195–198
Shalikashvili, John, 181
Sharpton, Al, 174
Shawcross, William, 129
Showalter, Elaine, 188–189
Simpson, Wallis, 7–8
Sinatra, Frank, 148
60 Minutes, 124
Spacey, Kevin, 226
Speakes, Larry, 142
Spencer, Diana. See Diana, Princess
　　of Wales
Springsteen, George, 98–99
Sputnik I, 27–28
Stanley, Thomas, 26
Stedman, Phyllis Lady, 124
Stewart, Jon, 228–229
Stoneman, William H., 84
The Sun, 241
The Sunday Times, 180
Susman, Louis, 223

Taro Aso, 215
Tatum, "Big Jim," 31–32
Taylor, Elizabeth, 72
Taylor, James, 263
Tfank, Barbara, 224
Thatcher, Margaret, 139, 141, 144,
　　153–154, 162–163
Thomas-Ellis, Aeronwy, 131
Time magazine, 207
The Times (London), 73, 119–120,
　　131, 143, 198, 205, 236,
　　264–265
Travolta, John, 155
Trend, Burke, 76–77
Trudeau, Justin, 253
Truman, Bess, 15
Truman, Harry S.

Churchill and, 13, 19
Elizabeth and, 15–17, 20, 213
George VI and, 15, 18–19, 20
Truman, Margaret, 13–14, 15
Trump, Donald
background, 236
ban on travel by Muslims,
　　237–239, 247
Brexit and, 241, 243
Camilla and, 246, 249–50
Charles and, 245, 246, 249–50
Churchill bust and, 237
comments by British ambassador
　　and, 251–252
Elizabeth and, 236, 240–241,
　　242, 243–244, 245,
　　248–249, 250–251, 252,
　　253, 274–275, 276
Boris Johnson and, 241, 251,
　　252, 253
Khan and, 238, 239, 241–242
May and, 237, 239–240, 241,
　　250, 252
Meghan and, 245–246
Philip and, 249
protocol and, 242–243, 251
trade with Britain and, 237
Trump, Donald, Jr., 247
Trump, Eric, 247
Trump, Ivanka, 247
Trump, Melania, 238, 242, 245,
　　247, 252
Trump, Tiffany, 247
Truss, Liz, 268
Turner, Ted, 173
Two Champs (Jackson), 113–114

Van Buren, John, 3–4
Van Buren, Martin, 3
Vance, Cyrus, 125
Victoria, 3–6
The Victoria Daily Times, 35
Vidal, Gore, 52, 53
Vietnam, 63, 65, 70–71, 76–77, 78

Waging Peace (D. Eisenhower), 40
Walker, Diana, 152–153
Wallace, George, 84–85
Wallace, Margaret, 17
Walters, Barbara, 88–89, 91
Warren, Earl, 69
Warwick, Dionne, 148
Washington, Walter, 133
The Washington Post, 123, 278–279
The Washington Times-Herald, 16
Westmacott, Sir Peter, 229–230
While England Slept (Churchill), 49
Why England Slept
        (John Kennedy), 48
William, Duke of Cambridge, 224,
        229, 262, 272, 279
William IV, 3

Wilson, Harold
    Elizabeth and, 85–86
    Johnson and, 63, 64, 65, 70–71, 78
    Nixon and, 85
    royal finances and, 90–91
Wilson, Woodrow, 6–7
Winternitz, Robin, 171
Woodward, Jack, 41
Wright, David, 118
Wright, Sir Oliver, 147

Young, Sir Edward, 267

Zantzinger, Amy, 211
Ziegler, Philip, 94